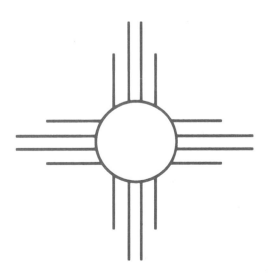

The proceeds from *Savoring the Southwest* will be used by the Roswell Symphony Guild in its support of the Roswell Symphony Orchestra.

Additional Copies of *Savoring the Southwest* may be obtained by writing or calling

ROSWELL SYMPHONY GUILD PUBLICATIONS
P.O. BOX 3078
ROSWELL, NEW MEXICO 88202-3078
(505) 623-7477

First Edition	September 1983	15,000 copies
Second Edition	November 1984	15,000 copies
Third Edition	September 1988	10,000 copies
Fourth Edition	February 1992	10,000 copies
Fifth Edition	February 1994	15,000 copies

Design by Donna Messick
Photography by Richard L. Faller
Title by Karole Frankenfield

Printed in the USA by

WIMMER
The Wimmer Companies, Inc.
Memphis • Dallas

About the Artwork on the Cover

SKY DANCE, 1988

Angus Macpherson

34" x 54" acrylic on canvas

Angus Macpherson decided on a career in art when he was still a young teenager. A decade later, in 1975, he loaded up some of his paintings and traveled to San Patricio, New Mexico, for a visit with Peter Hurd. Within weeks after that inspiring visit, Macpherson quit his job with the Albuquerque newspapers and began to paint full-time.

"I paint the way one writes a story," says Macpherson. "I have an idea, or some kind of sensory memory, and I try putting together a lot of random elements which interrelate to tell my story. I get great joy out of seeing how nature herself puts together the seemingly random elements of the landscape in New Mexico."

Macpherson was born in 1952. A third-generation New Mexican, he graduated from the University of New Mexico in 1974. He now lives with his wife and two daughters in Albuquerque.

Savoring the Southwest is the culmination of a three-year project in which members of the Roswell Symphony Guild collected, culled, typed, tested, proof-read, edited and indexed the more than 500 recipes contained in this book. Although the Guild has other fund raisers, the proceeds of which go to the Roswell Symphony Orchestra, this unique cookbook is the most ambitious.

The guild was organized in 1961 for the purpose of supporting the newly formed orchestra whose first season, 1960-61, consisted of three concerts. The orchestra now annually performs five subscription concerts and, as a gift to the community, a summer open-air concert. Also, realizing the importance of the exposure of "live" symphonic music to young people, the orchestra has performed as many as five free youth concerts a year.

The orchestra has progressed from volunteer musicians to one of professional status with renowned conductor, John Farrer, who commutes from Bakersfield, California to conduct the Roswell Symphony. Soloists of national acclaim and young guest artists perform annually with the Symphony. The very existence of a symphony orchestra in a town of less than 50,000 is unusual, and to have one of such high caliber is a miracle. Roswell is located in southeastern New Mexico, a distance of 200 miles from any major city.

In addition to fund raising, Guild members develop, organize and conduct the season ticket drive, provide housing for out-of-town orchestra players, refreshments for rehearsals, ushering at concerts and office assistance. In addition, the Guild provides youth scholarships and develops educational programs for youth in the community.

More than a cookbook, Savoring the Southwest reflects not only the rich and colorful heritage and mystique of New Mexico, but the dedication of those who believe that beautiful music should be a part of the cultural legacy of a community.

About the Southwest

by Paul Horgan

In tribute to the Roswell Symphony Orchestra, its leader, its players, its supporters—these lines are adapted from an earlier essay to offer a wide view of the Southwest land where throughout history, right into the present, people have according to their times worked to bring the graces of life into being.

A French map in the year 1678 showed the new land explored as far as the "terra incognita" of present-time Utah. The groaning wagons and horses had tried the terrain of Nueva Granada, that embraced everything we know now as New Mexico, Texas, Arizona, and part of Oklahoma. The Rio Grande, according to the heroic cartographer who sent his map to Paris for engraving, flowed from the north into the Pacific Ocean. Mountains, in the light of later accuracies, were a little carelessly disposed. But the yellowing water-laid paper carried a fiber of mankind that was ambitious, tough, and wild enough to follow blind riverbeds to the north. The shifts of sunlight on our yellow horizons could easily dazzle a mapper and put his rivers and his mountains out of accuracy. But nothing made him turn back. His chart of what he found suggests that we use his name for the territory, since it so easily indicates the boundaries of the Southwest as we now regard it.

In area, then, Texas, New Mexico, Arizona, and Oklahoma will constitute the Southwest of our time. America's regions seem to divide themselves into those of New England, the East (Atlantic states), the South, the Middle West, the Southwest, the West (mountain states), the Northwest, and California.

The Southwest is large enough to include the widest varieties of terrain, and thus of weather and of human pursuits. It is a country of one of two characters: either there are immense plains, flat alike to the tempests and the endless days of sunlight, or there are mountains that challenge the zenith with the power of a legend. Only in the littlest local sense are there pastoral regions, with bounding green hills and sustained valleys. This meant that, looking for natural securities and havens, the early people found none; and the resultant exercise of human ingenuity and faith produced that crew of pioneers whose philosophy so often seemed almost geological in its simplicity and its strength. The great river, Rio Grande, went slowly and widely down to the Gulf of Mexico, hardly oozing enough water in summer to slake a traveled animal train, going brown and reedy in the winter under its red banks, tearing away from the course of mountains in the spring, and changing the face of the deserts through which it went with the high breast of flood. So, either sleepy and endlessly peaceful, or sudden and terrible with storm and change, the life in the valley of the Rio Grande affords an easy figure for the life of the entire region.

In a land where gold was the temptation from the first rumors of the cities of Cibola, water was immensely more valuable. Its only sources were the mountain streams that made the rivers and the heavy thunderheads that gathered like a doom in El Greco. When the clouds broke and the plains were harried by the quick passing lines of the rain, the water sheeted down the brown spotted hills into the low runs where the arroyos were cut; and the sandy walls of the arroyos were dragged and broken by the red water as it flowed. A party of travelers, crossing such an arroyo to the south, where it might be sunny and dry, could hear a roar of mysterious quality and suddenly perceive the flood wall, dirt-red, advancing between the blue shadowed walls of the bed upon their fording party. The foam on the water would be light tan, whipped up from the surface mud. Yet the whisper of gravel, rolling under the pour, the scamper of prairie animals, the hurry of the travelers to mount the firm ground while the flood went by, and wait for the fall of the water, and the final seep of the red earth under the sun — these things marked the land but rarely. For the rest of the time, there was the sun overhead, and there lay the distance, changing in the heat and never dropping its challenge.

The surface of the ground was hard and resistant, with unfriendly plants and stones. The salty white of alkali was exposed, and the chalky sharp stone of gypsum. Under the shadow of the mountains, where they might be encountered, lay hills that offered protection. Safer from sunlight, they were neither baked nor blinding. Farms might be set up in such places, if the river country was too insecure with flood and shift.

To the south, near Mexico, the wild plants blossomed with furious color, scarlets and whites, high yellows and flashing greens. Over the whole of the territory when the spring had been soaked by the skies, the white and lavender verbena came to purfle the ground. It was one of the few times when a sense of something intimate, like a little wild flower, pervaded the land and gave it, besides its terrible beauty and mysterious wonder of distance and newness, some friendly aspect, much needed by men in a place where the only change from a flat brown plain was a sudden butte, hard and disdainful in its abrupt walls and unseen top.

The things that lived there required no conditions that were not common. Up the river valleys lived the Indians in houses built of the earth. Wild animals found their food in the endless life-process of stalking and killing, with the high vultures sailing until the feast was done and the refuse abandoned. Snakes dwelt with the secrecy of plants, and in the mountains the cat watched for the antelope, and the coyote whimpered after dark on the desert.

Buffalo wandered under the changing months, governed by solstices and the species of food. Their paths were never constant; nothing charted the huge spaces for the pioneers but the courses of rivers and the steadfast sign of stars. The interruption of a northward course by a canyon, long ago eaten down by an irresistible water, would cause weeks of search for a crossing or a ford. A mountain range, with flanks rearing back for miles of approach, must have been resistant to the search for a pass, over or around. There were dangers from everything, from the very distance, from the very passage of time. A young man could easily die from natural causes before a mission was completed. A climate, tropical in the daytime and cold at night because of the steady rise of the ground with the advance away from the sea, could of itself produce a need for a new philosophy. To the European eye, the eloquent strangeness of this country of Nueva Granada must have offered first fancy, and then fact, as a basis for legend. Travelers that return from new lands bring exactly enough information and have suffered exactly enough terror and hardship and excitement to let the several kinds of experience mingle in their reports. And so legend is born, is transmuted in passing from person to person, and a social force too strong to be resisted is put in motion. The quality of this sort of legend that makes it both dangerous and splendid is its constant change: while the serene legend from which myth grows, the legend that is devised without author and accepted without apostasy, is so slow to change that dogma seems really safe and the gods truly reliable.

But men put upon a new country at once bring about marvels too full of meaning for silence. History breaks the silence of the past.

About Paul Horgan

Musician, playwright, historian, essayist, artist, short story writer and novelist, Paul Horgan, twice winner of the prestigious Pulitzer Prize, was born August 1, 1903, in Buffalo, New York. From 1919 through 1923, Mr. Horgan was a student at New Mexico Military Institute. He left the Institute to study music and dramatics but returned in 1926 when reasons of health forced him to resign from the staff of the Eastman Theatre of Rochester, New York. He held the position of N.M.M.I. librarian until 1942 when he was commissioned as Captain, AUS Specialists Corps. He rose to LTC, Chief Army Information Branch and was awarded the Legion of Merit.

Eugene Jackman in his unpublished doctorate thesis quotes the ROSWELL DAILY RECORD, February 26, 1965:

> When Institute men speak of Horgan, they invariably associate him with Peter Hurd, his classmate at N.M.M.I. and fast friend since the beginning of the 1920's. Lon Tinkle, a book critic of the DALLAS MORNING NEWS, has recently called the pair probably the two most famous Southwesterners in the creative arts who are still living.

In 1933, Mr. Horgan received national acclaim when his novel, THE FAULT OF ANGELS, garnered the Harper Prize.

He is the recipient of many awards including the Pulitzer Prize, Bancroft Prize of Columbia University, Texas Institute of Letters, Champion award of Catholic Book club, Laetare medal, University of Notre Dame, Bronze medal Smithsonian Institute, medal National Portrait Gallery.

He has served on the board of directors of the Roswell Museum (president), Roswell Public Library, Santa Fe Opera (chairman); advisory board of the Guggenheim Foundation; honorary trustee of the Aspen Institute for Humanistic Studies; past member of the National Council of Humanities; member of the American Catholic Historical Association (president); founding trustee of the Lincoln County (New Mexico) Heritage Trust.

Both the N.M.M.I. library and an addition to The Roswell Museum and Art Center bear his name.

To honor this gifted writer and humanitarian, the Chaves County Historical Foundation sponsors an annual Paul Horgan Award Dinner. The recipient is an individual from the community who has contributed to the historical heritage of this area.

Some of Mr. Horgan's many works are: MAN OF ARMS, 1931; THE FAULT OF ANGELS, 1933; NO QUARTER GIVEN, 1935; THE RETURN OF THE WEED, 1936; NEW MEXICO'S OWN CHRONICLE (with Maurice Garland Fulton), 1937; A TREE ON THE PLAINS, AN AMERICAN OPERA (music by Ernst Bacon), 1942; YOURS, A. LINCOLN (drama), 1942; THE DEVIL IN THE DESERT, 1952; ONE RED ROSE FOR CHRISTMAS, 1952; GREAT RIVER: THE RIO GRANDE IN NORTH AMERICAN HISTORY (Pulitzer and Bancroft Prizes, Texas Institute of Letters award), 1954; THE SAINTMAKER'S CHRISTMAS EVE, 1955; THE CENTURIES OF SANTA FE, 1956; GIVE ME POSSESSION, 1957; A DISTANT TRUMPET, 1960; CITIZEN OF NEW SALEM, 1961; CONQUISTADORS IN NORTH AMERICAN HISTORY, 1963; PETER HURD: A PORTRAIT SKETCH FROM LIFE, 1965; ENCOUNTERS WITH STRAVINSKY, 1972; LAMY OF SANTA FE, HIS LIFE AND TIMES (Pulitzer Prize, Texas Institute of Letters), 1975; MEXICO BAY, 1982.

He is now author in residence at Wesleyan University, Middletown, Connecticut, and is at work on another book.

Foreword

For those who know the Southwest well, the City of Roswell is a unique community with a long tradition of civic and community responsibility. Separated by nearly 200 miles from a city of like or larger size, it has been forced to draw on its own inner resources to develop a cultural pattern that would do credit to many a larger city.

The Roswell Museum, now nearly 50 years old, The Carnegie Library and The Woman's Club are all early examples of the large number of organizations which now dot the City. The Shakespeare Club may well be the oldest of all and it still continues with its monthly meetings. The Roswell Symphony Orchestra is a more recent addition, although it is now going into its 25th season.

My family and I have had the good fortune to be part of this great community and to those who peruse this volume, I can promise that the culinary arts are first and foremost among Roswell traditions.

Robert O. Anderson
Roswell, New Mexico
April 22, 1983

Robert O. Anderson

Robert Orville Anderson, petroleum executive, rancher and civic leader, has been active in the oil industry since his graduation from the University of Chicago in 1939 with a Bachelor of Arts degree.

Mr. Anderson served Atlantic Richfield Company (formerly known as Atlantic Refining Company) as its Chief Executive Officer for 17 years, as Chairman of the Board for 21 years, and as a member of the Board of Directors for 23 years. He retired from the company in 1986 to form an independent oil and gas company. Currently he is President and Chief Executive Officer of Hondo Oil and Gas Company, Roswell, New Mexico. In the past 50 years his business endeavors have included, in addition to the exploration, production, refining and marketing of oil, cattle raising and feeding operations, mining and milling and general manufacturing.

He is Chairman of the Board of United New Mexico Financial Corporation and has been an officer and/or director of numerous business, civic, charitable, educational and cultural organizations. He has been the recipient of numerous honorary degrees and awards, recognizing his extensive interest in public and charitable affairs. He has served as Chairman of the Board of the Federal Reserve Bank of Dallas, and on the Board of Directors of the Chase Manhattan Bank and Columbia Broadcasting System.

He was born in Chicago on April 13, 1917, and has been active for many years in political affairs, having served as a member of the Republican National Committee. He and his wife, Barbara, have seven children and nineteen grandchildren.

About the sculpture: Mrs. Barbara Phelps Anderson commissioned artist Mr. Rogers Aston to do a sculpture of her husband fishing — his favorite sport.

Rogers Aston

With a Bachelor of Arts degree in the creative arts, Mr. Aston has long been associated with various phases of different media. In the late forties, he began wood carving as a hobby. A few years ago he became interested in the lost wax method of sculpturing and now works exclusively on figures to be cast in bronze. His bronzes are in the collections of New Mexico State University, Las Cruces, New Mexico; Lubbock Christian College, Lubbock, Texas; United States Military Academy at West Point; the United States Cavalry Museum at Fort Riley, Kansas; Texas Tech Museum, Lubbock, Texas; Permian Basin Museum, Midland, Texas; State of New Mexico Collection, Santa Fe, New Mexico; New Mexico Military Institute, Roswell, New Mexico; Arizona Historical Society, Tucson, Arizona; Arizona Historical Foundation, Tempe, Arizona; Roswell Museum and Art Center, Roswell, New Mexico; and many private collections throughout the United States.

In May 1980, Mr. Aston received an Honorary Doctor of Laws Degree from New Mexico State University, Las Cruces, New Mexico. Other awards include:

Service to Mankind Award from New Mexico and El Paso District of Sertoma International,

Outstanding Citizen of the Year Award from Roswell Junior Chamber of Commerce.

God and Country Award from Lubbock Christian College, Lubbock, Texas.

Mr. Aston says about his sculpture, "I have such a deep admiration for the hardy souls who carved a mighty nation out of a rough and unforgiving wilderness. I hope to catch the vitality and the dedication of the free spirits who made America . . . I realize that I must observe with great accuracy as I work; I feel that I must be aware of not only the physical composition of my work, but, equally, I must look for a spiritual quality."

Contents

ABOUT THE VIGNETTES - In keeping with the charm of the material taken directly from the following old newspapers, the content has not been edited for spelling or punctuation: December 14, 1894 - April 3, 1915 Roswell Record; Roswell Register; Roswell Daily Record; Roswell Register-Tribune; The Roswell Evening News. The advertisements have been framed to simulate their appearance in those early papers.

About the Art

Sidney Redfield, **LINCOLN TOWN,** 1967
watercolor, 28" X 40"
Courtesy of Mr. and Mrs. Ralph Burnworth

Rogers Aston, **R.O.A.,** 1980
bronze sculpture, 12" X 29"
Private collection

Pancho McKnight, **EAST GRAND PLAINS MORNING,** 1981
water color, 14½" X 21½"
Courtesy of Mr. and Mrs. Kenneth Eakins

Henriette Wyeth, **DONA NESTORITA,** 1940
oil on canvas, 46" X 37"
Permanent collection, The Roswell Museum and Art Center

Peter Rogers, **MUSE LOOKING FOR A LOST ARTIST,** 1978
ARTIST LOOKING FOR A LOST MUSE, 1978
acrylic on birch wood, 44" X 34"
Courtesy of Mr. and Mrs. Thomas K. Denton

Donald B. Anderson, **UNTITLED,** 1972
oil, 48" X 48"
Private collection

Peter Hurd, **THE GATE AND BEYOND,** 1972
egg tempera, 47" X 90"
Permanent collection, The Roswell Museum and Art Center

Jane Davisson, **LAS FLORES,** 1972
oil on canvas, 30" X 40"
Private collection

Michael Hurd, **THE GREY,** 1978
oil on canvas, 30" X 36"
Courtesy of Helen Hayes

Carol Hurd, **THE JOKER,** 1980
acrylic on paper, 18" X 24"
Courtesy of Wiggins Gallery of Art, Roswell, New Mexico

Bruce Connor, **THE PICNIC,** 1975
casein, 28½" X 34½"
Courtesy of Mr. and Mrs. S. H. Cavin

Suzanne Mulkey, **SCHIZOPHRENIC COFFEECUP,** 1972
oil on canvas, 30" X 36"
Courtesy of Mr. and Mrs. Jimmy J. Hooper

Dorothy Peterson, **JUSTICE OF THE PEACE,** 1983
mixed media, 40" X 40"
Private collection

Savoring the Southwest

ROSWELL REGISTER   FEBRUARY 14, 1902

MERCANTILE LIFE OF ROSWELL
Mrs. Mary P. Cobean

While battling for the possession of Mexico, Cortez constantly heard of a fair land, far to the north and setting out to discover it, found this, our land, New Mexico, a country of wonderful resources. The river Pecos, rising high in the Rocky mountains, about 100 miles northwest of Las Vegas, twists and winds about for 300 miles, where it emerges into an open country a good sized river. Flowing on again between high bluffs and foothills in a narrow valley until past the longitude of El Capitan mountains when its bluffs sweep back and its valley broadens out into the most fertile and beautiful of New Mexico - this our beloved Pecos Valley.

This was a favorite hunting and resting ground of the Comanche and Apache Indians, as the buffalo and other animals roamed here, nourished by the succulent grasses which grew so luxuriantly; so much so, that the first white men found that their cattle kept in a marketable condition the year round and readily sold to buyers coming here from Colorado.

But the fame of the land went abroad and vast herds were driven in, which soon depleted the fine growth of grass. The stockmen tell us that the supply of water has never varied from what it was fifteen years ago as the springs seem to be never failing.

In 1800, this was the geographical center without touching a railroad of an area of 400 miles and Roswell was the longest distance from the railroad of any town in the United States.

ROSWELL REGISTER-TRIBUNE   OCTOBER 12, 1909

Roswell has six saloons which pay an annual license of $2000, and the number of saloons cannot be increased until there is a material increase in population.

While nominally in the center of the so-called semi-arid west, Roswell is noted for the number of luxuriance of its shade trees. It is estimated that there are more than 2,000 shapely cottonwoods in Roswell, and the number is being constantly added to.

Roswell is the seat of the New Mexico Military Institute, the great school for boys in all the southwestern country. This is a teritorial institution looked after by the government, and is maintained at such high efficiency that it is rated as first class under the exacting requirements of the war department.

Roswell is 206 miles from Amarillo, 474 miles from Dallas, 377 miles from El Paso, 765 miles from Kansas City, 1023 miles from St. Louis, 1220 miles from Chicago, 681 miles from Denver, 2200 miles from New York, 106 miles from Torrance by automobile, 75 miles from Carlsbad and only half a mile from heaven in the spring time.

Southwest Contents

Gringo Glossary

Albondigas	meatballs
Arroz	rice
Arroz con pollo	rice with chicken
Bizcochitos	anise flavored cookies
Bolillos	hard rolls
Bunuelo	a fried bread sprinkled with cinnamon and sugar
Burritos	rolled flour tortillas with a variety of fillings
Calabacitas	squash
Caldo	stew
Capirotada (sopa)	bread pudding
Carne adovada	pork marinated in red chile sauce
Carne asada	grilled marinated steak
Chile con queso	melted cheese with green chile
Chile (green)	a long mild green pepper
Chile jalapeno	a small, shiny, dark green hot chile
Chile manzano	a yellow-green chile similar to jalapeno but milder
Chile (red)	a green chile allowed to ripen, usually dried and used as a basic in seasoning Mexican food
Chile relleno	a green chile stuffed with cheese, dipped in batter and deep fried
Chile serrano	a tapered bright green chile usually canned, pickled or packed in oil; fairly hot
Chimichanga	a stuffed flour tortilla, sometimes deep fried
Chorizo	a spicy Mexican sausage
Cilantro	fresh coriander resembling parsley; the same as Chinese parsley
Comino (cumin)	aromatic seed
Coriander	round, pale yellow to brown seed of coriander plant; may be used to grow fresh plants for cilantro
Enchiladas	flat or rolled corn tortillas filled with meat or cheese and covered with red or green chile sauce
Empanadas	small turnovers stuffed with meat, mushrooms or fruit
Ensalada	salad
Escabeche	pickled in vinegar or marinade
Flan	custard
Flautas	a variety of taco
Frijoles	beans
Frijoles refritos	refried beans

Garbanzos	chick peas
Gazpacho	a cold vegetable soup
Guacamole	avocado salad or dip, usually mashed avocado with seasoning
Huevos	eggs
Indian fry bread	deep fried bread round, usually served with honey
Jicama	a large root vegetable with gray brown skin; the crisp white meat has the appearance of a potato, texture of a water chestnut and the flavor of a mild radish; usually served peeled and raw
Masa	corn meal used to make tortillas and tamales
Masa harina	commercially prepared corn meal
Molletes	anise-flavored buns
Nachos	tortilla chips covered with melted cheese
Natillas	custard pudding
Pastelitos	pastry crust filled with dried fruit
Pepitas	toasted and salted pumpkin seeds
Picante	sharp, hot, highly seasoned
Picadillo	meat and almond stew; also used as a dip
Pollo	chicken
Posole	hominy and pork stew, garnished with red chile or green
Quesadilla	a deep fried corn tortilla stuffed with cheese
Quelites	fresh greens or spinach with pinto beans
Ristra	a string of red chiles
Salsa	sauce
Salsa picante	a very hot sauce made from fresh chiles and tomatoes
Sopa	bread pudding
Sopaipillas	puffy, deep fried "pillow" of dough, traditionally served with honey
Taco	a folded corn tortilla, fried crisp and stuffed with a variety of meat, cheese, beans and garnishes
Tamale	shredded pork in red chile, encased in masa, wrapped in a cornhusk and steamed
Taquitas	rolled tacos, deep fried
Tostados compuestos	a crisp corn tortilla cup, stuffed with a variety of fillings
Tostados	crisp corn tortilla chips
Tortilla	a flat bread made of white flour or corn flour

Tumbleweeds

+ Never handle chiles without gloves as they contain volatile oils which irritate the skin.

+ Place avocado seeds in the middle of guacamole and cover with the mixture to prevent darkening as it stands. Lime or lemon juice will also help.

+ To keep tortillas hot for several hours, wrap tightly in foil and place in an insulated bag or wrap the foil package in layers of newspaper.

+ To reheat and soften tortillas, place on an ungreased surface and rub each lightly with a damp hand before heating a few seconds. Wrapping in a damp towel and heating in the microwave 20 seconds will also soften the tortilla.

+ To keep tortillas hot at the table serve between two heated plates.

+ Don't add cold water to beans while cooking, it causes them to break open. The addition of salt toughens the skins.

+ To freeze chiles without loss of flavor, blister them and leave the skins on; they will come off easily when thawed.

+ Longhorn cheese is best for enchiladas; Monterey Jack for chiles rellenos.

+ A chile with a pointed tip will be hotter than one that is rounded.

+ The real heat in a chile is in the seeds and veins; their removal will lessen the heat.

Preparation of Fresh Green Chiles

Wash and drain chiles and place on a hot grill or in broiler; turn frequently, and roast until skin is blistered. Remove the chiles from grill or broiler and cover with a damp towel for 10-15 minutes. Chiles may then be frozen unpeeled. To use in a recipe, thaw and prepare by peeling skin, starting at stem end and pulling downward. Slit open and remove seeds and veins.

Preparation of Dried Red Chiles

Wash chiles and remove stems. Slit open and remove seeds and veins and any blemishes. Place chiles on a cookie sheet in 250° oven; bake for 10-12 minutes. Remove from oven and cover with damp towel; allow to steam for 5 minutes. Chiles are now ready to use in making red chile sauce.

Green Chile Sauce #1

2 tablespoons vegetable oil
2 cloves garlic, minced
4 tablespoons minced onion
2 tablespoons flour
2 cups water
½ teaspoon salt
2 cups diced green chiles

Over medium heat, saute onion and garlic in oil until tender. Blend in flour and brown lightly. Add remaining ingredients, simmer for 5 to 6 minutes. Use in recipes calling for green chile sauce. *Yields about 1 quart.*

Green Chile Sauce #2

6 to 8 green chiles, freshly roasted
water
¼ teaspoon salt
½ teaspoon garlic salt
½ teaspoon oregano

Peel and remove seeds from the chiles. Put 3 to 4 chiles in blender. Cover with water and add the spices. Process on low speed. Add remainder of chiles and more water, continuing to blend on low speed until mixture is fairly thick. Remove sauce from blender and simmer in saucepan over low heat for 30 minutes. Use fresh sauce for green enchiladas, or allow to cool and freeze in small cartons, and use as needed. *Yields about 1 quart.*

Red Chile Powder

Remove the stems from 8 dried red chile pods. Place half the chiles in blender and process on low speed until completely powdered. Repeat process. Store in tightly covered jar. *Yields 1 cup.*

Red Chile Sauce

10 to 12 red chile pods, freshly roasted, stems removed
⅛ teaspoon oregano
1 clove garlic
1 teaspoon salt
water

Place 5 to 6 chiles in blender, cover with water and add the spices. Process on low speed. Add remainder of chiles and more water, continuing to blend on low speed, until sauce is of good consistency and skins are completely blended. Remove sauce from blender, strain and simmer in saucepan for 15 to 20 minutes. *Sauce may be frozen. Yields about 1 quart.*

Salsa Picante

16 large tomatoes, chopped
2 fresh green chiles, chopped
2 fresh red chiles, chopped
4 onions, chopped
2 hot peppers, chopped
2 tablespoons salt
1 cup vinegar
½ teaspoon celery salt
½ teaspoon mustard seed

Place all ingredients in large kettle and simmer over low heat for 2 hours, or until of a good sauce consistency.
Yields about 3 quarts.
May be frozen in small containers and used as needed.

Mexican Seasoning

⅓ cup dry minced onion
¼ cup parsley flakes
1 tablespoon instant chicken bouillon granules
1 tablespoon chili powder
2 teaspoons crushed red pepper
1 tablespoon oregano
¼ teaspoon garlic powder
½ teaspoon salt

Put all ingredients in a pint jar and shake well.
Use to season hamburgers, tacos or any Mexican dish. Shake well before using. Good on anything!

Chile Con Queso de Marcos

1 large onion, chopped fine
2 cloves garlic, minced
2 tablespoons butter
6 fresh green chiles, chopped, or 2 cans (4 ounce) chopped green chiles, drained
2 large tomatoes, chopped
1 or more teaspoons ground cumin
1 or more teaspoons oregano
1 pound pasteurized process cheese, cubed
1 pound Monterey Jack cheese, grated
Tabasco sauce

Saute the onion and garlic in butter until transparent. Add tomatoes and chiles. Add spices. Simmer about 10 minutes until the vegetables are soft. Add cheeses. Stir constantly until cheese is melted. Add Tobasco sauce to taste.
Serve warm with tostados or chips. This dish is best when made one day before serving.

Chile con Queso y Crema

1 pound Velveeta cheese
½ medium size onion, chopped
1 can (4 ounce) chopped green
   chiles
1 fresh tomato, peeled and chopped, or 1 canned tomato
3 drops Tabasco sauce
¼ teaspoon garlic salt
¼ cup whipping cream

Place all ingredients except cream, in double boiler. Cook until cheese is melted and onions are tender. Keep warm in double boiler or chafing dish. Just before serving, add ¼ cup cream. *Serve with fritos or tostados.*
Serves 20.

Chile Cheese Puffs

½ cup margarine
2 cups grated sharp Cheddar
   cheese
1 cup flour
½ teaspoon salt
1 can (4 ounce) chopped green
   chiles

Preheat oven to 375⁰. Cream margarine, stir in cheese, flour and salt. Add green chiles and mix well. Form dough into ¾ inch balls and place on greased cookie sheet. Bake 12-15 minutes. Serve warm. Puffs may be made in advance and frozen. Do not thaw; increase baking time to 18-20 minutes.

Ceviche

1 pound flounder or other white fish
  - fresh or frozen
1 tablespoon salt
¼ teaspoon garlic salt
¼ teaspoon tarragon
1 large onion, chopped
4 fresh green chile peppers (canned
   chopped chile may be
   substituted)
juice from 6 limes
lemon juice to taste

Cut fish into bite size pieces, add next 5 ingredients. Pour lime juice over and marinate in refrigerator for 24 hours. Add lemon juice for additional flavor.
Serves 4.

Cinco Dip

Mix together for layer #1:
1 can (16 ounce) refried beans
1 package (1¼ ounce) taco mix or 2
  tablespoons salsa casera

Mix together for layer #2:
3 avocados, mashed
3 tablespoons sour cream
2 tablespoons lemon juice
¼ teaspoon garlic salt

Mix together for layer #3:
1 can (4 ounce) chopped green
  chiles
4 green onion tops, chopped

Mix together for layer #4:
½ pound Cheddar cheese, grated
½ pound Monterey Jack cheese,
  grated

Mix together for layer #5:
12 pitted ripe or green olives, sliced
1 large tomato, seeded and cubed

Toppings:
chili powder
parsley

In a 2-quart crystal or glass bowl with straight sides, layer in the following order: the bean mixture, the avocado mixture, the chile and onion mixture, the cheeses, and last the olives and tomato. Sprinkle the top lightly with chili powder and garnish with parsley. Refrigerate. Serve as a dip with tortilla chips.
Serves 20-25 as a dip, 8-10 as a salad.

Quesitas

1 package (8 ounce) cream cheese
12 ounces Cheddar cheese, grated
  fine
2 cans (4 ounce) chopped green
  chiles, drained
1 cup ground pecans

Combine grated Cheddar and softened cream cheese, mixing well. Stir in green chiles and mix thoroughly. Form into bite-sized balls and roll in pecans. Chill until firm.

Tostados

1 dozen corn tortillas
vegetable oil
salt

Cut the tortillas into 8 pie-shaped wedges and fry in hot oil until crisp. Lift out with slotted spoon and drain on paper towels. Sprinkle with salt and serve with dips or salsa picante.

Empanaditas por Cocteles

Pastry:
2¼ cups flour
¾ cup cornmeal
1 teaspoon salt
1 teaspoon chili powder
½ cup butter or margarine
⅓ cup vegetable shortening
½ cup plus 1 tablespoon cold
  water

Filling:
1 pound ground beef
4 ounces Cheddar cheese, grated
1 medium tomato, diced
¼ cup onion, diced
1 hard-cooked egg, chopped
½ cup raisins
1 teaspoon salt
⅛ teaspoon Tabasco red pepper
  sauce

For pastry: In a large bowl, combine flour, cornmeal, salt and chili powder. Cut in butter and shortening until mixture resembles coarse crumbs. Add water very gradually, stirring until mixture forms a ball.

For filling: Brown meat, drain off any fat. Add remaining ingredients and set aside. Roll out ½ the pastry to ⅛ inch thickness on floured surface. Cut with 3¼ inch round cutter (mayonnaise jar lid is right size). Place 1 tablespoon filling on half of each circle and fold in two, moistening edges with a bit of water; crimp with tines of fork. Repeat with remaining dough and filling. Heat oven to 425°. Grease 2 cookie sheets and place empanaditas on them. Brush tops with melted butter and bake 15-20 minutes or until golden brown. Serve piping hot, with salsa picante or salsa casera, if desired.

If desired, substitute 3 medium size zucchini for the ground meat. Slice and boil in small amount of water for 5 minutes, drain, then chop fine. Add remaining listed ingredients to zucchini for filling. Yields 24 to 30.

Green Chile O'

1 can (4 ounce) green chiles
1 pound longhorn cheese, grated
3 eggs
3 tablespoons water

Line bottom of greased glass dish (8 x 10 x 2 inch) with green chiles. Pile longhorn cheese on top. Beat eggs with 3 tablespoons water and pour over top. Bake 45 minutes at 350°. Cool 10 minutes. Cut into squares, and serve on a square cracker, such as a Triscuit.

Guacamole

3 large avocados, peeled and seeds removed
1 medium tomato, chopped fine
1 tablespoon minced or grated onion
2 tablespoons lemon juice
½ teaspoon garlic salt
12 drops (or more) Tabasco pepper sauce

In a medium size bowl, mash the avocados. Add remaining ingredients and mix well. This may be used as a topping or garnish for tacos or enchiladas.
Serves 4 to 6 as a salad.

Guacamole Picante

1 tablespoon chopped onion
1 pod yellow chile, seeded
3 ripe avocados
1 hard-boiled egg
1 ripe tomato
1 teaspoon lemon juice
1 teaspoon salt

Mash avocados, chop egg, tomato and chile. Combine all ingredients and serve on toasted or deep-fried tortilla chips. Green chile instead of yellow chile is milder. Leave avocado pit in dip until last minute to preserve color. Very easily made in processor.
Yields about 2 cups.

Guadalajara Dip

2 pounds ground beef
1 teaspoon salt
1 teaspoon pepper
1 teaspoon garlic salt
1 teaspoon onion salt
1 can (1 pound 15 ounce) refried
   beans
1 pound American or mozzarella
   cheese, grated
1 jar (16 ounce) picante sauce
guacamole salad using 6 avocados
1 pint sour cream

Brown the ground beef; add salt, pepper, garlic salt and onion salt. Line a 9 x 13 inch casserole dish with the meat mixture; spread refried beans over the beef. Layer the cheese over the beans and pour over all the picante sauce. Top with guacamole salad, and heat in 350° oven for 30 minutes. Before serving, spread with sour cream. Serve with tostados or chips.
Serves 30 to 40.

Nachos

36 tostados (tortilla chips)
9 ounces Monterey Jack or mild
   Cheddar cheese, grated
3 jalapeno chiles, sliced

Preheat oven to 400°. Arrange tostados on cookie sheet and put cheese on tostados. Place a slice of jalapeno on each and heat in oven just until cheese is melted. These may be made in a microwave oven, using microwave dish; heat on high for about 30 seconds.
Yields 3 dozen.

Party Chile-Cheese Appetizers

10 eggs
½ cup flour
1 teaspoon baking powder
⅛ teaspoon salt
½ cup melted butter or margarine
1 can (8 ounces) chopped green
   chiles
1 pint cottage cheese
1 pound Monterey Jack cheese,
   shredded

Beat eggs slightly. Blend in flour, baking powder and salt. Add melted butter, green chiles and cheeses. Mix just enough to blend. Spread batter in greased 9 x 13 x 2 inch glass baking dish. Bake at 400° for 15 minutes, then reduce heat to 350° and bake 35-40 minutes more. Cut into bite-size squares.
Best served on small square cracker, or tostado.
Yields 60 to 100 1 inch squares.

Ricardo's

6-8 corn tortillas
1 avocado
6-8 teaspoons salsa picante
Mexican seasoning (see index)

Butter tortillas and warm in oven until soft. Mash a slice of avocado on one side of tortilla with a fork. Put 1 teaspoon salsa on avocado, sprinkle with Mexican seasoning. Roll up (as a jelly roll) and secure with a toothpick. Pop back in oven until hot. Serve at once. Good as an appetizer or served with soups and salads.

Shrimp Coriander

3 dozen small cooked shrimp, peeled and deveined
½ cup lime juice
2 medium tomatoes, chopped
1 large avocado, peeled and cubed
1 can (4 ounce) chopped green chiles
2 tablespoons finely chopped coriander leaves
3 tablespoons vegetable oil
salt and pepper to taste

Toss the shrimp with all the rest of the ingredients. Serve immediately with tortilla wedges.

Sopa Merida

3 corn tortillas
2 tablespoons corn oil
1 clove garlic, minced
1 tomato
½ onion
6 cups chicken broth
1 hard-boiled egg
½ teaspoon ground cumin
pepper
1 cup grated Monterey Jack cheese
1 avocado, sliced

Cut tortillas in narrow wedges, and fry in oil. Drain. Process garlic, tomato, and onion in processor, and saute in oil, stirring, for 3 minutes. Add the chicken broth, egg, cumin, and pepper. Simmer for 15 minutes. Place tortillas in soup bowls, sprinkle with ¼ cup cheese each, and spoon the soup over this. Top with sliced avocado.
Serves 4.

Albondigas

Meatballs:
1½ pounds ground beef
1 cup bread crumbs or 6
  tablespoons corn meal
2 eggs
2 cloves garlic, minced
2 teaspoons ground coriander
1 teaspoon salt
1 teaspoon pepper
½ onion, diced

Soup:
2 tablespoons butter, shortening or
  bacon grease
2 tablespoons flour
4 cups hot water
8 sprigs cilantro or parsley,
  chopped
2 teaspoons salt
3 potatoes, peeled and cubed

Combine all ingredients for the meatballs and mix thoroughly. Shape into balls of desired size. Melt the shortening in large soup kettle, and brown flour in it. Do not allow it to burn! Add hot water and seasonings. When soup mixture is boiling, add meatballs and potatoes. Lower heat and simmer until meat is cooked through and potatoes are tender, about 30-40 minutes.
When serving, the addition of a teaspoon of green chile salsa per meatball may be desired, since this is a mild dish.
Serves 8.

Arroz con Pollo

1 cooking chicken, 4 to 5 pounds
¼ teaspoon pepper
1 teaspoon salt
2 tablespoons cooking oil
12 ripe pitted olives, sliced
1 small onion, chopped
2½ cups canned tomatoes
1 teaspoon chili powder
1 cup rice
2½ cups boiling water
1 teaspoon salt

Cut chicken into serving pieces. Sprinkle with salt and pepper. Heat oil in large skillet and add the chicken, olives, onion, tomatoes and chili powder. Cover and cook until chicken is almost done. Add the rice to the skillet. Add the salt to the boiling water and pour over rice and chicken. Cover and cook until chicken is done and rice is tender but still moist.
Serves 6.

Budin Mexicano

1 dozen corn tortillas, softened in oil
4 large green chile peppers, fresh, canned or frozen
2 chicken breasts, cooked, boned and cut into pieces

Tomato Sauce:
8 medium size tomatoes, chopped fine
1 small onion, diced
2 cloves garlic, diced
1 teaspoon salt
chicken broth (from cooked chicken)

1 pound Monterey Jack cheese, grated
1 can (13 ounces) evaporated milk or 1 pint half and half

Make tomato sauce: blend the tomatoes with the onion, garlic, salt and chicken broth in large saucepan, cooking and stirring occasionally until sauce is bright orange in color. Prepare the peppers: seed, devein and cut in thin strips. In a 9 x 13 inch greased ovenproof glass dish, layer the ingredients, starting with the tortillas folded in half, then the chicken, chili strips, tomato sauce, grated cheese and cream. Repeat, ending with cream and cheese. (You must have enough tomato sauce so that the budin will not dry out in baking.) Bake in a preheated 350º oven for 30-40 minutes.
Serves 6 generously.

Calabazas

1 onion, chopped
2 cloves garlic, minced
2 tablespoons oil or butter
3 fresh green chiles, chopped
2 summer squash, cut into 1 inch pieces
2 zucchini, cut into 1 inch pieces
2 crookneck squash, cut into 1 inch pieces
3 tomatoes, quartered
8 sprigs cilantro, chopped fine
3 sprigs mint
1 can (12½ ounce) goats' milk
3 ears fresh corn, cut in 2 inch rounds
1½ teaspoons salt
1 cup goats' cheese, or ricotta

In a large kettle, saute the onions and garlic in oil or butter. Add the chiles and saute 1 minute longer. Add the squash, tomatoes, cilantro and mint; cook 6 to 8 minutes. Add the goats' milk, cover and cook on reduced heat for 20 minutes. Add the corn and cook 5 minutes longer. Add the salt, sprinkle with goats' cheese or ricotta. Turn off heat and allow to stand 20 minutes. (Flavor develops during standing time.)
Serves 8 to 10.

Camille's Posole

Part I:
2 pounds frozen posole
3 quarts water
meaty ham hock
1 large onion, chopped
2 cloves garlic, minced
1 tablespoon salt
1 tablespoon pepper
2 tablespoons crumbled dried red
   chile
1 can (7 ounce) tomato and green
   chile salsa
2 tablespoons beef or chicken
   bouillon granules

In large soup kettle bring all ingredients to boil. Lower heat and simmer, covered, about 3 hours until posole is tender but not mushy. Stir occasionally and add water and more seasonings if taste tells you it's necessary. (Chiles vary in degree of hotness.) Remove bone from ham hock when cooked and chop ham into mixture.

Part II:
3 tablespoons cooking oil
4 pounds lean pork and/or beef,
   chopped in 1" cubes (pork roast
   or round steak)
1 tablespoon salt
1 tablespoon pepper
2 cloves garlic, minced
2 large onions, chopped
1 pint fresh green chiles, roasted,
   peeled and chopped, or frozen
   green chiles
1 can (28 ounce) or 2 cans (16
   ounce) tomatoes undrained, and
   chopped
1 quart water
beef or chicken bouillon if
   necessary for flavor

In a large, oiled Dutch oven, over high heat, stir meat, salt, pepper and garlic until meat is gray and juices are sealed. Add onion and chile. Continue stirring over HIGH heat. Add tomatoes and water while stirring. Lower heat and cover. Simmer about 1-2 hours, stirring occasionally. Add more water and bouillon if necessary. It should not be dry.

Combine Parts I and II into the larger pan. Serve immediately or let cool, removing fat from the top. This will keep several days refrigerated or may be frozen. It is best to divide into smaller containers when storing to prevent spoilage. Serve posole as you would soup, in bowl, with tostados or warmed flour tortillas, and a guacamole salad, and allow for LOTS of seconds. *Serves 12.*

Carne Adovada

4 pounds lean pork, sliced thin
2 teaspoons salt
2 cloves garlic, minced
2 teaspoons whole leaf oregano
1 quart red chile sauce (see Index)

Sprinkle meat with salt. Add garlic and oregano to chile sauce and pour over the meat. Marinate in refrigerator overnight, stirring occasionally so meat is evenly covered. Cook slowly on top of stove or in a 350º oven for 1-1½ hours, or until meat is tender. Potatoes, sliced thick, may be added to marinade and cooked with meat. May be rolled in warm flour tortillas and served with the hot chile sauce.
Serves 8.

Carne Casera

2 pounds lean stew beef or pork shoulder, cut in 1 inch cubes
4 tablespoons flour
1 teaspoon salt
½ teaspoon pepper
2 tablespoons vegetable oil
2 cloves garlic, minced
2 medium size onions, chopped
1 cup hot water
1 cup (8 ounces) green chile sauce
¼ teaspoon ground cloves
½ teaspoon cinnamon
4 tablespoons slivered blanched almonds
¼ cup raisins
8 ounces prepared green chiles, cut in strips

In a bag, shake together the meat, flour, salt and pepper. In a large skillet, heat oil and brown meat. Add garlic, onion, water and green chile sauce. Cover and simmer 1 hour or until meat is tender. Add remaining ingredients and simmer 15 minutes. Serve over rice.
Serves 6 to 8.

Chalupas

1 dozen corn tortillas
vegetable oil
carne adovada, shredded chicken, refried beans or Mexican meat filling
½ pound mild cheese, grated

Toppings:
chopped tomatoes
guacamole
shredded lettuce
sour cream

Place tortillas, one at a time, in 1 inch of hot oil. Hold a spoon in the center of tortilla, so it will curl up and form a cup. Fry until crisp and drain on paper towels. Fill center with any of the meats or beans and sprinkle with cheese and other toppings, such as chopped tomatoes, guacamole, shredded lettuce and sour cream.
Serves 6.

Chili Con Carne de Edythe

2 tablespoons salad oil
3 medium onions, chopped (about 2½ cups)
2 cloves garlic, crushed
2 pounds ground beef
1 can (28 ounce) tomatoes, undrained
1 can (6 ounce) tomato paste
1 can (4 ounce) chopped green chiles
3 tablespoons chili powder
1 tablespoon ground cumin
1 bay leaf
2½ teaspoons salt
6 whole cloves
¼ teaspoon cayenne pepper
2 cans (15 ounce) red kidney beans, drained

In a Dutch oven heat salad oil. Add onions and garlic, saute until tender, about 5 minutes, stirring occasionally. Add ground beef and cook until browned, breaking up pieces with a spoon. Skim off fat. Add the tomatoes, tomato paste, chiles and seasonings. Simmer, covered, over low heat, stirring occasionally, for about 2 hours. Add drained beans to chili. Cook until just heated through. *Yields 10 cups.*
Can be prepared in advance. Cover and refrigerate up to 24 hours. Can be frozen and stored up to 2 months. If frozen, thaw in refrigerator overnight. Cook over low heat about 30 minutes, stirring occasionally until heated through.

Cheese Tacos

1 small onion, chopped
2 tablespoons vegetable oil
1 can (10 ounce) tomatoes and green chile
½ teaspoon crushed oregano
8 ounces Monterey Jack or longhorn Cheddar cheese
12 taco shells
1 large avocado, peeled and cut into 12 wedges
¼ head lettuce, shredded
2 small tomatoes, diced
1 cup sour cream

Cook onion in oil until transparent. Stir in the tomatoes and chile, and oregano. Simmer until thick, about 20 minutes, and keep warm. Cut the cheese into 12 strips and place one strip in each taco shell. Place on a baking sheet and heat in 350º oven for 7-8 minutes, or until cheese starts to melt. Top the cheese with the hot tomato mix, wedge of avocado, lettuce and tomato and a dollop of sour cream.
Serves 6.

ROSWELL REGISTER   APRIL 25, 1902

Newspapers soaked in a solution made of cayenne pepper and water, and thrust into mice holes, will free the house from mice.

Chicken Enchilada Casserole

1 3 to 4 pound chicken
1 carrot, cut in 1 inch slices
1 sprig parsley
1 stalk celery, cut in 1 inch slices
1½ teaspoons salt
½ teaspoon pepper

Sauce:
4 tablespoons olive oil or vegetable oil
1 small onion, chopped
1 clove garlic, diced
5 cans (4 ounce) chopped green chiles
¼ teaspoon cumin
½ teaspoon salt
¼ teaspoon pepper
2 to 3 cups broth from cooked chicken

cooking oil
18 corn tortillas

1 pound Cheddar cheese, grated
½ pound Monterey Jack cheese, grated
1 pint (16 ounces) sour cream
1 can (2¼ ounce) pitted ripe olives, sliced

Place chicken in large kettle along with carrots, parsley, celery and seasonings and add water to cover. Bring to boil, reduce heat and simmer until chicken is tender, 1-1½ hours. Cool, remove chicken from bones and cut into bite-size pieces. Discard the carrot, parsley and celery. Heat olive oil in large skillet. Saute onion and garlic lightly. Add green chiles, cumin, salt, pepper and chicken broth. Simmer 20 minutes, then set aside. Heat cooking oil until very hot. Fry tortillas, one at a time, until limp, ½ minute on each side, turning with tongs. Drain well on paper towels. Reserving ⅓ of the cheese, layer in a large casserole tortillas, chicken and sauce. Spread sour cream over top, sprinkle with remaining cheese and olive slices. Bake in 350° oven 45 minutes to 1 hour. Serve lettuce and tomatoes in bowls as garnish.

Chile Kabobs

1½ pounds beef, boneless and cubed
1½ pounds zucchini, parboiled and cut in 1 inch slices
1 pound cherry tomatoes (about 32)
1 can (8 ounce) whole green chiles, cut crosswise into 1 inch pieces

Using 16 skewers, on each skewer arrange beef, zucchini slice, cherry tomato and chile slice, repeating until skewer is filled. Continue arranging ingredients until all the skewers are filled. Broil over hot coals on barbecue grill until done. Serve on rice, if desired. For microwave oven: Place 4 skewers at a time in large browning dish, set dial on roast or medium high and microwave for 4 minutes. Turn skewers over and rotate dish ¼ turn; microwave an additional 3 to 4 minutes. While remainder of kabobs are cooking, keep the first ones warm on a cookie sheet in a 250° oven. *Serves 8.*

Chili Pecos

3 cloves garlic, minced
3 medium onions, chopped
2 tablespoons olive oil
2½ pounds beef, coarsely ground
1 tablespoon salt
1-2 teaspoons pepper
1 tablespoon ground cumin
1 teaspoon oregano
1 teaspoon coriander
1-2 tablespoons white flour
3-4 tablespoons chili powder
2 cups beef bouillon

Brown onions and garlic in sufficient olive oil to keep from sticking to pan (about 2 tablespoons). Add beef and brown after the onions are cooked to transparent. Add salt, pepper, coriander, cumin, oregano and chili powder. Sprinkle lightly with the flour and mix well with fork. Add beef stock and simmer 1-2 hours on low heat. Serve over half a bowl of frijoles.

FRIJOLES:
2 cups frijoles (pinto or Mexican beans)
1 onion, chopped
⅓ pound salt pork cut into small pieces

Pick over beans carefully and soak overnight. Drain and cover with fresh soft cold water. Fry salt pork until it is brown and crispy. Drain off half the grease. Add onions and slightly brown. Add the beans and water and boil 4-6 hours. As water boils away, add boiling water; never cold. Frijoles may be served just as they come from the pot or with chili con carne.
Serves 12.

Cliff Allen's Hoosier Style Gringo Chili

1½ pounds ground beef
1 can (28 ounce) stewed tomatoes, cored and chopped (reserve 1 cup liquid)
1 medium white onion, chopped
1 can (23 ounce) Ranch Style Beans
2 tablespoons red chili powder
1 teaspoon cumin seed
1 tablespoon granulated sugar
3 teaspoons salt
½ teaspoon garlic powder
water

Cook ground beef slowly in large kettle, stirring and turning frequently, just until meat is no longer red. Drain and discard liquid. Add remaining ingredients plus the reserved tomato juice. Mix thoroughly and add enough water to make desired consistency (approximately 3 cups). Place on low heat and simmer 1 hour.
This recipe won first place in the First Annual New Mexico De Vargas Mall chili cook-off in Santa Fe, New Mexico.
Serves 6 to 8.

Pancho McKnight

Pancho was born February 3, 1951. He was reared thirty miles west of Roswell on his parent's farm/ranch and attended school at Hondo, New Mexico. He graduated from the New Mexico Military Institute, Roswell, New Mexico, in 1969.

After graduation, he began pursuing an art career by studying with area artists and later attending Pennsylvania Academy of Fine Arts in Philadelphia, Pennsylvania. He returned to the Roswell area and built his studio on the McKnight farm where now he lives with his wife, Cindy.

EAST GRAND PLAINS MORNING was painted in 1981 for Mr. and Mrs. Kenneth Eakins on their farm at East Grand Plains just southeast of Roswell. They also have many meticulous working drawings of this scene which preceded the final execution of this watercolor.

Pancho's paintings are represented in numerous private collections in and around Roswell.

EAST GRAND PLAINS MORNING
Artist - Pancho McKnight
14½" X 21½"   1981
watercolor
Courtesy of Mr. and Mrs.
Kenneth Eakins

Chile Verde (Meat stew with green chiles)

1 tablespoon olive oil
1 onion, chopped
3 cloves garlic, chopped
3 pounds pork shoulder, cut in 1 inch cubes, fat trimmed
1 can (28 ounce) tomatoes
2 cans (4 ounce) chopped green chiles
1 cup beef stock, or water
1½ teaspoons salt
3 large potatoes, peeled and cubed (optional)

Saute onion and garlic in olive oil in Dutch oven. Remove onion and garlic and brown meat in same pan. Add onion and garlic to meat, along with all other ingredients. Cook slowly for 1½-2 hours or until meat is tender.
This is best when prepared a day ahead.
Serves 6.

Chiles Rellenos

8 green chiles, roasted and peeled, seeds removed (see Index)
1 pound lean pork
water
1 clove garlic
1 teaspoon salt
4 eggs, separated
flour
vegetable oil

Prepare the chiles. Cover pork with water and add the garlic and salt. Boil until tender. Cut into strips. Stuff chiles with the meat and hold together with a toothpick. Beat the egg whites until very stiff, fold in slightly beaten yolks. Roll chiles in flour, dip in egg batter and deep fry in hot oil until golden.
Serves 4.

Chiles Rellenos con Queso

1 dozen long green chiles, roasted and peeled (see Index)
½ pound Monterey Jack or Asadero cheese (the best)
3 eggs, separated
2 tablespoons flour
2 tablespoons milk
1 teaspoon sugar
1 teaspoon baking powder
vegetable oil

Prepare the chiles. Cut cheese into 12 strips and stuff each chile. Beat egg whites until very stiff. Beat yolks until creamy and add flour, milk, sugar and baking powder to yolks. Mix well. Blend yolk mixture with egg whites using a wire whisk. Heat oil about 1½ inch deep in skillet. Dip chiles into batter and fry until golden brown.
Chiles can be roasted, frozen in plastic bags, and peeled as needed.
Serves 4.

Chile Relleno Pie

1 pound ground beef (optional)
1 green pepper, chopped
1 medium onion, chopped
¼ teaspoon oregano
1 garlic clove, minced
salt and pepper
1 can (7 ounce) green chiles
½ pound Monterey Jack cheese, grated
½ pound sharp Cheddar cheese, grated
4 eggs, slightly beaten
1 cup half and half
1 tablespoon flour
1 can (8 ounce) tomato sauce

Brown meat with the pepper, onion, oregano, garlic and salt and pepper. Seed chile peppers, and spread on bottom of greased baking dish. Cover with browned meat. Sprinkle with cheese. Combine eggs, cream and flour and pour over top. Bake at 375° in a 9 x 13 inch pan for 45 minutes. Pour tomato sauce on top and bake for 10 minutes longer. *This pie is equally delicious omitting the beef.*
Serves 6-8

Chile Casserole with Cheese

5 or 6 cans (4 ounce) whole green chiles, or 6-8 roasted and peeled fresh green chiles
¾ pound Cheddar cheese, grated
¾ pound Monterey Jack cheese, grated
4 eggs, separated
1 can (13 ounce) evaporated milk
2 tablespoons flour
½ teaspoon salt
¼ teaspoon pepper

Preheat oven to 350°. Grease 10 x 10 inch or 9 x 13 inch casserole. Pick over the chiles to remove veins and seeds and cut into strips lengthwise. Put half the chiles in casserole dish. Sprinkle with half of the cheeses. Repeat. Beat the egg yolks until fluffy; add and beat in the milk, flour and seasonings. Beat egg whites until stiff and fold into yolks. Pour the egg mixture over the layered chiles and cheese. Bake 45 minutes or until set.
Serves 10 to 12.

Chimichangas

12 flour tortillas (large size)
6 cups Mexican meat mix (see p. 41)
cooking oil

Toppings:
shredded lettuce
green chile salsa
chopped tomatoes
guacamole
sour cream
ripe black olives, sliced

Warm the tortillas on an ungreased griddle. Put ½ cup meat mixture on lower part of tortilla. Fold the bottom edge over the meat, fold both sides toward the center and roll into a cylinder, securing with a toothpick. Heat oil in large skillet, and fry chimichangas, 2 or 3 at a time, until golden brown and crisp. Drain on paper towels. Serve hot over layer of shredded lettuce, garnished with any or all of the toppings.

Enchiladas Verdes

Chicken filled tortillas with green tomato sauce

2 whole chicken breasts (about ¾ pound each)
1 cup chicken stock
6 ounces cream cheese
2 cups heavy cream
¾ cup finely chopped onions
4 large or 6 medium fresh green peppers
1 can (10 ounce) Mexican green tomatoes (Tomatillos), drained
2 cans (6 ounce) chopped green chiles
2 to 3 teaspoons ground coriander
1 egg
1½ teaspoon salt
¼ teaspoon freshly ground black pepper
3 tablespoons lard or vegetable oil
12 corn tortillas
½ cup freshly grated Parmesan cheese

Cook chicken in stock for 20 minutes or until tender. Shred the meat into small pieces. In a large mixing bowl, beat the cream cheese with a wooden spoon until smooth. Beat in ½ cup of cream, 3 tablespoons at a time. Stir in the onions. Add the shredded chicken, mix well and set aside. Prepare peppers, (see Index for Preparation of Fresh Green Chiles). Chop the peppers coarsely and place them in a blender or food processor. Add the tomatillos, chopped green chiles, coriander and ¼ cup of the reserved chicken stock. Blend at high speed until contents are reduced to a smooth puree. Pour in the remaining 1½ cups of cream, the egg, salt, pepper, and blend for 10 seconds. Scoop the puree into a large bowl.

Preheat the oven to 350º. In a heavy 8 to 10 inch skillet, melt the lard or heat the oil over moderate heat until a light haze forms. Dip a tortilla in the chile tomato sauce, drop into the skillet and fry it for a minute or so on each side until limp. Transfer the tortilla from the pan to a plate and place ¼ cup of the chicken filling in the center. Fold one side of the tortillas over the filling, then roll up completely into a thick cylinder. Place the tortilla seam side down in a shallow 8 by 12 inch baking dish. Fry and fill the remaining tortillas in the same manner, replenishing the lard or oil as needed. Pour the remaining chile-tomato sauce over them and sprinkle the top evenly with the grated Parmesan cheese. Bake on the middle shelf of the oven for 15 minutes or until the cheese melts and the enchiladas brown lightly on top. Serve at once.
Serves 6.

Enchilada Casserole

1½ pounds ground beef
1 large onion, chopped
1 teaspoon chili powder
1 teaspoon salt
1 teaspoon pepper
1 can (10¾ ounce) cream of
   mushroom soup
1 can (10¾ ounce) cream of
   chicken soup
1 can (4 ounce) chopped green
   chiles
1 can (4 ounce) taco sauce
1 can (10 ounce) enchilada sauce
1 package (12 count) corn tortillas
¼ pound Cheddar cheese, grated

Brown ground beef in skillet. Add onion, chili powder, salt and pepper, and mix well. Add remaining ingredients, except the tortillas and cheese, and simmer 6 to 8 minutes. In a greased 9 x 13 inch baking dish, place one layer of tortillas, and pour over some of the meat mixture. Repeat until all the tortillas and meat mixture are layered. Sprinkle cheese over top and bake at 350° for 30 minutes.
Serves 8 to 10.

Flautas

1 large onion, chopped
2 cans (4 ounce) chopped green
   chiles
2 tablespoons vegetable oil
3 cups cooked chicken, shredded
1 teaspoon salt
12 corn tortillas
vegetable oil or fat for frying
½ pound Cheddar cheese, grated
½ pint (8 ounces) sour cream
1 large tomato, diced
lettuce, shredded

Saute onion and chiles lightly in oil. Add chicken and salt and heat thoroughly. Fill the center of each tortilla with mixture and roll into a tight tube. Fry in deep fat, a few at a time, until lightly browned. Serve with sour cream and cheese, lettuce and tomatoes.
Serves 4.

Green Chile Lamb Stew

2 cups lean lamb, cubed
1 large onion, diced
cooking oil
1 tablespoon flour
8 to 10 cups hot water
½ teaspoon chili powder
1 garlic clove, crushed
salt and pepper
1 can (4 ounce) green chiles,
   chopped
4 large potatoes, diced

In heavy pan, brown lamb and onion in a little cooking oil. Stir in flour. Cover with hot water. Add chili powder and garlic. Salt and pepper to taste and simmer 20 minutes. Add chiles and potatoes, cook on low until stew is tender, 45 minutes to an hour. Serve with warm flour tortillas.
Serves 6 to 8.

Corn Green Chile

1 package (8 ounce) cream cheese
½ cup milk
2 tablespoons butter
2 cans (12 ounce) whole kernel
   corn, drained
1 can (4 ounce) diced chiles
¼ teaspoon garlic powder
½ teaspoon salt

Melt cream cheese, milk and butter over very low heat. Add remaining ingredients. Mix well and pour into buttered casserole. Bake in 350° oven for 30 minutes.
Serves 5 to 6.

Huevos Rancheros

1 cup red or green chile salsa
2 tablespoons margarine or butter
6 eggs
6 flour tortillas, warmed
½ pound Monterey Jack cheese,
   grated

Heat salsa to boiling, then keep warm over low heat. In a large skillet, melt the margarine, and fry eggs over easy. Place one egg on each tortilla, spoon salsa over each, and sprinkle with cheese.
Serves 6.

Mexican Meat Mix (for Chimichangas, Tacos, or Enchiladas)

Meat mixture:
5 pounds beef roast
3 tablespoons cooking oil
2 onions, chopped
1 can (4 ounce) chopped green
   chiles
2 cans (7 ounce) green chile salsa
¼ teaspoon garlic powder
4 tablespoons flour
4 teaspoons salt
1 teaspoon cumin
juices from roast

Place roast in a pan with tight cover and roast in 350° oven 2½ hours or until well done. (Time in oven may be reduced by roasting meat partially and then removing to pressure cooker, adding 1 cup water and cooking until well done.) Drain the meat, reserving juices. Cool the roast, then remove fat and bones. Shred the meat and set aside. Heat oil in a large skillet, add onions and green chiles. Saute 1 minute. Add salsa, garlic powder, flour, salt and cumin. Cook 1 minute. Stir in reserved meat juices and the meat. Cook 5 minutes or until thick.
May be frozen.
Yields approximately 9 cups.

Mexicali Steak

⅓ cup flour
2 pounds round or Swiss steak,
   trimmed and cut into serving size
   pieces
2 tablespoons cooking oil
½ teaspoon basil
½ teaspoon pepper
1 clove garlic, minced
2 cups green chile sauce

Dredge meat with flour and brown well in oil in large hot skillet. Stir in remaining ingredients. Lower heat, cover, and simmer about 1 ½ hours or until meat is tender.
Serves 6.

New Mexico Green Chile Stew

1½ pounds beef, cubed
1 tablespoon vegetable oil
1 cup hot water
3 cans (4 ounce) chopped green
   chiles or 8 fresh roasted and
   peeled chiles, chopped
2 small onions, chopped
1 can (8 ounce) stewed tomatoes
1 teaspoon salt
1 cup pinto beans (fresh cooked or
   canned)
¼ teaspoon cumin
¼ teaspoon oregano
1 clove garlic, minced

Brown meat in oil in a heavy pot. Add hot water, cover pot and cook until meat is tender. When done, add remaining ingredients and simmer for 30-35 minutes.
The medium hot roasted and peeled chiles give a better taste, but if unavailable, the canned may be used. Freshly cooked pintos are excellent; however, canned (plain) are also effective.
Serves 6 to 8.

Pork Chops Veracruz

6 center cut pork chops, trimmed of
   fat
salt
pepper
1 onion, sliced
1 clove garlic, minced
12 ounces green chile sauce
sour cream (optional)

In a large skillet, brown the pork chops and season each with salt and pepper. Add remaining ingredients; lower heat, cover and simmer about 1 hour, or until meat is tender. Serve with sauce, topped with sour cream, if desired.

Quiche New Mexico

2 unbaked pie shells (9 inch)
½ cup bacon bits
4 eggs, well-beaten
2 cups half and half
2 tablespoons chopped onion
½ pound Swiss cheese, grated
1 can (4 ounce) chopped green
chiles
⅛ teaspoon nutmeg
½ teaspoon salt

Sprinkle half of bacon bits on bottom of each pie shell. Mix together remaining bacon bits and the rest of the ingredients. Pour half of this mixture into each pie shell. Bake in 350⁰ oven 40-45 minutes or until golden brown and knife inserted comes out clean.
Serves 12.

Southwestern Quiche

Crust:
½ package (11 ounce) pie crust mix
1 teaspoon chili powder
2 tablespoons cold water

Filling:
¾ cup grated Cheddar cheese
½ cup grated Monterey Jack
cheese
3 large eggs, lightly beaten
1 teaspoon salt
¼ teaspoon white pepper
1½ cups half and half
1 can (4 ounce) chopped green
chiles
1 can (2¼ ounce) ripe olives, sliced
2 tablespoons finely chopped green
onions

Preheat oven to 350⁰. In bowl blend pie crust mix and chili powder. Add water. Mix with fork until dough holds together. With hands form into smooth ball. Roll out on floured surface until 1½ times larger than inverted 9 inch pan. Ease into pan and flute edges. Mix cheeses together and spread on bottom of pastry shell. In medium size bowl beat the eggs; add remaining ingredients. Pour over cheese covered pastry. Bake 40-45 minutes or until knife inserted comes out clean. Serve at once as an hors d'oeuvre or main course.
Serves 6.

ROSWELL REGISTER   MARCH 1, 1901

Frank D. Parks has been in town this week from the sheep ranch, while J. S. Lea, his partner remained at the camp to look after their herd of wooly money makers.

Posole Pronto

1 to 2 onions, chopped
1 tablespoon cooking oil
2 pounds pork shoulder, cubed
1 cup hominy
1 cup red chile sauce
1 teaspoon salt
1 clove garlic, minced (optional)

In a large saucepan, saute onions in oil, then brown the pork. Add remaining ingredients and simmer, covered, until pork is tender, about 4 hours. Serve in bowls, as soup, with crackers or warmed flour tortillas.
Serves 6 to 8.

Tacos

12 corn tortillas
shortening or vegetable oil for
    frying
Mexican meat mixture, heated (see
    Index)
1 small onion, chopped (optional)
½ large head of lettuce, shredded
3 tomatoes, chopped fine
½ pound mild cheese, grated
red or green chile sauce (see Index)

In a skillet, melt shortening until very hot. Place one tortilla at a time in shortening, and fry, folding in center. Drain on paper towels. Place 2 table-spoons of hot meat mixture in center; sprinkle with lettuce, tomatoes and cheese. Spoon on chile sauce, if desired.
Serves 4 to 6.

Tamale Pie

¼ cup milk
¾ cup yellow cornmeal
1 pound ground beef
1 onion, diced
1 green pepper, diced
3 tablespoons oil
1 can (8 ounce) tomato sauce
½ teaspoon salt
2 tablespoons sugar
2 teaspoons chili powder
1 can (12 ounce) whole kernel corn
1 jar (5 ounce) green olives, sliced,
    plus juice
1 cup hot water

Mix milk with cornmeal and set aside. Saute beef, onion and pepper in oil. When browned add tomato sauce, salt, sugar, chili powder, corn and olives. Simmer 20 minutes. Remove from heat; add cornmeal mixture and 1 cup hot water. Pour into 9 x 9 inch baking dish. Cover and bake 1½-2 hours in 350⁰ oven. Remove cover last half hour.
Serves 4 to 6.

Sheepherders' Sandwich

1 medium onion, chopped
2 large tomatoes, chopped
1 can (8 ounce) chopped green
   chiles
1 cup orange juice
2 tablespoons brown sugar
6 large flour tortillas
½ pound Monterey Jack cheese,
   grated
1 pound ham or corned beef, thinly
   sliced

Mix onion, tomatoes, chiles, orange juice and brown sugar together. Refrigerate overnight. Drain. Layer meat, cheese and sauce on warmed tortillas and roll up. Delicious with pinto beans and guacamole.
Serves 6.

Taco Salad

1 pound lean ground beef
1 can (8 ounce) taco sauce, divided
1 head lettuce, torn
1 cup vinegar and oil dressing
2 tomatoes, peeled and diced
1 onion, chopped
2 avocados, sliced
1 package (10 ounce) tortilla chips,
   slightly crushed

Brown ground beef. Drain. Cook 2 minutes more in 4 ounces of taco sauce. Toss lettuce with ground beef and dressing. Place the remaining ingredients in individual serving bowls and pass.
Serves 4 to 6.

ROSWELL REGISTER   MARCH 1, 1901

Haddix, the photographer, is at work on some very fine pictures for Mr. Geo. Slaughter, which consist of several views taken of cattle on the ranch one and a half miles east of town, and the central picture of the group is to be a view taken of a large herd of Whitefaces on Main Street here. When finished and framed in groups they will make a most handsome advertisement for Mr. Slaughter, and will be hung in different hotels throughout the valley.

Cheese Grits Ole

1 cup grits
2 teaspoons salt
4 cups water
½ cup butter
1 can (4 ounce) chopped green
  chiles
4 eggs, beaten
1 cup milk
1 teaspoon Worcestershire sauce
½ cup grated sharp cheese

In large saucepan, add grits and salt to boiling water. Cook until thick, stirring occasionally. Cool slightly and mix in the remaining ingredients, reserving half the cheese. Pour the mixture into a greased 9 x 13 inch or 10 x 10 inch ovenproof casserole dish. Sprinkle reserved cheese over top and bake in 350º oven for 1 hour.
Serves 12.

Frijoles Refritos

3 cups cooked pinto beans
3 tablespoons bacon fat
2 cloves garlic, minced
1 teaspoon cumin
1 teaspoon oregano
1 tablespoon chili powder
Salt and pepper to taste

Place 3 tablespoons bacon grease in a large frying pan. Saute minced garlic in fat. Over low heat, put about a cup of beans at a time in the fat and mash with a potato masher or fork until beans are creamy and have formed a heavy paste. Keep adding beans and mash until all are used. Add spices. Beans can be mashed in a food processor first. Once pureed, follow the same frying directions. Serve with grated longhorn or Cheddar cheese on top of each serving. Normally eaten with a tostada dipped into the beans.

Quelites

2 packages (10 ounce) frozen
  spinach
1 tablespoon bacon grease
½ small onion, chopped
1 clove garlic, minced
¼ teaspoon chili powder
1 teaspoon salt
2 cups cooked pinto beans

Cook spinach as directed on package and drain well. Saute onion and garlic in bacon grease until transparent. Add the spinach and remaining ingredients and heat thoroughly.
Serves 8.

Colache

2 tablespoons butter
4 small zucchini or yellow squash,
  sliced
1 small onion, chopped
1 bell pepper, seeded and diced
½ cup water
1 large tomato, peeled, seeded and
  diced
1½ cups corn (3 or 4 ears) freshly
  cut
salt and pepper

Heat butter in large frying pan. Stir in squash, onion, bell pepper and water. Cover and cook 6 minutes over high heat, stirring often. Mix in tomato and corn. Cover and cook 5 minutes more or until vegetables are tender but not overcooked. Add water if needed. Season with salt and pepper.
½ teaspoon sugar and a sprinkle of oregano may be added.
Serves 6.

Chili Bean Salad

¼ cup cooking oil
2 tablespoons chili powder
1 cup chopped onion
2 tablespoons sugar
3 tablespoons vinegar
3 tablespoons catsup
2 cans (15 ounce) kidney beans,
  rinsed in cold water and drained
½ cup mayonnaise
1 teaspoon salt
½ teaspoon black pepper
1 large head lettuce
green pepper garnish
1 cup chopped black olives
1 cup shredded cheese, Cheddar or
  Monterey Jack

Put oil in skillet, add chili powder and let simmer 2 to 3 minutes. Add chopped onion, sugar, vinegar and catsup. Simmer for 10 minutes. Add beans and mayonnaise to the onion mixture and refrigerate for 1 hour. Add salt and pepper. Tear lettuce; pour beans over lettuce. Toss well, garnish with cheese, olives and green pepper.
This salad could be used as a supper main dish by adding slices of cooked ham to the salad.
Serves 12 to 15.

Peggy's Hominy

1 can (29 ounce) hominy, drained
1 can (8 ounce) chopped green
  chiles
1½ cups grated Cheddar cheese
8 ounces sour cream

Mix all together. Pour into greased ovenproof dish. Bake at 350º for 30 minutes.

Jalapeno Corn Bread

1 cup yellow cornmeal
1 cup cream style corn
1 cup sour cream
2 teaspoons baking powder
1 teaspoon salt
½ cup salad oil
2 eggs, lightly beaten
2 cups grated Cheddar cheese
3-4 hot jalapeno peppers, chopped
1 onion, diced

Combine ingredients and mix well. Bake in greased hot iron skillet or in bundt pan at 350⁰ for 1 hour.
Serves 10 to 12.

Mexican Cornbread

½ teaspoon soda
1 cup cornmeal
½ teaspoon salt
1 cup buttermilk
2 eggs
¼ cup bacon grease or vegetable oil
2½ cups cream style corn
½ pound cheese, grated
1 can (4 ounce) chopped green chiles
3 tablespoons chopped onion

Sift together soda, cornmeal and salt. Add buttermilk, eggs, oil and corn. Pour ½ corn batter (first 7 ingredients) into a well-greased and heated iron skillet. Over this sprinkle the grated cheese mixed with green chile and onion. Pour on remaining batter. Bake at 400⁰ for 30-40 minutes.

Navajo Fry Bread

3 cups flour, either all white or half whole wheat
1⅓ cups warm water
1 teaspoon baking powder
¼ teaspoon salt

Mix flour, baking powder and salt. Add warm water and knead until dough is soft but not sticky. Tear off one piece at a time and stretch and pat dough until thin and round (about 6 inches across). Poke a hole through the middle of the round piece of dough and drop into kettle of sizzling cooking oil. Brown the bread on both sides by turning it over in the hot oil with a large cooking fork. Serve hot with honey or jam. One can toast it later for breakfast.
¡Poking the center of the bread to make a hole lets the evil spirits out!

Pan De Los Reyes

1 cup butter or margarine
¾ cup sugar
3 large or medium eggs
¼ cup milk
4 tablespoons candied orange peel
  or 2 tablespoons freshly grated
  orange peel
3 cups flour
¾ cup golden raisins
¾ cup currants
4 tablespoons diced citron
4 tablespoons chopped almonds
1 teaspoon cinnamon
¼ teaspoon powdered allspice
1 bean or dried pea

Cream butter and sugar until fluffy. Add eggs one at a time and beat well. Add milk and beat thoroughly to keep fluffy texture. Coat raisins, currants, citron and orange peel with a little flour. Sift remaining flour with spices and fold into batter. Add floured fruits and almonds and stir until well mixed. Put in bean or dried pea. Bake in ring mold or form into a circle with hands. Grease mold and line with waxed paper or bake on greased baking sheet on waxed paper. Arrange foil loosely over cake to retain moisture. Bake in 275⁰ oven for two hours. Place baked cake on serving plate or tray and ring outside with juniper sprigs. Melt a little wax and attach Christ Child candle of white wax to center of server. Space one brown, one yellow and one black candle and insert in cake for the Three Kings. Serve with wine. If there is a celebration, the recipient of the bean or dried pea presides over the festivities. For random callers, it is a token of special blessings. In New Mexico the Dia de los Tres Reyes is celebrated on January 6.
Serves 15 to 20.

Sopaipillas

4 cups flour
2 teaspoons baking powder
1 teaspoon salt
4 tablespoons shortening (solid)
¾ cup warm water
vegetable oil
honey, or cinnamon and sugar

Combine dry ingredients and cut in shortening until the mix resembles cornmeal. Add water and mix until dough is smooth. Turn out onto lightly floured surface and knead 1 minute. Cover dough and allow to rest 20-30 minutes. Roll into a rectangle of ⅛ inch thickness, and cut into 3 inch squares. Heat oil in deep fat fryer to 370⁰ or 380⁰. Drop squares into oil, turning at once so they will puff evenly. Brown on both sides and drain on paper towels. Traditionally, sopaipillas are served warm with honey, or they may be rolled while hot in a mixture of ½ cup sugar mixed with 1 teaspoon cinnamon.

Flour Tortillas

4 cups flour
1½ teaspoons salt
1½ teaspoons baking powder
4 tablespoons shortening or lard
1½ cups warm water

In mixing bowl combine dry ingredients. Cut in shortening. Add warm water, a small amount at a time, to form a dough. Knead dough until smooth and elastic. Cover and let stand 10 to 15 minutes. Divide dough into 12 egg-sized balls, and flatten with hands. On floured surface, roll each ball into a 6 inch circle, about ⅛ inch thick. Cook on a hot ungreased griddle about 2 minutes on each side, until lightly brown. Cover to keep warm and soft until served. Tortillas may be allowed to cool, wrapped in plastic bags and frozen until needed.
Yields 12.

Quick Wheat Tortillas or Sopaipillas

(Santa Fe Recipe)

1 cup whole wheat flour
1 cup biscuit mix
¾ cup warm water or milk

Mix together the flour and biscuit mix. Add water or milk slowly. Stir and then knead until dough is easy to handle. Divide into 8 balls, roll into thin pancakes and bake on medium hot griddle on both sides until speckled (about 2 minutes each side). Makes 8 tortillas. For sopaipillas, roll the pancakes ½ inch thick, cut into 4 pieces and let stand for 5 minutes. Deep fry in hot oil, turning once. These will puff and be hollow. Serve with honey.
Yields 8 tortillas or 32 sopaipillas.

Tortillas de Maiz

2 cups cornmeal, fine white or blue
1½ cups warm water

Mix meal and water until dough is not sticky. Form into balls about 1¾ inches in diameter and roll out between wax paper or pat out with hands to 6 inches in diameter. Cook on moderately hot dry griddle, turning frequently until flecked with brown.

Jalapeno Jelly

4 large bell peppers, seeded and
    chopped
8 jalapeno peppers, seeded and
    chopped
6½ cups sugar
1½ cups cider vinegar
1 bottle (6 ounce) liquid fruit pectin
green food coloring

Put the bell peppers and jalapeno peppers through a food chopper. Place in large saucepan or kettle and add sugar and vinegar. Bring to a rolling boil and cook until mixture is transparent, about 30 minutes. Remove from heat and allow to stand 5 to 10 minutes. Add fruit pectin and stir well. Add food coloring to give desired color. Pour through a strainer into hot sterilized jars and seal. This is especially good with cornbread, or may be used with cream cheese on crackers. *Yields 6 cups.*

Red Chile Jam

12 large fresh red chiles
cider vinegar
2 lemons, quartered
3 cups sugar

Remove stems and seeds from chiles. Put chiles through food chopper. Put in saucepan, cover with water, and boil 5 minutes. Drain. Cover with vinegar and add the lemons. Simmer 30 minutes. Remove the lemons and add the sugar. Boil 10 minutes. Pour into sterile jars and seal or cover with paraffin. Good accompaniment for meat. *Yields 3 pints.*

ROSWELL RECORD   DECEMBER 18, 1894

$1,500
Will buy a lot on Main Street with 4-room frame house, a lovely shade tree; already rented for $25.00 per month. A good investment.

E.L. Wildy

Henriette Wyeth

Much has been written about Henriette Wyeth, the daughter of the famous artist, N.C. Wyeth, and wife of Peter Hurd. Paul Horgan, her life-long friend, has written a book on her life. The book was written for the exhibition at the Brandywine River Museum in Chadds Ford, Pennsylvania. Her famous father, N.C. Wyeth, trained his children to become artists extraordinaire. Henriette lived and painted in Chadds Ford until she married Peter Hurd in 1927. They lived and worked in Chadds Ford until they moved to the Sentinel Ranch in San Patricio, New Mexico, in 1941. The Hurds have three children, Peter, Carol and Michael.

Henriette's paintings are in permanent collections at the following museums across the country: Art Institute of Chicago, Chicago, Illinois; Brandywine River Museum, Chadds Ford, Pennsylvania; Carnegie Institute, Pittsburgh, Pennsylvania; Delaware Art Museum, Wilmington, Delaware; Columbus Gallery of Fine Art, Columbus, Ohio; Metropolitan Museum of Art, New York City, New York; The Museum at Texas Tech University, Lubbock, Texas; The New Britain Museum of American Art, New Britain, Connecticut; The Roswell Museum and Art Center, Roswell, New Mexico; and Smithsonian Institution, Washington, D.C.

About the painting, DONA NESTORITA: Dona Nestorita was blind and did not speak English. Henriette thought that she had an intriguing face and wanted to paint her. While she posed every day, she wished to stand because this was the most comfortable position for her arthritic condition. As Henriette painted, Dona would sing old Mexican songs to her.

DONA NESTORITA
Artist - Henriette Wyeth
46" X 37"   1940
oil on canvas
Permanent Collection of
Roswell Museum and Art Center

Bizcochitos (Mexican Cookies)

2 cups lard or shortening
1 cup sugar
1 teaspoon anise seed
2 eggs
6 cups sifted flour
3 teaspoons baking powder
1 teaspoon salt
¼ cup water or white wine or dry sherry
½ cup sugar
1 teaspoon cinnamon

Cream shortening thoroughly. Add sugar and anise seed. Add eggs to mixture and beat until fluffy. Sift flour with baking powder and salt; add to first mixture. Add water and knead until well-mixed. Roll ¼ inch thick on lightly floured board and cut in fancy shapes. May be put through cookie press. Mix together the cinnamon and sugar, and sprinkle on top of cookies. Bake in 350⁰ oven 8-10 minutes, until lightly browned. *Yields 4 to 6 dozen cookies.*

Capirotada (Bread Pudding)

8 slices bread, toasted lightly
2 cups water
1 cup sugar
1 teaspoon cinnamon
½ teaspoon nutmeg
½ teaspoon cloves
¼ teaspoon salt
1 cup grated Cheddar cheese
1 cup raisins
3 tablespoons butter
½ cup red wine (optional)
whipped cream (optional)

Break the toasted bread into 2 inch pieces. In saucepan make a syrup of water, sugar, spices and salt. Bring to a boil, reduce heat, and simmer 10 minutes. Grease a 2-quart baking dish. Layer bread, cheese, raisins and wine. Dot each layer with butter. Pour syrup over bread mixture and bake at 350⁰ for 20 minutes, or until syrup is absorbed. Serve warm or cold with whipped cream. *Serves 8.*

Mexican Wedding Cookies

1 cup butter, softened
1 cup powdered sugar
2 cups sifted flour
1 cup ground nuts
1 teaspoon vanilla

Preheat oven to 350⁰. Mix together all the ingredients. Shape into 1 ½ inch balls. Bake for 10-15 minutes or until set. Roll in powdered sugar while still warm. *Yields 3 dozen.*

Dessert Empanadas

Pastry:
1 cup butter, softened
2 packages (3 ounce) cream cheese
2 cups sifted all-purpose flour
2 teaspoons lemon zest
cinnamon
sugar

Filling:
mincemeat
apricot or other fruit jam

In electric mixer on medium speed, cream butter and cream cheese until light and fluffy. At low speed, add flour. Add lemon zest. Shape dough in a ball, wrap in aluminum foil and refrigerate overnight. Take out of refrigerator 1 hour before rolling out on a bread board. Roll to ⅛ inch thickness. Cut in 2-2½ inch circles or squares. Place 1 teaspoon mincemeat or jam in center, and fold over in half, dampening edges with a little water, and seal with a dampened fork. Sprinkle with cinnamon and sugar, place on cookie sheet, and bake in a 375⁰ oven for 15-20 minutes.

Flan

½ cup sugar
4 eggs
1 can (14 ounce) Eagle Brand Condensed Milk
1 can (13 ounce) evaporated milk
2 cups whole milk
2 teaspoons vanilla, Mexican, if available

In heavy skillet, melt sugar until caramelized, stirring constantly. Pour into 2-quart mold. Beat eggs until lemon colored. Add milks and vanilla. Pour into mold. Place mold in pan with water in it (water bath) and bake about 1 hour at 350⁰. *Serves 6.*

Natillas (Boiled Custard)

4 eggs, separated
¾ cup sugar
¼ cup flour
⅛ teaspoon salt
4 cups milk
nutmeg

Beat egg yolks and stir in sugar, flour and salt. Mix until smooth. Put milk and yolk mixture in a saucepan; cook over medium heat until mixture thickens to a soft custard consistency. Remove from heat and cool to room temperature. Beat the egg whites until stiff and fold into the custard. Spoon into individual dishes; chill. Sprinkle with nutmeg before serving.
Serves 8.

Pinon Fudge

3 cups sugar
1 can (13 ounce) evaporated milk
1 teaspoon vanilla
½ cup pinon nuts

Melt 1 cup of the sugar in a heavy skillet (such as cast iron), stirring with a wooden spoon, until sugar is caramelized. Add remaining 2 cups of sugar and evaporated milk, stirring constantly. Cook to hard ball stage (250°-266°). Remove from heat. Add vanilla and beat until creamy. Add nuts. Pour into well buttered 8 inch pan. Cut into squares.

Pumpkin Flan

1⅔ cups sugar
3 cups half and half
2 cups canned pumpkin
1 teaspoon salt
¼ cup dark rum
6 eggs

In heavy skillet melt one cup sugar over low heat. When sugar is caramelized pour into ring mold, tilting mold to cover with caramel.

Mix together half and half, pumpkin, salt, ⅔ cup sugar, and rum. Add eggs, one at a time, beating well. Pour into ring mold. Place in pan of water and bake in 350° oven for 1 hour. Allow to cool, then invert on round serving dish.
Serves 6-8.

Para Mi Amante

4 cups strawberries
2 cups tequila

Wash strawberries; drain; hull berries. Cut each strawberry in half and place in air-tight jar. Pour tequila over berries and seal the jar. Refrigerate for at least 3 weeks. When ready to serve, strain into small stemmed glasses. Serve very cold.

Margarita Cocktail

1½ ounces Tequila
½ ounce Triple Sec
Juice of ½ lime

Stir with crushed ice. Rub rim of 3 ounce cocktail glass with rind of lime, dip rim in coarse salt, pour and serve.

Tequila Sour

Juice of ½ lemon
1 teaspoon powdered sugar
2 ounces Tequila

Shake well with cracked ice and strain into glass. Decorate with a half-slice of lemon and a cherry.

El Sueno (The Dream)

1 scoop lemon ice
1½ ounces rum

Pour rum over ice, stir together, and serve in your prettiest cocktail glass with a short straw plunged into the ice.

Black Charro

1½ ounces Kahlua
1½ ounces Tequila

Mix together and serve on the rocks.

Chocolate Mexicano

4 ounces Mexican chocolate (or 4 ounces sweet American chocolate)
4 cups milk
1 teaspoon ground cinnamon

Combine all and cook over a low heat, stirring constantly, until mixture is blended and all the chocolate has melted. Beat to a froth before serving.
It's fun to do as the Mexicans do when serving chocolate. Pour it in a large earthenware jug and bring it to the table steaming and foaming.

Savoring
Appetizers
& Beverages

A TOWN OF CLUBS

A town of clubs, societies, organizations - call them what you will - is usually one of intelligence. The old idea, that a woman should not be a club member, is dead, and today the good mother is the progressive mother.

Woman's Club

Roswell boasts of a number of these organizations and worthy of first mention is the "Woman's Club." To this club the town will stand indebted for its library.

The Cecilia is a musicial auxiliary of this club. The membership is limited to musicians. Mrs. D. M. Downes is the leader. The Shakespeare Club is also an auxiliary of the Woman's Club.

Shakespeare Club

The original plan of the club was for all of the Woman's Club who felt so disposed, to meet fortnightly and read Shakespeare. There was no constitution to govern its meetings, no officers to be responsible for the lessons.

The end of this organization was inevitable. It soon passed into its seventh act, sans members, sans interest, sans meetings, sans everything.

On Friday, March 21, 1902, the permanent organization was effected at the home of Mrs. C. E. Mason. Mrs. Mary E. Thorne, Mrs. Chas. Norvell, Mrs. J. A. B. Bear, Mrs. and Miss Marie Holt were present. Officers were elected and a constitution adopted. All who had attended the meeting of the old club were elected members of the new, and the membership limited to twenty. As the constitution stipulates that no officer shall serve for a longer period than one year, during the three years of the club's existence, it has been presided over by three presidents - Mrs. Thorne, Mrs. Mason and Mrs. Hill. This year and last the club has published Year Books outlining its course of study which has been exclusively Shakespeare and Parliamentary Law.

For the year 1904-1905 the lessons are from Macbeth, Twelfth Night and Julius Caesar. All the meetings of the club are conducted according to the strictest usage of parliamentary law.

The Social Circle

The oldest social organization in Roswell is known as the Social Circle.

There were seven charter members namely, Mrs. James Garrard, Mrs. Nathan Jaffa, Mrs. Joe Jaffa, Mrs. D. A. Starkweather, Mrs. W. S. Prager, Mrs. E. A. Cahoon and Mrs. Sidney Prager.

The ladies had met to do honor to one of their friends on her natal day. The afternoon proved so enjoyable an affair that they decided among themselves to make it a permanent social gathering.

Other ladies, numbering twelve in all the first year were invited to join. The name of the club was adopted, and it was agreed to meet every alternate Wednesday at the home of one of the members, where the time was to be spent in social intercourse.

Light refreshments were to be served and it was to be an entirely informal affair. There were no rules nor regulations but this was an unwritten law, that there was to be no unkind gossip about anyone.

Old members have dropped out and new ones have filled their places.

The number has been limited to fourteen members for several years. No new person is admitted unless a vacancy by resignation or as in two instances where loved members have joined the Social Circle in the great beyond.

Anna's Crab Ring

1 teaspoon unflavored gelatin
¼ cup cold water
2 packages (8 ounce) cream cheese
2 tablespoons sherry
¾ teaspoon seasoned salt
1 jar (2 ounce) pimientos, chopped
   and drained
1 can (6 ounce) crab meat, drained
   and flaked
⅛ teaspoon ground black pepper
¼ cup parsley, snipped

Sprinkle gelatin over cold water to soften. Then stir gelatin over hot water until dissolved. Beat cream cheese until smooth. Stir in sherry, seasoned salt, pimientos, crab meat, pepper and parsley. Put into a 3 cup mold. Refrigerate 4 hours until set. Unmold, garnish with parsley. Serve with club crackers or waverly wafers.

Beer Nuts

2 cups raw peanuts
1 cup sugar
½ cup water
salt

Slowly bring to low boil the first 3 ingredients until all water is gone and sugar is crystallized. Stir constantly. Spread peanuts on pan and salt. Bake 15 minutes in 300⁰ oven. Stir, salt again. Bake another 15 minutes. Cool completely before storing in tight container.

Brussels Sprouts with Bombay Dip

2 pounds fresh Brussels sprouts or
   one package (8 ounce) frozen
   sprouts
½ teaspoon salt
1 cup water

Bombay Dip:
1 cup mayonnaise or salad dressing
2 tablespoons lemon juice
2 teaspoons grated onion
2 teaspoons sugar
1 teaspoon curry powder

orange slices to garnish

Add ½ teaspoon salt to 1 cup water. Heat to boiling. Add Brussels sprouts. Cover and heat to boiling. Cook 6-8 minutes until crisp and tender. Drain, refrigerate. Mix remaining ingredients except orange slices to make dip in small bowl. Cover. Refrigerate at least 2 hours. To serve, arrange Brussels sprouts on orange slices around dip.

Carrot-Cashew Pate

2 tablespoons butter or margarine
1 small onion, sliced
1 clove garlic, minced or pressed
2 cups thinly sliced carrots
½ teaspoon curry powder
¾ teaspoon salt
⅔ cup water
1 cup cashews, salted and roasted
1½ to 2 tablespoons salad oil

In a wide frying pan, melt 2 tablespoons margarine over medium heat. Add onion and garlic. Cook, stirring occasionally, until onion is soft. Add 2 cups carrots, curry powder, salt and water. Cover tightly and cook, stirring occasionally, until carrots are tender, 6-8 minutes. Set aside. In blender, whirl ¾ cup salted roasted cashews until finely ground. Continue blending, gradually adding 1½ to 2 tablespoons salad oil until creamy and smooth. Add carrot mixture and whirl until smooth. Stir in ¼ cup chopped salted roasted cashews. Serve pate at room temperature with salted crackers or raw vegetables.
If made ahead, cook, cover and refrigerate. Yields 1½ cups.

Caviar Mousse

2 tablespoons lemon juice
2 tablespoons water
1 envelope unflavored gelatin
1 cup mayonnaise
1 teaspoon Worcestershire sauce
1 teaspoon onion powder
3 anchovies, minced or 1 teaspoon anchovy paste
6 hard-boiled eggs, sieved
1 jar (4 ounce) red caviar

Soften gelatin in lemon juice and water. Heat until gelatin dissolves. Mix anchovy paste with mayonnaise, onion powder, sieved eggs and Worcestershire sauce. Mix with gelatin. Carefully fold in caviar just to blend. Put in oiled mold. Chill overnight. Serve with crackers.
Serves 10 to 12.

Cheddar Cheese Ball

2 pounds Swiss cheese
1 pound sharp Cheddar cheese
5 tablespoons mayonnaise
¼ teaspoon garlic salt
½ medium onion, grated

Grate cheeses and mix all ingredients thoroughly. Shape and roll in paprika, chopped pecans or finely chopped parsley.
Serves 18.

Cheese Ball

3 packages (8 ounce) cream cheese
1 package Good Seasons Italian
   Dressing
¾ cup pecans, toasted
freshly ground pepper

Mix all ingredients well. Roll in cracked freshly ground pepper (will be black).
Keeps well - may be made 2 or 3 days ahead. Serves 10 to 12.

Macademia Cheese Ball

3 packages (8 ounce) cream cheese,
   softened
1 cup Macademia nuts, chopped
2 tablespoons Lawry's Seasoned
   Salt
1 can (12 ounce) crushed pineapple,
   drained
2 tablespoons onions, finely
   chopped
½ cup bell pepper, coarsely
   chopped
1 cup walnuts, finely chopped

Mix first 6 ingredients and refrigerate overnight. Roll in chopped walnuts before serving.

Chutney Pie

1 package (8 ounce) cream cheese,
   softened
1 teaspoon curry powder
2 tablespoons sherry
small jar (9 ounce) Major Grey's
   Chutney
1 bunch green onions, sliced thin

Mix cheese, curry powder and sherry. Pat mixture into greased 9 inch pie plate. Chill until 1 hour before serving. Turn onto platter and cover with chutney and green onions. Serve at room temperature with wheat crackers.

Dill Dip

1 cup mayonnaise
2 teaspoons Beau Monde seasoning
2 tablespoons minced chives
1 cup sour cream
2 teaspoons dill weed
1 teaspoon minced parsley

Mix all ingredients and stir well. Store for 24 hours in refrigerator. Serve with fresh raw vegetables.
Yields 2 cups.

Dip for Fresh Fruit

1 pint sour cream
½ cup brown sugar
1 teaspoon vanilla

Mix sour cream, brown sugar and vanilla. Place in bowl. Sprinkle 1 to 2 teaspoons brown sugar over top.
Place bowl of dip in center of a large round glass plate. Arrange fruit around it.

Camille's Spinach Dip

1 package frozen chopped spinach
½ cup chopped fresh parsley
¾ teaspoon salt
1 tablespoon sugar
¾ teaspoon Beau Monde seasoning
¼ cup chopped green onions
½ teaspoon dill weed
1 tablespoon lemon juice
1 cup mayonnaise
1 cup sour cream

Thaw and drain spinach. Combine all ingredients. Chill several hours before serving. Serve with fresh vegetables or chips.
This is good on baked potatoes or other cooked vegetables such as broccoli. Use in your chicken, egg or tuna salad. Recipe may be doubled - omitting the spinach until ready to use, since the spinach is the only ingredient that loses its color after several days. The rest will keep several weeks covered in the refrigerator.

Cocktail Ring Pate

1 can (10½ ounce) beef bouillon
1 envelope (one tablespoon)
  unflavored gelatin
1 package (8 ounce) cream cheese
1 package (8 ounce) liverwurst
½ tablespoon Worcestershire sauce

Soften gelatin in bouillon. Heat bouillon with gelatin until gelatin is dissolved. Pour ¾ of bouillon mixture into mold and refrigerate until firm. Blend cheese, liverwurst and Worcestershire sauce together until smooth. Spread this mixture over the firm mixture in mold. Pour the remainder of the bouillon mixture over the mold. Guide down around side of the mold with a wet knife. Refrigerate until firm, at least ½ hour before serving. Remove from mold and serve with crackers.
Serves 10 to 12.

Ham Stuffed Celery

2 tablespoons prepared horseradish
2 tablespoons mayonnaise
½ teaspoon seasoned salt
1 teaspoon Worcestershire sauce
⅛ teaspoon pepper
1 package (8 ounce) cream cheese
6 thin slices boiled ham
1 bunch celery

Process horseradish, mayonnaise, salt, sauce, pepper and cream cheese. Add boiled ham and process briefly. Stuff 4 inch stalks of celery and serve on platter.

Smoked Oyster Dip

1 package (8 ounce) cream cheese
1½ cups mayonnaise
4 drops hot sauce
1 tablespoon lemon juice
1 can (4½ ounce) black olives,
  chopped
1 can (3.66 ounce) smoked oysters,
  drained and chopped

Combine first 4 ingredients, mixing well. Stir in olives and oysters. Serve with raw vegetables or crackers.

Chicken Liver Pate

½ pound butter
1 pound fresh chicken livers
¾ cup coarsely chopped onion
½ cup finely chopped celery
1½ cups chicken broth
½ teaspoon paprika
salt and pepper
1 clove garlic, crushed
½ cup brandy
1 envelope unflavored gelatin
1 cup chopped toasted almonds
2 hard-cooked eggs, chopped
  coarsely

In heavy enameled saucepan, melt butter, add chicken livers, onion, and celery and saute gently for about 10 minutes, or until livers are browned but pink in the center, and onions and celery softened. Add half the chicken broth to pan, and paprika, salt, pepper, and garlic. Simmer a few minutes, then remove from heat and add brandy. In a separate saucepan, dissolve gelatin in rest of chicken broth. Then slowly bring it to a simmer until all the grains disappear. Turn off heat and let it stand. Process until smooth; stir in gelatin stock, almonds, and hard-cooked eggs. Pour into 6-cup mold and refrigerate overnight. *Yields 6 cups.*

Liver Sausage Spread

Mix #1:
1 pound liver sausage
¼ teaspoon garlic salt
½ teaspoon sweet basil
3 tablespoons minced onion
½ cup mayonnaise to spread

Mix #2:
1 package (8 ounce) cream cheese
⅛ teaspoon garlic salt
⅛ teaspoon Tabasco sauce
½ cup mayonnaise or cream to
  spread (cream is better)

Mold mix #1 in a small round bowl and chill. Unmold and frost with cream cheese mixture, mix #2. Sprinkle with minced parsley or chives. Serve with crackers or rounds of rye bread. Can be made a day ahead. Cover with plastic wrap and refrigerate. Add chives or parsley just before serving.
Serves 15 - 20.

THE ROSWELL REGISTER   APRIL 25, 1902

TO KILL THE MOTH

Mr. C. W. Haynes has a method for killing the moth that produce the catarpillars that will soon be marring the beauty of the foliage on our trees. Mr. Haynes recommends the hanging of a lantern in the trees under which is placed a bucket or pan of water. The moths will be attracted to the light and striking the lantern will fall into the water.

Liver Pate

1 pound chicken livers
½ cup chopped onion
1 package (3 ounce) cream cheese
3 tablespoons Madeira wine
⅛ teaspoon crushed thyme
1 teaspoon salt
freshly ground pepper to taste

Cook chicken livers until soft but still pink inside. Combine with other ingredients and blend or process until smooth. Spoon into a bowl and cover with plastic wrap and refrigerate at least 24 hours. Serve with crackers.
Yields 2½ cups.

Mushrooms Mario

1 pound large mushrooms
5 tablespoons butter, divided
8 ounces chicken livers
3 ounces cream cheese
salt and pepper
¼ teaspoon tarragon

Remove stems from mushrooms and chop. Saute caps for 5 minutes in 3 tablespoons butter. Remove from pan. Add to pan and brown 2 tablespoons butter and the chicken livers. Cool and chop. Cream the cream cheese, liver mixture, salt, pepper, tarragon; place into mushroom caps and chill thoroughly.

Mushroom Spread Capitan

⅔ cup finely chopped fresh
   mushrooms
3 teaspoons butter
1 tablespoon finely chopped chives
   or onions
1 teaspoon paprika
dash Tabasco
1 teaspoon lemon juice
1 package (3 ounce) cream cheese,
   softened
2 tablespoons mayonnaise

Saute mushrooms in butter. Add chives and seasonings. Remove from heat and blend in the remaining ingredients. Serve at room temperature on small crackers.

Marinated Mushrooms

2 pounds small fresh mushrooms
⅔ cup wine vinegar
½ cup oil
2 cloves garlic, sliced or crushed
2 teaspoons salt
½ cup parsley, chopped
1 tablespoon Dijon mustard
2 tablespoons brown sugar

Wipe mushrooms. Heat vinegar, oil, garlic and salt, parsley, mustard and sugar. Bring to a boil. Add mushrooms. Simmer 15 minutes. Allow to cool in liquid. Refrigerate. Drain and serve with cocktail picks.

Salmon Mousse

1 envelope unflavored gelatin
¼ cup cold water
½ cup boiling water
½ cup mayonnaise
2 tablespoons lemon juice
1½ tablespoons grated onion
½ teaspoon Tabasco
1½ teaspoons salt
2 tablespoons finely chopped
    capers
½ teaspoon paprika
2 cups salmon, drained and mashed
½ cup whipping cream

Soften gelatin in cold water. Add hot water and stir to dissolve. Cool. Fold remaining ingredients, except cream, together. Add gelatin and mix well. Whip the cream and fold into mixture. Pour mixture into an oiled fish mold or individual molds. Refrigerate until set. Unmold and top with Dill Dressing. Serve with crackers.
Serves 8.

DILL DRESSING:
¾ teaspoon salt
¼ teaspoon white pepper
1 teaspoon grated lemon rind
2 cups sour cream
3 tablespoons finely chopped fresh
    dill or 1 tablespoon dill weed

Mix well and chill.

Shrimp Cheese Stack

2 packages (8 ounce) cream cheese
2 tablespoons Worcestershire sauce
¼ teaspoon lemon peel
1 tablespoon lemon juice
½ cup thinly sliced green onion
⅛ teaspoon liquid hot pepper
  seasoning
12 ounce bottle tomato-based chili
  sauce
1 tablespoon horseradish
¾ pound small cooked shrimp
assorted crackers

Beat together the first 6 ingredients until smooth. Spread on a 10-12 inch rimmed serving plate. Cover and chill if made ahead. To serve: Stir together the chili sauce and horseradish. Spread over cheese mixture. Top with the shrimp. Serve with assorted crackers.
Serves 12 to 16.

Shrimp Marinade

1 pound jumbo shrimp, cooked and
  peeled (leave shell on tail)
1 onion, thinly sliced
2 packages Good Seasons Italian
  Dressing, mixed according to
  directions on package
2 tablespoons horseradish
4 teaspoons dry mustard
2 cloves garlic, minced

Place shrimp in a shallow glass bowl. Scatter onions over shrimp. Mix next four ingredients well. Pour dressing over shrimp, covering all shrimp. Refrigerate overnight. Serve chilled.
Serves 10-12.

Jada's Shrimp

5 pounds shrimp, cleaned and
  deveined
4 packages (8 ounce) cream cheese
1½ cups mayonnaise
juice of 4 lemons
1 large onion, finely grated
2 tablespoons sour cream
dash Tabasco
4 teaspoons Worcestershire sauce

Boil shrimp according to directions or until shrimp turns pink, cool, peel, and devein. Have cheese at room temperature. Make sauce by combining all ingredients except shrimp. Mix until smooth. Then add cool shrimp. Remove from refrigerator ½ hour before serving.
Serves 25 to 30.

Spinach Sandwich Filling

2 cups mayonnaise
½ cup parsley sprigs
½ small onion, chopped
1 small clove garlic
1 tablespoon lemon juice
¼ teaspoon pepper
1 package (10 ounce) frozen
   spinach, thawed, drained on
   paper towels
1 package (8 ounce) cream cheese

In covered blender or food processor blend all ingredients at high speed just until finely chopped. Cover; refrigerate at least 4 hours.
Can be made one or two days before serving.
Yields 3 cups.

Artichoke Quiche

2 jars (6 ounce) marinated artichoke
   hearts. Reserve the marinade
   from 1 jar
1 small onion, finely chopped
1 clove garlic, minced
4 eggs
¼ cup fine dry bread crumbs
¼ teaspoon salt
⅛ teaspoon pepper
⅛ teaspoon oregano
⅛ teaspoon Tabasco
½ pound sharp Cheddar cheese,
   shredded
2 tablespoons minced parsley

Drain artichokes, reserving liquid from 1 jar. Put liquid in a skillet. Put artichokes in a food processor and chop. To liquid in skillet add onion, garlic and saute until limp, about 5 minutes. In a bowl, beat eggs, bread crumbs, salt, pepper, Tabasco and oregano. Stir in cheese and parsley. Add artichoke and onion mixture. Put into a well greased baking pan 7 inch x 11 inch or 9 inch square and bake at 325° for 30 minutes or until knife inserted in middle comes out clean. Cut into squares. Serve warm or cold.
Serves 8 to 10.

Cheese Straws

1 cup sifted flour
½ teaspoon baking powder
1 cup grated Cheddar cheese
½ cup butter
3 tablespoons cold water

Mix together to form dough. Place in cookie press. Press onto cookie sheet and bake in 400° oven for 8-10 minutes.
Yields 3 dozen.

Cheese Puffs

1 package frozen puff pastry,
  thawed
1 recipe pate a chou, note below
1½ cups freshly grated Parmesan
  cheese, divided
⅜ teaspoon cayenne pepper
1 egg
2 tablespoons milk
½ cup grated Gruyere cheese

On a floured surface roll puff pastry into a square ¹⁄₁₆ inch thick. Cut with a pastry wheel into 2½ inch squares. Make pate a chou and combine it with 1 cup Parmesan cheese and cayenne pepper. Place 1 tablespoon on each pastry square. Combine egg with milk to make a wash. Brush edges of squares with the wash and the tops of the puffs. Sprinkle tops with mixture of Gruyere cheese and remaining ½ cup of Parmesan cheese.
Bring 4 corners of the squares up over the puffs to center and pinch them together to seal them. Brush the pastries with remaining egg wash. Bake in the middle of a preheated 400° oven for 20 to 25 minutes. Immediately remove from baking sheet to rack and serve warm. The cheese puffs can be frozen and reheated at 375° for 10 minutes.
Yields 16.

Pate a Chou:
1 cup water
½ cup butter, cut into pieces
¼ teaspoon salt
1 cup flour
3 eggs

In a heavy saucepan over high heat, bring water, butter, and salt to a boil. Reduce heat and add flour all at once. Beat the mixture with a wooden spoon until it leaves the sides of the pan and forms a ball. Transfer the dough to the bowl of an electric mixer and mix at high speed. Add eggs, one at a time, beating well after each addition. The batter should be thick enough to hold soft peaks.

Toasted Cheese Squares

½ pound Cheddar cheese, grated
12 tablespoons butter, softened
2 egg whites
1 large sandwich loaf of unsliced
  bread

Mix together cheese, soft butter and egg whites; then beat in mixer until fluffy. Remove crusts from bread and cut bread into 1 inch squares. Frost on all but bottom side with cheese mix. Cook at 400° for 10-12 minutes or until edges brown, or place on cookie sheet and freeze. Then place in freezer bags and store. (Frozen squares will take a few minutes longer to cook . . . 12-15 minutes.)

Ham Crescents

Filling:
10 ounces ham, diced small
1¼ cups butter, well chilled
2 tablespoons flour

Pastry:
3½ cups flour
1 envelope dry yeast
1 teaspoon sugar
¼ teaspoon salt
½ cup butter
pepper
nutmeg
1 egg
1 tablespoon milk
1 egg yolk

Mix ham, butter and flour. Roll into a rectangle of 8 x 11 inches and put into the refrigerator on a wooden board. For pastry, put flour in mixing bowl, add yeast, sugar, salt, butter, pepper, nutmeg, and egg. Pour 1 cup lukewarm water over mixture and make dough. Let rest in warm place for 12 to 15 minutes. Punch down and work into a ball and refrigerate for 10 minutes. Roll into 12 x 16 inch rectangle. Put the ham and butter rectangle on the right side of the pastry rectangle, fold left side over, press sides together. Roll on floured work surface into a 14 x 18 inch rectangle. Fold one-third of pastry leaf over and fold other one-third on top, pressing slightly. Cover and refrigerate for 10 minutes. Roll into 14 x 22 inch rectangle, again folding, pressing slightly and refrigerating for 10 minutes. Then roll to a 14 x 23½ inch rectangle. Cut into triangles 2 x 2 x 3 inches. Brush with water, roll up, and form into crescents. Put on lightly buttered baking sheet, and brush with egg yolk and milk mixture. Bake in middle of preheated 425⁰ oven for 20-25 minutes. Serve warm.
Can be frozen and reheated at 375° for 10 minutes.
Yields 40 crescents.

Helen's Cocktail Meatballs

½ pound ground smoked ham
¾ pound ground beef
¾ pound ground pork
1 cup milk
2 cups wheat flakes, crushed
2 eggs, unbeaten
1 teaspoon salt

Combine and shape into small marble-size balls.

Sauce:
1¼ cups brown sugar
½ cup red cider vinegar
1 cup water
1 teaspoon dry mustard

Make sauce and pour over meatballs. Bake at 350⁰ for 1¼ hours.
Can be frozen and re-heated.

Hot Crabmeat Appetizer

1 package (6 ounces) frozen
   crabmeat, defrosted
1 package (8 ounces) cream cheese
2 tablespoons milk
1 teaspoon horseradish
dash liquid hot pepper seasoning
¼ teaspoon salt
2 tablespoons finely minced onion
paprika
minced parsley

Remove cartilage from crabmeat. Flake. Blend together cream cheese and milk. Add crabmeat along with horseradish, hot pepper seasoning, salt and onion. Stir well. Put into small casserole. Heat in 375º oven for 15 minutes or until bubbly and hot. Remove from oven. Sprinkle with paprika and chopped parsley. Serve hot with crackers.

Hot Broccoli Dip

2 packages (10 ounce) frozen
   broccoli, chopped
½ cup butter or margarine
1 cup green onions, sliced with
   tops
1 cup chopped celery
1 cup fresh chopped parsley
2 tablespoons flour
1 can (10¾ ounce) mushroom soup,
   undiluted
1 can (4 ounce) sliced mushrooms
1 roll garlic cheese, cubed
1 teaspoon creamy style
   horseradish

Cook broccoli as directed on package, cool. In skillet melt margarine, add onions, celery and saute until tender. Add parsley and flour; stir until smooth. Stir in soup, mushrooms, cheese cubes and horseradish. Heat until cheese melts. GENTLY fold in broccoli. Serve in chafing dish. Serve with sliced French bread or crackers.
Yields 5 cups.

Hacienda Artichoke

1 can (14 ounce) artichokes in water
1 cup mayonnaise
1 cup grated Parmesan cheese

Drain artichokes. Cut in quarters. Place in small greased flat baking dish. Mix mayonnaise and cheese. Spoon on top of artichokes and bake in 350º oven for 20 minutes until cheese melts. Serve hot with rye crackers.
Serves 10-12.

Hot Mushroom Dip

4 slices bacon
½ pound fresh mushrooms, sliced
1 medium onion, finely chopped
1 garlic clove, minced
¼ teaspoon salt
⅛ teaspoon freshly ground pepper
1 package (8 ounce) cream cheese,
  cut into small pieces
2 teaspoons Worcestershire sauce
2 teaspoons soy sauce
½ cup sour cream
assorted crackers or breadsticks

Fry bacon until crisp. Drain, reserve 2 tablespoons drippings in pan. Add mushrooms, onions, garlic and cook over medium heat until tender and liquid from mushrooms has evaporated. Add salt, pepper, cream cheese, Worcestershire and soy sauce. Stir until cheese is melted. Remove from heat and stir in sour cream and crumbled bacon. Serve warm in chafing dish.
Yield: 2½ - 3 cups.

Hot Clam Mushroom Ripple

1 pound fresh mushrooms, sliced
2 tablespoons butter
1 package (8 ounce) cream cheese
4 green onions, chopped
1 can (6½ ounce) minced, drained
  clams
1 teaspoon Worcestershire sauce
1 teaspoon soy sauce
1 teaspoon lemon juice

Saute mushrooms in butter until tender. Blend in next 6 ingredients which have been creamed together. Heat and keep warm in chafing dish. Serve with crackers or chips.

Hot Shrimp Dip

2 packages (8 ounce) cream cheese
1 medium fresh ripe tomato,
  chopped fine
1 medium onion, chopped fine
2 to 3 jalapeno peppers, chopped
  fine
1 to 2 large size banana peppers,
  chopped fine
1 to 2 cloves garlic, chopped fine or
  put through garlic press
1 cup cooked shrimp, chopped

Combine above ingredients and heat over hot water (double boiler) until mixture can be blended well with spoon. Keep hot. For a milder taste, you may use 1 jalapeno pepper and 1 banana pepper.

Chafing Dish Meatballs

1 pound ground steak
salt and pepper to taste
1 egg, slightly beaten
1 tablespoon heavy cream
1 or 2 tablespoons flour
2 tablespoons butter
1 cup chili sauce
½ cup grape jelly
juice of ½ lemon

Mix meat, salt, pepper, egg and cream. Add enough flour just to hold meatballs together. Make very small. Melt butter in skillet. Brown meatballs at 325°, turning carefully to avoid piercing. Mix chili sauce, grape jelly, and lemon juice in small saucepan. Heat to boiling to dissolve jelly. Pour over meatballs and simmer for 30 minutes.

Fingerlings

2½ pounds chicken wings
1 cup mayonnaise
1 cup cornflake crumbs
¼ cup Parmesan cheese
salt and pepper to taste

Cut off and discard tips of chicken wings. Divide each wing in half at joint. Brush chicken well with mayonnaise. Mix cornflake crumbs with Parmesan cheese. Roll chicken in crumb mixture. Arrange in single layer in baking pan. Bake 45 minutes at 375°.
Serves 10.

Ham Nuggets

½ pound ground fully cooked ham
½ pound ground fresh pork
¼ cup green onions, chopped
   including tops
1 can (5 ounce) water chestnuts,
   drained and finely chopped
1 egg, slightly beaten
1 tablespoon milk
1 small clove garlic, crushed

Thoroughly mix all ingredients and chill. Form into marble-size meatballs. Brown slowly on all sides in small amount of hot shortening. Continue cooking, turning frequently, until meat is cooked through. Serve hot with hot mustard or horseradish sauce.
Yields 5 dozen.

Mushroom or Shrimp Turnovers

Dough:
4 ounces cream cheese
½ cup butter
1 cup flour

Cream cheese and butter. Add flour and work until smooth. Chill 2 hours. Roll dough to ¼ inch thickness on floured surface. Cut into rounds with a 2 inch cookie cutter. Place teaspoon of filling in center. Fold dough over. Place on ungreased cookie sheet. Bake at 400° 15-20 minutes or until brown.

Mushroom Filling:
1 large onion, chopped
1 teaspoon margarine
¼ pound mushrooms, chopped
¼ teaspoon thyme
salt and pepper
2 tablespoons flour
¼ cup cream

Cook onion in butter until soft. Add mushrooms and cook 5 minutes. Add remaining ingredients. Cook, stirring until all liquid is evaporated. Cool before spreading on pastry.

Shrimp Filling:
1 can (6½ ounce) or 1 cup frozen tiny shrimp, cooked and diced
2 tablespoons mayonnaise
½ teaspoon lemon juice
2 to 3 tablespoons green onions, chopped

Combine with mayonnaise, lemon juice and green onions.

Rich Cream Cheese Dough for Tarts

2½ cups flour
½ teaspoon salt
½ cup butter
½ cup margarine
8 ounces cream cheese
⅓ cup cream
⅛ cup water

Mix flour and salt. Combine butter, margarine and cream cheese. Cut in flour. Whip cream and water together and add to other mixture. Mix thoroughly; chill 2 hours. Make small balls and press into individual tart tins. Fill with Cheese Quiche Tarts.
See Index.

Cheese Quiche Tarts

1 cup grated Swiss cheese, divided
2 eggs
1 cup heavy cream
1 teaspoon Dijon mustard
½ teaspoon dry mustard
⅛ teaspoon freshly grated nutmeg
¼ teaspoon salt
⅛ teaspoon white pepper

Place cheese in bottom of pastry tart. Combine eggs, cream, mustard, nutmeg, salt and pepper. Mix thoroughly and add filling to pastry. Then sprinkle more cheese on top. Bake in 350° oven for 15 to 20 minutes or until crust is slightly brown.

Oriental Rumaki

Marinade:
½ cup maple blended syrup
⅓ cup soy sauce
2 tablespoons vinegar

Appetizer:
12 chicken livers
2 cans (5 ounce) water chestnuts, drained
18 bacon slices, cut in half

For marinade, combine syrup, soy sauce and vinegar. Cut each chicken liver in thirds. Cut water chestnuts into ¼ inch slices. For each appetizer, wrap a piece of liver and a slice of water chestnut together in a half slice of bacon. Secure with a wooden toothpick. Place appetizer in marinade, cover and refrigerate overnight. Place on rack in pan. Bake at 400° for 20 minutes; drain. *Yield: 36 pieces.*

Rumaki

¾ pound chicken livers, washed, drained and cut in half
1 can water chestnuts
½ pound bacon
½ cup soy sauce or teriyaki sauce
1 small clove garlic, crushed
1 to 2 drops Tabasco
toothpicks

Wrap liver around water chestnut. Wrap in half slice of bacon and fasten with toothpick. Mix soy sauce, garlic and Tabasco. Marinate livers in sauce for several hours. Drain and place on rack in shallow pan and broil 5-7 minutes, turning once. Bacon should be crisp. *Serves 18.*

Spinach Puffs

2 packages (10 ounce) frozen
  spinach, chopped
2 cups herb stuffing mix
1 onion, finely chopped
6 eggs, beaten
¾ cup butter, melted
½ cup grated Parmesan cheese
1 teaspoon garlic salt
½ teaspoon thyme
½ teaspoon black pepper
1 tablespoon MSG (monosodium
  glutamate)

Cook spinach according to directions on package. Drain well. Add all remaining ingredients and mix. Roll into balls. Sprinkle with additional Parmesan cheese; freeze. Bake 20 to 25 minutes at 350⁰.
Yields 75 balls.

Sandia Oysters

2 dozen medium size oysters
½ cup chili sauce
1 tablespoon chopped bell pepper
1 tablespoon chopped green chile
1 tablespoon Worcestershire sauce
6 slices uncooked bacon, finely
  diced
¾ cup Parmesan cheese

Place oysters, well drained, in ovenproof casserole. Combine chili sauce, bell pepper, green chile and Worcestershire sauce; pour over oysters. Put in 350⁰ oven for 5 minutes, or until oysters begin to puff. Sprinkle with bacon and cheese; continue baking for 10 minutes. Transfer to chafing dish for serving.

Sesame Toast

2 tablespoons sesame seeds
2 tablespoons butter

Herb Butter:
6 tablespoons butter
¼ teaspoon basil
¼ teaspoon rosemary
¼ teaspoon marjoram
1 small loaf thin sliced bread

Brown sesame seeds in 2 tablespoons butter. Blend 6 tablespoons butter and herbs. Let stand overnight. Trim crusts from bread. Cut each bread slice into thirds. Spread with herb butter. Bake 20 minutes at 300⁰ or until browned. These can be prepared ahead of time.

Sauerkraut Balls

4 tablespoons butter or margarine
1 medium onion, finely chopped
1⅓ cups ham, finely chopped
½ garlic clove, finely chopped
4 tablespoons flour
1 tablespoon parsley, finely
   chopped
3 cups sauerkraut, finely chopped,
   drained well
½ cup sauerkraut juice (from
   drained sauerkraut)

Breading:
1 egg
1 pint milk
2½ cups flour
2 cups bread crumbs

Brown onion in butter; add ham and garlic and brown slightly. Stir in flour; cook thoroughly. Add sauerkraut and parsley. Mix thoroughly. Cook until stiff; cool. Form into balls one inch in diameter. Beat egg and milk together. Roll balls in flour, egg mixture and bread crumbs. Fry in deep fat. *Excellent served with cocktails. Can be prepared ahead. Can be frozen after frying. (Reheat in 425° oven for 15 minutes or until crispy.) Yields 50.*

Baked Stuffed Mushrooms

16 large fresh mushrooms
2 tablespoons butter
salt
pepper
¼ teaspoon thyme
¼ teaspoon oregano
1 clove garlic, minced
¼ cup finely chopped parsley
4 teaspoons grated Parmesan
   cheese
2 teaspoons bread crumbs
peanut oil

Wash mushrooms and remove stems. Chop stems very fine and saute in butter over low heat until dry. Add remaining ingredients, adding enough oil to moisten. Stuff mushroom caps with mixture. Bake in greased pan 15 to 20 minutes at 375°. Baste with butter. Serve hot. *These can be frozen after they are baked. To serve, be sure they are heated thoroughly and piping hot.*

Won Tons

1 pound lean ground pork
1 can (6 ounce) water chestnuts
4 green onions, thinly sliced
2 tablespoons soy sauce
¼ teaspoon garlic salt
2 tablespoons dry Sherry
1 tablespoon cornstarch
1 package (1 pound) Won Ton skins
1 egg, beaten
salad oil

Cook pork until brown and crumbly. Stir in drained and chopped water chestnuts, onion, soy sauce and garlic salt. Mix sherry with cornstarch and add to pork mixture; cook for 3 minutes. Cool filling before wrapping and frying Won Tons. Serve with hot mustard for dipping.
Procedure for making Won Tons:
Put 1 teaspoon filling in the corner of skin, moisten with egg, fold egg moistened corner over filling, rolling to tuck point under. Moisten both corners of filling ends with egg, bring these corners together and pinch slightly to seal. Continue until all Won Ton skins are filled. Heat 2 inches of oil and fry Won Tons until golden.
Can be frozen and reheated in 350° oven for 15 minutes.
Yields 6 dozen.

Salmon Stuffed Pasta Shells

1 package (12 ounce) large conch
   shaped pasta shells
2 eggs, beaten
2 cups ricotta cheese
½ cup chopped green pepper
¼ cup chopped onion
¼ cup snipped fresh parsley
¼ cup milk or light cream
½ teaspoon shredded lemon peel
½ teaspoon salt
¼ teaspoon ground mace
1 can (15 ounce) salmon, drained,
   boned and flaked
⅓ cup fine dry bread crumbs
⅓ cup grated Parmesan cheese
2 tablespoons butter or margarine,
   melted

Cook pasta in boiling water 9 minutes or until just tender. Drain. Rinse with cold water, drain and set aside. Combine all other ingredients except bread crumbs, Parmesan cheese and butter. Spoon mixture into shells. Place filled side up in 13 x 9 x 2 inch dish. Add 2 tablespoons water to dish. Cover, bake at 350º for 30 mintues. Combine remaining three ingredients and sprinkle over shell. Bake uncovered 5 minutes or until crumbs are browned. Serve hot. Garnish with lemon or lime wedges, if desired.
Shells can be filled ahead of time, covered and refrigerated, then baked as needed.
Great for party hors d'oeuvres or serve several together on a plate as a first course.

Spinach Feta Strudel

2 pounds spinach (fresh or frozen)
¼ cup butter
12 green onions, minced
6 ounces feta cheese, coarsely chopped
½ cup bread crumbs
½ cup minced parsley
4 egg whites
2 tablespoons dried dill weed
salt and freshly ground pepper
¾ pound phyllo leaves
1 cup unsalted butter, melted

Cook spinach for 5 minutes. Put in colander and press out all moisture. Puree in food processor or blender. Cook onions in ¼ cup butter for 5 minutes. Combine spinach puree, onions, feta cheese, 2 tablespoons bread crumbs, parsley, egg whites, dill, salt and pepper in food processor and blend well.

Cover phyllo leaves with wax paper and wrap in damp towel until ready to use. Place a damp towel on counter. Put first phyllo leaf on towel and brush with some of the melted butter, sprinkle with 1 teaspoon bread crumbs. Place second leaf on top of first leaf. Repeat brushing with butter and sprinkling bread crumbs. Repeat this process with 2 more leaves. Spread ⅓ of spinach mixture on phyllo and roll up tightly. Place on a buttered baking sheet. One strudel is now complete. make two more strudels repeating the above process. Brush strudels with melted butter and bake in a 375⁰ oven for 30-35 minutes; cut into 1 inch slices.
Serves 40.

THE ROSWELL DAILY RECORD   DECEMBER 6, 1904

Chafing Dish Clubs

The Chafing-Dish Club was organized in October, 1902, in a very informal way and has always been informal. The charter members were:

Mesdames Pruit, Stone, Morrow, Earle, Veal, N. Jaffa, H. Jaffa, McGaffey, Willson, Joyce, Poe and Slaughter.

Music, cards, fancy-work or darning are the amusements. The refreshments are always prepared on the Chafing-Dish. The hostess in each instance showing the members how to prepare the things served. The club adjourns for the summer in June.

There is also a Chafing-Dish club of young ladies who meet for a jolly good time, good things to eat and for learning an art that may be of use in the future.

Other Clubs

There is a Polo Club, Tennis Club, Golf Club, a good baseball organization, and numberless smaller social and literary clubs. One of Roswell's possibilities is an organization of Daughters of the Revolution; one of her needs is a humane society.

Apricot Liqueur

1 pound dried apricots
1 quart vodka
1 cup sugar

In large container, combine all ingredients; cover loosely. Let stand 7 weeks, stirring once every two weeks. Serve as after-dinner liqueur.

Apricots may be removed from liqueur and used: fold into vanilla pudding, bread pudding, rice pudding, Christmas fruit cakes and fruit balls. Stuff brandied apricot with cream cheese. Serve with toothpick. Apricots can be dipped in candy-making chocolate and given as gifts along with the liqueur.

Bourbon Slush

1 can (12 ounce) frozen lemonade
1 can (6 ounce) frozen orange juice
6 cups water
½ cup sugar
2 cups brewed strong tea
1½ cups bourbon

Mix all ingredients and freeze. Stir after 2-3 hours and repeat if necessary to avoid having all the slushy bourbon on the bottom and hard ice on top. Make 24 hours ahead.
Serves 25.

Cappuccino

1 package sweet chocolate mix
1 ounce Cognac
6 ounces hot coffee
heavy cream, whipped

Mix chocolate and cognac. Add coffee, stir well, top with whipped cream.
Serves 1.

THE ROSWELL REGISTER   APRIL 3, 1896

A. M. Robertson has a car-load of Manitou Water which is the best of all American mineral waters. It is a splendid drink for women and children, and then it is the most palatable solution with which to wash down straight whiskey, or use in a long toddy.

Hot Buttered Rum #1

Ice Cream Mixture:
1 quart vanilla ice cream, softened
1 pound butter, softened
1 pound powdered sugar
1 pound brown sugar
½ teaspoon cinnamon
½ teaspoon nutmeg
1½ ounces rum per cup
boiling water as needed

Mix first 6 ingredients together. Store in large sealed container in refrigerator. To serve add together in large mug: 1½ scoops of ice cream mixture, 1½ ounces rum and fill the remainder of cup with boiling water.
Can be frozen.

Hot Buttered Rum #2

½ cup butter
1 pound dark brown sugar
¼ teaspoon ground cinnamon
¼ teaspoon nutmeg
¼ teaspoon cloves
dark Puerto Rican Rum

Cream butter with dark brown sugar. Mix cinnamon, nutmeg and cloves thoroughly into batter. To store, refrigerate in covered container.

The drink:
Into each cup or mug place 1 heaping tablespoon of batter. Add 1½ ounces rum. Fill with boiling water, stir and serve.

Coffee Liqueur

2 cups sugar
1¼ cups distilled water
4 tablespoons instant coffee
½ cup distilled water
2½ tablespoons pure vanilla extract
½ pint (190 proof) grain alcohol

Bring water and sugar to boil until sugar is dissolved. Add 4 tablespoons instant coffee, mix well. Add ½ cup distilled water; cool. Add vanilla extract. When completely cool, add ½ pint 190 proof grain alcohol. Add enough distilled water to make 1 quart.
Yields 1 quart.

THE ROSWELL REGISTER   APRIL 3, 1896

Choice imported and domestic wines are to be obtained at the Legal Tender.

Frozen Strawberry Daiquiri

1 package (10 ounce) frozen sliced
   strawberries
1 can (6 ounce) frozen daiquiri mix
¾ cup light rum
3 cups ice cubes

Thaw strawberries enough to cut the block into cubes. In blender container, place strawberry cubes, frozen mix, and rum. Cover and blend. While blender is running, add ice cubes, a few at a time, blending until ice is melted. Pour into 2 refrigerator trays or a half-gallon plastic container. Cover and freeze several hours or overnight. Mixture will not freeze firm. To serve, spoon into cocktail or sherbet glasses. Garnish with whole, fresh strawberries, if desired. Store any unused portion in covered container in freezer. *Serves 5.*

Glogg

2 teaspoons dried orange peel
1 teaspoon whole cloves
4 whole cardamon, cracked
3 short sticks cinnamon
2 bottles (⅘ quart size) Burgundy
1 cup dark raisins
1 package (8 ounce) dried apricots,
   cut in small pieces
1 bottle (⅘ quart size) Vodka
¾ cup sugar
1 cup whole blanched almonds

Place spices and orange peel in a cheesecloth bag. Put Burgundy and fruits in a pan and simmer 30 minutes. Remove from heat and discard spices. Stir in remaining wine, Vodka, sugar and cover. Let stand overnight. To serve, heat, but *do not boil.* Stir occasionally. Optional: Carefully ignite mixture with a match. Let burn a few seconds. Serve in a punch bowl.
Serves 20 — ½ cup servings.

Mexican Mocoa

¼ cup cocoa
3 tablespoons sugar
dash of salt
⅓ cup water
3 cups milk
2 tablespoons Kahlua
whipped cream, flavored with a
   dash of Kahlua

In a saucepan, mix together the first four ingredients. Bring to a boil and boil gently two minutes, stirring constantly. Add the milk and immediately lower heat. Keep over low heat, stirring gently until heated through. Take off the heat and stir in the Kahlua. Serve in cups or mugs topped with the whipped cream.
Yield: 4 cups.

Fruit Punch Favorite

1 cup sugar
1 cup lime juice, freshly squeezed
1 cup orange juice, freshly squeezed
1 cup grape juice
2 cups cold water or ginger ale

Combine all ingredients in a large pitcher or bowl. Stir briskly until sugar dissolves. Chill until ready to serve and pour over crushed ice.

Orange & Pineapple Punch

3 cups sugar
9 cups water
6 cups orange juice
4 cups pineapple juice
1 cup lemon juice
4 cups orange pekoe and black pekoe tea, combined
4 quarts ginger ale

Cook sugar and water together until sugar dissolves. Keep other ingredients cold until ready to mix. Mix all ingredients together and serve in punch bowl.
Serves 42.

Symphony Punch

1 quart pineapple juice
1 quart orange juice
1 quart lemonade
1 to 2 bottles champagne or ginger ale

Combine first 3 ingredients. Add the champagne or ginger ale just before serving.
Yield: 1 gallon.

White Sangria

1 bottle (750 ml.) dry white wine
½ cup Curacoa
¼ cup sugar
1 orange, thinly sliced
1 lemon, thinly sliced
1 lime, thinly sliced
4 or 5 large strawberries, sliced
1 bottle (10 ounce) club soda
ice

Combine wine, Curacoa, and sugar in a pitcher and stir until sugar is dissolved. Add sliced fruits. Cover and chill in refrigerator at least 1 hour to allow flavors to blend. Before serving, add club soda and ice. Serve in stemmed glasses.
Serves 6.

Banana Smoothie

1 banana, sliced
½ cup plain yogurt
½ cup orange juice
3 tablespoons honey
nutmeg

Put all ingredients except nutmeg into blender and blend until smooth. Pour into tall glass. Sprinkle with nutmeg.
Serves 1.

Cantaloupe Frappe

1 cantaloupe, peeled, seeded and cubed
2 scoops vanilla ice cream
sprig of mint

Put cantaloupe and ice cream into blender and blend until smooth. Pour into tall glass and garnish with a sprig of mint.
Serves 2.

Milk Punch

½ gallon coffee ice cream
½ gallon milk
2 cups bourbon
nutmeg

Place ice cream in punch bowl. Combine milk and bourbon; pour over ice cream. Stir to break up ice cream. Sprinkle lightly with nutmeg.
Serves 15-20.

Mint Tea

4 cups boiling water
2 "family size" tea bags
12 sprigs mint
juice of 2 lemons
¾ cup sugar
6 cups water

Pour 4 cups boiling water over tea bags and mint. Allow to steep 10 minutes. Combine lemon juice, sugar, and 2 cups of the remaining water. Heat, stirring until sugar dissolves. Remove tea bags and mint. Combine tea and sugar mixture, plus remaining 4 cups water. Stir to mix well. Serve over ice with mint to garnish.
Serves 8.

MUSE LOOKING FOR A LOST ARTIST
Artist - Peter Rogers
acrylic on birch wood 44" X 34"
Courtesy of Mr. and Mrs. Thomas K. Denton

ARTIST LOOKING FOR A LOST MUSE
Artist - Peter Rogers
acrylic on birch wood 44" X 34"
Courtesy of Mr. and Mrs. Thomas K. Denton

Peter Rogers

Peter Rogers was born in London, England, in 1933. He attended Sherborne School in Dorset and St. Martins School of Art in London. He trained as a guardsman in the Welsh Guards and was commissioned in the Queens Royal Regiment. He was elected a member of the Royal Society of British Artists.

He moved to France and then Spain, where he met his wife, Carol Hurd. They later married and subsequently moved to San Patricio, New Mexico.

He painted a 35 foot by 13 foot mural in the State Archives and Library Building in Austin, Texas, in 1964. Next he painted a series of 48 paintings of Alaska for the Atlantic Richfield Company in 1971. In 1974, he completed a 40 foot by 17 foot mural in the Museum of Texas Tech University, Lubbock, Texas.

In 1975, Peter moved to Santa Fe and continued his painting career in that community. In 1983, he moved back to the Sentinel Ranch in San Patricio with his wife, Carol.

Savoring Soups

THE WOMAN'S CLUB
"Growth in Population and Items of Special Interest in the Valley"
BY MISS M. M. HOLT

Fortunately there was no grants of land given to the Spaniards in the Pecos Valley. It was the hunting and fighting grounds of the fierce Indian tribes who made raids here as late as 1878, so when white men came, here was the virgin prairie ready for them to make of it what they would. Early in the sixties Americans began coming to the Valley seeking their fortunes, and one, Van Smith by name, "unmarried and of gentlemanly appearance," came here. He named the town Roswell for his father, Roswell Smith, and built the house on Main street in which Captain Lea, now resides, and an adobe building which stood on the site of the new Peeler building. At about the same time the three Chisum brothers came and built at what is known as the Chisum ranch, an adobe house around a court with the outer walls forming a high breastwork above the flat roof and having loopholes through which they could defend themselves against the Indians. The corral was also made with high walls and securely locked at night. These were the only buildings between Seven Rivers, sixty-five miles south and the Bosque Grande, thirty miles north, for many years. Mr. John S. Chisum, the oldest brother, was called "The Cattle King of New Mexico." His herds were estimated to number from forty to eighty thousand, and ranged up and down the Rio Pecos from Ft. Sumner to below the Texas line. There were smaller cattleowners in the Valley who charged Mr. Chisum with monopolizing the range, and that at each round-up the Chisum herd carried with it hundreds of cattle belonging to others, while Mr. Chisum claimed that these smaller proprietors had combined to round-up and drive away cattle bearing his brand and mark, which was known as "The Jingle Bob." This quarrel grew and caused "The Lincoln County War," in which Wm. H. Bonney, better known as Billy the Kid, took such a prominent part. The reckless daring, unerring aim and unrivaled horsemanship of "the Kid" rendered his services a priceless acquisition to the faction which could secure them. At first he was against the Chisum faction, but after a few months he joined it and frankly notified the other side of his change. The Chisum ranch was now the stronghold of defense. Marion Turner, who preempted Smith's place on Main street, had been a staunch friend of Mr. Chisum, but became his bitterest enemy. Mr. Turner had a sheriff's power over the Pecos Valley. The Kid, with fourteen men, was at the Chisum ranch when Turner, with between thirty and forty men, went there to arrest him, but the house was built for defence and fourteen determined men could hold it against an army, and Turner retreated. The Kid then went to Lincoln to McSween's; Turner followed and there was a fierce fight. It has been said that Mrs. McSween encouraged her wild garrison by playing inspiring airs upon her piano, but Mrs. McSween and three lady friends left the house before the fight commenced. It is also true that she requested permission to return to the house for some purpose; the firing ceased, she went in, returned almost immediately, and the firing was resumed. The magnificent piano was struck several times and sent forth discordant sounds, which gave rise to this story. The Kid escaped from the burning building under cover of darkness but Mr. McSween and six others were killed. After this the Kid appealed to John Chisum for assistance, was refused and he organized a band of men as lawless as himself and inaugurated a system of plunder which baffled all resistance. At one time they took 118 of Mr. Chisum's cattle which they sold to Colorado beef buyers, telling them that they were "employed in settling up Chisum's business." From this time the Kid led a fugitive life. There are many citizens of Roswell who can give you personal reminiscences of the Kid which I have no room for.

(continued on page 112)

Beef Stock

3 **pounds of beef bones with some meat attached**
2 **onions, coarsely chopped**
2 **carrots, washed and sliced**
2 **stalks of celery, sliced**
3 **quarts water**
3 **sprigs parsley**
1 **teaspoon thyme**
1 **teaspoon peppercorns**

Place bones in a heavy roasting pan and roast them without any liquid in a preheated 400° oven, for 20 minutes. Add the vegetables and brown them with the bones for an additional 15 minutes. Discard fat and transfer all ingredients to a pot. Add the water, parsley, bay leaf, thyme and peppercorns. If the water doesn't cover, add enough additional water to cover. Adjust the lid on the pot so the pot is almost covered, allowing about an inch for the evaporation of steam. Simmer for 6 hours. Strain through a colander, discard bones and vegetables. Do not press vegetables or broth will become cloudy. Chill broth and discard fat. Season to taste. The broth will keep for 4 or 5 days, can be frozen.
Yields 2 to 3 quarts.

Chicken Stock

1 **(2-3 pound) chicken, cut up**
1 **large onion, sliced**
1 **carrot, peeled and sliced**
1 **stalk of celery with top, sliced**
1 **teaspoon peppercorns**
4 **or 5 sprigs fresh parsley**
1 **bay leaf**
8 **cups water**

Place all ingredients in a pot. Adjust lid so pan is ¾ covered. Simmer 45 minutes. Remove chicken when cool enough to handle. Remove chicken from bones. Return bones and skin to pan. Simmer an additional 1½ hours. Strain broth, cool and chill at least 8 hours. Discard fat. *You now have a great stock. The chicken can be used in a number of ways or return to stock with noodles, chopped onion and carrots for a good chicken soup. Two tablespoons of lime or lemon juice is a good addition to soup. Stock can be frozen. Can be stored in refrigerator for 2 weeks but should be simmered for 10 minutes every 4 or 5 days to keep from going sour. Freezes well.*
Yields about 6 cups of stock - About 3 cups of chicken.

Fish Stock

3 pounds fish bone, head and
   trimmings
2 onions, coarsely chopped
2 carrots, coarsely chopped
2 stalks celery with leaves, chopped
3 quarts cold water
3 sprigs parsley
2 bay leaves
1 teaspoon peppercorns

Place all ingredients in a pot and bring to a boil. Reduce heat, cover pot and allow about 1 inch adjustment of lid to allow for evaporation of steam. Simmer gently for 20 minutes. Strain through colander, discarding all but broth. Season to taste. The broth will keep 2 or 3 days in the refrigerator or can be frozen.
Yields 2 to 3 quarts.

Bavarian Split Pea Soup

½ pound knockwurst cut into ½
   inch slices
½ cup chopped celery
½ cup chopped carrots
¼ teaspoon marjoram leaves,
   crushed
3 tablespoons butter
2 cans split pea soup
1½ cups water
2 tablespoons prepared mustard
1 package (10 ounces) frozen peas
   with pearl onions

In a large skillet, brown knockwurst, cook celery and carrots with marjoram and butter. While the first ingredients are cooking, place remaining ingredients in a deep well crockpot and set heat on low. When carrots and celery are tender pour skillet mixture into crockpot. Cook on low for 3 to 4 hours or until frozen peas are tender.
This is a very hearty soup and can be frozen. Serves 4 to 6.

Hearty Black Bean Soup

2 cups dried black beans, soaked
   overnight in eight cups of water
1 bay leaf
3 tablespoons butter or oil
2 onions, chopped
2 stalks celery, sliced
2 carrots, diced
2 cloves garlic, minced
1 tablespoon lemon juice
½ teaspoon cumin seed
½ teaspoon oregano
4 cups tomato juice

Bring the beans, water and bay leaf to a boil in a large kettle. Lower the heat and simmer until the beans are soft - a full hour. Meanwhile, heat the butter or oil in a large skillet, and add the onions, celery, carrots and garlic. Stew over low heat for 10 minutes or until tender. When the beans are soft, add the vegetables to the kettle, along with the lemon juice, cumin, oregano and tomato juice. Bring to a boil. Discard the bay leaf and serve.
Serves 8 to 10.

Bouillabaisse in New Mexico

½ cup butter
6 stalks celery with leaves, coarsely
  chopped
2 onions, coarsely chopped
1 large bell pepper, chopped
5 cloves garlic, minced
3 tablespoons creole roux
3 tomatoes, coarsely chopped
8 cups fish stock (see index)
24 shrimp
1 pound scallops
12 oysters

Saute slowly celery, onions, and pepper in butter. Add the minced garlic cloves, creole roux and tomatoes. Cook for a few minutes, then add 2 cups of fish stock. Cook the shrimp, scallops and oysters in the remaining fish stock. Mix all the Ingredients together and serve at once.
Serves 4.

Creole Roux
3 tablespoons flour
3 tablespoons oil or bacon
  drippings

Blend together in a pot. Cook slowly over medium heat, stirring constantly until the mixture becomes a dark brown, not burned. It's the browning of the flour that gives the roux the distinctive flavor.

Broccoli Cheese Soup

2 packages (10 ounce) frozen
  broccoli, chopped
3½ cups chicken broth
20-30 fresh mushrooms, sliced
1 cup finely chopped celery
½ cup chopped green onion
2 tablespoons finely chopped fresh
  parsley
2 tablespoons butter
2 teaspoons garlic powder
½ teaspoon cracked pepper
½ teaspoon fresh pepper, grated
1½ cups grated mild or medium
  Cheddar cheese
½ cup sour cream
½ teaspoon Tabasco

Cook broccoli according to package directions. Drain. Puree in blender with 1½ cups chicken broth. In a medium size saucepan, simmer pureed broccoli with remaining chicken broth over medium heat while preparing the vegetables. In a skillet saute vegetables in butter until onions are transparent. Season with garlic powder and pepper, add to the broccoli. Cook covered over low heat for 30 minutes. Stir in grated cheese and sour cream. Season with Tabasco, serve when cheese is melted.
Serves 6.

Burmese Chicken Soup

1 can (10½ ounces) cream of
  chicken soup
1 soup can of half and half
2 teaspoons curry powder
2 tablespoons lemon juice
½ banana

Put all ingredients in blender and blend until smooth. Serve either hot or cold.
Serves 4.

Herbed Carrot Soup

4 tablespoons butter
1 pound carrots, cut in thin slices
5 green onions, chopped
2 or 3 shallots, minced
1 small potato, shredded
1 clove garlic, minced
1 teaspoon chervil
¼ teaspoon tarragon
pinch thyme
2 quarts chicken broth
1 cup cream, whipped
salt and pepper to taste

Melt butter. Add vegetables and seasonings and cook for about 15 minutes. Add 2 quarts chicken broth and cook another 15 minutes. Transfer to blender and puree. Return to pot. Add whipped cream and salt and pepper to taste. Serve hot or cold.
Serves 12.

Cheddar Cheese Soup

2 tablespoons butter
1 onion, finely chopped
1 carrot, chopped
¾ cup chopped celery
1 teaspoon dry mustard
1 tablespoon flour
5 cups chicken broth
1 cup grated Cheddar cheese
¼ teaspoon nutmeg
2 tablespoons white vermouth
⅓ cup heavy cream
1 cup croutons for garnish

Melt butter and saute onion, carrot and celery for 5 minutes until soft. Stir in mustard and flour. Add chicken broth. Cover and simmer for 20 minutes. Strain into another saucepan, discarding the vegetables. Stir in the grated cheese and add the other ingredients except croutons. Simmer until the cheese has melted and soup is very hot. Garnish with croutons.
Serves 6.

Chicken Egg Drop Soup

6 cups chicken broth
3 tablespoons cornstarch in 2
    tablespoons water
1 tablespoon soy sauce
½ teaspoon sugar
2 eggs, slightly beaten
salt and pepper to taste
2 scallions, diced

Bring broth to a boil. Combine cornstarch mixture with soy sauce and sugar. Add salt and pepper. Slowly stir into broth. Heat and continue stirring until thick and clear. Remove from heat. Gradually add eggs using a wide pronged fork. Stir with fork to separate eggs as they cook. Garnish with scallions and serve at once.
Serves 4.

Corn Chowder

4 medium sized mild onions, sliced
2 tablespoons butter or margarine
4 medium potatoes, cut in ½ inch
    pieces
4 tablespoons butter or margarine
2 cans cream corn (4 cups)
1 quart whole milk
½ cup light cream
1½ teaspoons salt
⅛ teaspoon pepper
⅛ teaspoon thyme
⅛ teaspoon marjoram
¼ teaspoon parsley flakes

Fry the onions until brown in the 2 tablespoons butter. Cook the cubed potatoes in simmering water for 15 minutes. Use ½ cup of potato water to rinse out the corn cans. Warm the milk and cream in a large pan and add onions, potatoes, corn, butter, herbs, salt, pepper and water. Heat mixture to piping hot, but do not boil. Set aside to cool for a couple of hours. Reheat to piping hot just before serving. Garnish with parsley flakes.
Serves 6 to 8.

Cold Cucumber Soup

2 tablespoons butter or margarine
¼ cup chopped onion or one leek,
    chopped
2 cups diced unpeeled cucumber
½ cup finely diced raw potato
2 cups chicken broth
2 sprigs parsley
½ teaspoon salt
¼ teaspoon pepper, freshly ground
¼ teaspoon dry mustard
1 cup heavy cream

Melt butter in a medium size saucepan; cook onion in it until transparent. Add remaining ingredients, except cream and garnish. Bring to a boil, and simmer 15 minutes or until potatoes are tender. Puree in blender or food processor. Taste for correct seasoning and chill. Before serving, add cream and garnish with chopped chives and radish.
Serves 4.

Cream of Asparagus Soup

1 pound fresh asparagus
2 cups beef bouillon
2 cups water
1 teaspoon sugar
2 tablespoons butter
2 tablespoons flour
2 tablespoons marinated red
   pimiento slices
1 egg yolk
2 slices white bread
1 egg
salt and pepper
1 tablespoon oil
chopped parsley for garnish

Peel asparagus, wash, cut into 2 inch long pieces and cook in bouillon and water with sugar for 20 minutes. Drain and reserve liquid. Melt butter, add flour and reserved liquid and bring to boiling. Add asparagus and pimiento slices. Mix egg yolk with a little liquid and return to soup. Do not boil anymore as egg yolk will curdle. Cut bread into cubes. Slightly beat egg with salt and pepper, turn breadcubes in egg mixture. Heat oil and fry breadcubes till golden. Sprinkle over soup with chopped parsley.

Cream of Celery Soup

3 cups finely chopped celery and
   leaves
2 cups chicken broth
2 cups boiling water
1 small onion, sliced
2 tablespoons butter
3 tablespoons flour
2 cups milk
1 cup half and half

In chicken broth and boiling water cook celery until soft. Set aside. Saute onion in butter, blend in flour and add milk. Combine celery mixture and liquid in which it was cooked with the onion mixture. Add cream and season to taste. Let cool. Put a little of the soup at a time in a blender or processor and puree well. Repeat until all the soup is well blended.
May be refrigerated and reheated when ready to serve.
Serves 10.

Curry Consomme

2 cans (10½ ounce) beef consomme
   with gelatin added
1 package (8 ounce) cream cheese
1 tablespoon finely minced green
   onion
1 teaspoon curry powder
watercress as garnish

Have all ingredients at room temperature. Blend 1 can consomme, cream cheese, onion and curry powder. Spoon into 8 cups or dishes. Refrigerate. When firm, spoon second can of consomme into dishes. Refrigerate and top with watercress.
Serves 8.

Farmer's Cheese Soup

3 tablespoons butter
1 cup finely chopped onion
1 cup chopped celery
¾ cup sliced carrot rounds
½ pound broccoli, separated into
    small flowerets (about 2¼ cups)
1 can (10¾ ounce) condensed
    chicken broth
3 cups milk
1 cup (4 ounces) shredded Cheddar
    cheese
6 to 8 slices French bread, toasted
    Gouda cheese, cut into thin
    wedges, two for each slice of
    bread
4 slices bacon, cooked and
    crumbled

In a 3 quart saucepan melt butter; add onion and celery. Stir and cook for 5 minutes. Add carrots, broccoli and broth. Cover, bring to a boil, then turn to simmer and cook for 15 minutes or until vegetables are tender. Add milk; bring to simmer. Add cheese, stirring until melted. Pour soup into 2½ quart casserole. Float bread slices on top of soup and cover each with two wedges of cheese to balance. Place under broiler for 2 or 3 minutes, until the cheese melts and turns a delicate brown. Sprinkle with crumbled bacon and serve.
Yields 7 cups.

Fish Chowder

2½ pounds haddock fillets, fresh or
    frozen
1 medium size onion, chopped
5 tablespoons butter or margarine
6 medium potatoes, cut in small
    cubes
¼ medium green pepper, finely
    chopped
1 quart whole milk, scalded
1 cup light cream, scalded
1½ teaspoons salt
⅛ teaspoon pepper
¼ teaspoon thyme
⅛ teaspoon oregano
¼ teaspoon parsley flakes

Cover fillets with water; bring to boil and simmer 7 or 8 minutes, or until fish is done. Drain. Save liquid. Skin fish, if not already done. Fry onion in 2 tablespoons of the butter. Boil potato cubes 5 minutes in the fish liquid. Add onions and green pepper. Cook until potatoes are tender. Place potatoes, pepper and onions in kettle. Add milk and cream (which has been scalded), fish, seasonings, herbs and other 3 tablespoons butter. Keep hot for 10 minutes, but do not boil. Set aside to cool and reheat to piping hot before serving.
Serves 10 to 12.

Lentil Soup

2 cups lentils
water
ham bone, the meatier the better
¾ cup onions
1 cup chopped celery with tops
1 cup chopped carrots
2 cloves garlic, cut in half
½ teaspoon red pepper
2 bay leaves
½ teaspoon rosemary
¼ teaspoon thyme
¼ teaspoon tarragon
1 can (16 ounce) tomatoes, drained
   and chopped or 2 medium fresh
   tomatoes peeled, seeded and
   chopped
1 tablespoon vinegar or 2
   tablespoons lemon juice

Cover lentils with water. Soak overnight or the length of time required according to package directions. Drain lentils, reserving liquid. Add enough additional water to make 12 cups. Return to pot with lentils. Add the ham bone. Cover and simmer 3½ hours. Add onions, celery, carrots, garlic, pepper, bay leaves, rosemary, thyme and tarragon. Cover and simmer ½ hour longer. Add tomatoes. Put soup through a sieve. Serve clear or with pureed vegetables. Just before serving add vinegar or lemon juice.
Yields about 2 quarts.

Monterey Jack Cheese Soup

2 cups chicken broth
1 cup finely chopped onion
1 cup peeled and diced tomatoes
1 can (4 ounce) chopped green
   chiles
1 teaspoon garlic, minced
6 tablespoons butter
6 tablespoons all-purpose flour
5 cups hot milk
½ teaspoon salt
⅛ teaspoon pepper
3 cups coarsely grated Monterey
   Jack cheese (¾ pound)

In a large saucepan mix chicken broth, onion, tomato, green chiles and garlic. Bring to boil over high heat; cover. Reduce to moderate heat and simmer 10 minutes or until vegetables are tender. In a medium size heavy saucepan melt butter over moderate heat. Remove from heat and stir in flour. Return to heat and cook 3 minutes, stirring constantly. Stir in 3½ cups hot milk, adding ½ cup at a time. Cook about 7 minutes, until smooth and thickened. Remove broth mixture from heat and stir into the milk mixture, ¼ cup at a time. Return to heat. Add remaining 1½ cups milk, salt, pepper, and cheese, stirring constantly until cheese is melted and soup is well-heated.
Serves 8.

Prairie Soup

2 cans (1 pound 14 ounces)
  tomatoes, chopped
¼ teaspoon garlic salt
¼ teaspoon vinegar
¼ teaspoon sugar or sugar
  substitute
1 pound ground round
2 bouillon cubes
4 cups hot water
1 cup finely chopped carrots or 2
  medium carrots
1 cup finely chopped celery or 4-5
  stalks celery
1 cup finely chopped green pepper
1 tablespoon dry parsley
1 cup finely chopped potatoes
1 medium onion, finely chopped

Simmer tomatoes, garlic salt, vinegar and sugar. Saute ground round slowly until brown, drain off any fat and add to tomatoes. Dissolve bouillon in hot water. Add bouillon and all vegetables to tomatoes. Add parsley and salt and pepper to taste. Simmer about 1 hour.

2 tablespoons of pasta or 2 tablespoons of barley can be added in place of the potatoes. This soup makes about 2 quarts.

Round-up Soup

1 pound hamburger
1 onion, chopped (about ½ cup)
1 cup chopped carrots
2 medium sized potatoes, unpeeled
  and thinly sliced
2 medium sized fresh tomatoes,
  chopped
1 can (10¾ ounce) tomato soup
¼ cup barley
8 cups water
salt and pepper to taste
1 package Vegetable Soup mix

Brown meat and drain off the fat. Add all ingredients except the soup mix. Simmer for 1 hour. Add soup mix and cook for 30 minutes more.

Red Wine Soup

5 cups beef consomme
2 large tomatoes, skinned and
   diced
½ cup dry sherry
½ cup Burgundy

Simmer tomatoes in consomme for 15 minutes. Add sherry and Burgundy just before serving. *Serves 8.*

San Juan Cocktail or Cold Soup

1 can (7 ounce) minced clams with
   juice
¼ cup diced tomato
2 tablespoons chopped onion
2 tablespoons chopped celery
¼ cup catsup
1 tablespoon Worcestershire sauce
⅛ teaspoon salt
dash Tabasco
1 avocado

Combine all ingredients except avocado and chill well. Just before serving, peel and slice avocado; add to top of each serving.
Serves 3 to 4 cocktails.

A Santa Fe Soup

1 avocado
8 ounces plain yogurt
1 can (14½ ounce) chicken broth, or
   homemade broth
1 clove garlic, pressed
12 sprigs cilantro, chopped or
   Chinese parsley, or regular
   parsley
juice of ½ lemon
1 small green chile or jalapeno,
   chopped
paprika

Put all ingredients in blender, excluding paprika. Blend well. Chill several hours. Serve with paprika sprinkled on top.
Serve with cucumber sandwiches. This will keep for several days. Do not freeze.
Serves 2 to 4.

Savory Borscht

3 tablespoons butter
¾ cup finely chopped onion
2 to 2½ pounds beets, peeled and
    cut into 2 inch strips
6 tablespoons red wine vinegar
1½ teaspoons sugar
3 tomatoes, peeled, seeded and
    coarsely chopped
salt and freshly ground black
    pepper
3 quarts beef stock (fresh, canned,
    or bouillon cubes dissolved in
    water)
¾ pound white cabbage, coarsely
    shredded
6 sprigs parsley, tied together with
    1 bay leaf
½ cup finely cut fresh dill or
    parsley
1 cup sour cream

In a large soup pot, melt the butter over moderate heat. Add onions and stirring frequently, cook 3 to 5 minutes or until they are soft but not brown. Stir in the beets, then add the wine vinegar, sugar, tomatoes, salt and pepper. Pour in 1 cup of the stock, cover the pan and simmer undisturbed for 1 hour. Pour the remaining stock into the pot and add the chopped cabbage. Bring to a boil. Submerge the parsley and bay leaf in the soup, and simmer partially covered, for 45 minutes. Remove parsley and bay leaf. Sprinkle with fresh dill or parsley. Accompany the soup with a bowl of sour cream, to be added at the discretion of each diner.
May be refrigerated and reheated just before serving.
Serves 10.

Spanish Gazpacho

3 ripe tomatoes, peeled
3 tablespoons olive oil
3 tablespoons vinegar
1 cup bread crumbs
1 clove garlic, minced
1 small onion
1½-2½ cups water, iced
save ½ cup water to dilute soup at
    serving time
salt to taste
garnishes:
    onions, tomatoes,
    cucumbers and
    croutons

Mix all ingredients in blender except water. Add water a little at a time. Refrigerate several hours. Before serving, dilute with reserved half cup water. To add to this, serve small dishes of chopped onion, tomato, cucumber, croutons and have each person put a teaspoon of each into the gazpacho.
Authentic recipe from Spain.
This is a soup to be served cold. Can be frozen.
Serves 3 cups.

Simply Superb Seafood Soup

1 pound fresh halibut
1 jar (10 ounce) shucked oysters; save liquid
1 cup cleaned shucked clams or 1 can of chopped clams; save liquid
¼ pound cooked shrimp or 4 ounces canned or frozen shrimp
2 large onions, chopped
4 ribs celery, cut diagonally
1 green pepper, coarsely chopped
1 small clove garlic, crushed
¼ pound butter
2 quarts water
2 teaspoons chicken seasoned stock base
1 teaspoon salt
½ teaspoon pepper
2 bay leaves
¼ teaspoon thyme
1 can (15 ounce) evaporated milk
1 can (1 pound) creamed corn
2 medium potatoes, cooked and cubed
1 jar (2 ounce) chopped pimiento, drained
chopped fresh parsley

Snip halibut, oysters, clams, and shrimp (if large) into pieces with scissors and reserve any liquid from oysters and clams. In a large kettle saute onion, celery, green pepper, and garlic in butter until soft on low heat. Add water, chicken stock base and all seasonings plus any seafood liquid. Simmer 20 minutes. Thicken with a paste of ½ cup flour mixed to a smooth paste with cold water. Add halibut and other raw seafood and cook 5 minutes. Add milk, corn, potatoes, pimiento, shrimp and any canned seafood, if used. Simmer 10 minutes. Serve in large soup tureen and sprinkle chopped parsley over top.
Serves 8.

Split Pea Soup

2¼ cups green split peas
1½ pounds meaty ham bone
2 quarts water
1 teaspoon salt
½ teaspoon pepper
¼ teaspoon marjoram
1½ cups sliced onion
1 cup diced celery
1 cup diced carrots

Cover peas with 2 quarts of cold water. Simmer gently for 2 minutes; remove from heat, cover and let stand 1 hour. Add bone, onions, salt, pepper and marjoram. Bring to boil, cover, reduce heat and simmer (do not boil) for 1½ hours. Stir occasionally. Remove bone, cut off meat and dice. Return meat to soup and add vegetables. Cook slowly uncovered for 30 to 40 minutes.
Serves 6 to 8.

Spanish Bean Soup

½ pound dried garbanzo beans
10 cups water
1 tablespoon salt
1 beef bone
1 ham bone
2 quarts water
¼ pound salt pork, chopped fine
pinch paprika
1 tablespoon shortening
1 chopped onion
1 pound potatoes, peeled and
   quartered
1 pinch saffron
1 chorizo Spanish sausage, cut in
   thin slices

In large pot place beans in salted water to soak overnight. Next day, drain water and place beans, beef, and ham bones and 2 quarts water in large pot. Place over low heat; simmer 45 minutes. Fry the chopped salt pork, add paprika and onion (plus 1 tablespoon shortening if needed) and cook until onion is tender. Add to beans, then add potatoes. Toast saffron on the cover of a casserole or in the oven and mash before measuring. Mix with a little hot stock from the pot and add to soup. Taste and season with salt and pepper. In about 15 minutes, when potatoes are done, put chorizo slices in soup and serve hot.
Serves 4.

Southwestern Corn Chowder

1½ pounds Polish or German
   sausage (pre-cooked), sliced
2 cans (17 ounce) cream style corn
3 cups milk or half and half
1 can (4 ounce) chopped green
   chiles
black cracked pepper
1 pound Monterey Jack or Gruyere
   cheese, cubed

Fry sausage until brown in a large pot. Add remaining ingredients, except the cheese and pepper. Cook slowly for 30 minutes. Season with pepper. Add the cheese and cook until cheese is melted.
Serves 6 to 8.

Steering Committee Potato Soup

2 cans (10¾ ounce) condensed
   cream of potato soup
21½ ounces half and half
2 cans (4 ounce) chopped green
   chiles
4 ounces or more Monterey Jack
   cheese

Combine soups, half and half and green chiles. Heat but do not boil. Cube cheese into ½ inch pieces and place in the bottom of soup bowls. Pour soup into bowls and serve.
Serves 4.
This recipe can be doubled or tripled easily.

Donald B. Anderson

Donald B. Anderson was born April 6, 1919 in Chicago, Illinois, where he attended the University of Chicago grammar and high schools. He is a graduate of Purdue University in Mechanical Engineering. During World War II, he served four years at sea in the U.S. Navy as a Deck and Engineering Officer.

In addition to his occupation as a painter, he is President of Anderson Oil Company and Chairman of the Board of Anderson-Myers Drilling Company. He is President of the Board of Trustees of The Roswell Museum and Art Center; serves The Smithsonian Institution as Commissioner of the National Museum of American Art; is a member of the Board of Managers of the School of American Research, Santa Fe, and is a Director of the Jargon Society Inc. of Highlands, North Carolina.

UNTITLED
Artist - Donald B. Anderson
oil
48" X 48"   1972
Private collection

Tomato Bisque

4 tablespoons butter
¼ cup diced onions
¼ cup diced celery
1 can (20 ounce or 2½ cups)
    tomatoes
1 cup chicken stock
salt and pepper
1 teaspoon basil
½ teaspoon thyme
½ teaspoon oregano
minced parsley

Saute onions and celery in butter. Add remaining ingredients and bring to simmer. Remove from heat. Place mixture in food processor or blender. Puree. Return to heat; simmer 20 minutes.

Tomato Cream Soup

2 cans (10½ ounce) tomato soup
1½ cups dry sherry wine
salt and pepper to taste
½ teaspoon thyme
½ teaspoon marjoram
½ teaspoon onion powder
½ teaspoon curry powder

Combine all ingredients. Heat in a saucepan until hot. Can be served hot or cold.
Serves 6.

Zucchini Soup

1 large onion, chopped
6 small zucchini, cubed
1 teaspoon curry powder
½ teaspoon dry mustard
3 cups chicken broth
3 tablespoons uncooked rice (not
    instant)
1½ cups milk
salt and pepper
chives for garnish

Simmer covered all ingredients except milk for 45 minutes. Cool and puree. Add milk. Reheat to boiling. Garnish with chives.

Graves-Gatewood Wedding

Most Elaborate Nuptial Event Roswell has Seen in Several Years

Couple on Honeymoon

The wedding of Mr. Robert L. Graves and Miss Lottie A. Gatewood held at the Southern Methodist Church last night was an affair of beauty as well as happiness and was easily the most elaborate nuptial event Roswell has witnessed in several years. Every detail was carried out with exactness - nothing was overlooked. It was an event long to be remembered.

For the occasion the church was decorated in a profusion of flowers never before witnessed there. Mr. Santheson, the florist, exerted his every means to make the plan beautiful, and his success was beyond measure. Upon entering the attention was first attracted by the immense bank of green that formed a background for the floral decorations in the front of the church. This bank was flanked with palms, ferns and rubber trees, potted plants and cut flowers and to the front was an immense arch, covered with greens that were sprinkled with carnations and other white flowers. The rail in front of the place usually occupied by the altar was covered with greens and cut flowers and decorated with palms and potted plants. From the immense arch hung ropes of roses and in the center was the wedding bell, made of seven hundred verbena. Below was a profusion of vari-colored flowers that made the attractive spot in the whole. The aisles were lined with greens and phlox, each seat having a large bouquet of these flowers. In this place of beauty, brightly lighted, was the crowd of invited guests filling the church to over-flowing. Hial Cobean, J. H. Mullis and R.F. Cruse acted as ushers to seat the immense audience.

At eight-thirty o'clock Mrs. J. M. Nelson, at the piano, and Miss Eva Nelson, with the violin, struck up Lohengrin's wedding march and to the strains of this music the bridal party moved forward. Down the left aisle were the groom and his best man, Willard Hurd, and other attendants, Ben Urton and Roscoe Graves, all dressed in black and white golves and waistcoats. On the right were the maid of honor, Miss Zella Graves, in light blue silk, and the bride's maids, Misses Laura Orr and Sadie Martin, both in white organdie, and all bearing bride's maid roses. In the center aisle marched the bride, at the arm of her father, Judge W. W. Gatewood. The bride was gowned in an exquisite creation of soft, white brocaded silk, with veil and carried a huge bouquet of bride roses. Her father was perfectly attired in black. Preceding the bride and her father were the flower girls, little Misses Pauline Wilson and Myra Martin, both dressed in white.

This party assembled before the bank of flowers, the bride and groom under the wedding bell and facing the audience. With the faint strains of "Hearts and Flowers" in the air, Rev. John Wesley Smith conducted the service, using the ring ritual ceremony of the Methodist church. The ceremony over, the party moved down the center aisle to the door. Mrs. Nelson and Miss Nelson playing Mendelsohn's march and the party preceded by the little girls, who strewed flowers in the pathway of the bride and groom.

The bridal party went from the church to the Gatewood home on North Lea Avenue, where refreshments were served and congratulations given and received.

By this wedding two of Roswell's most prominent families are united. The groom, the son of a leading cattleman, is at present studying law in the office of Judge Gatewood, the father of the bride and this alone is a guaranty the he will make a success in the legal world. The couple have a great many friends who have for them wishes for all success and happiness.

Savoring Salads & Dressings

(continued from page 92)

THE ROSWELL REGISTER   MARCH 7, 1902

One of our prominent business men was with Pat Garrett when he shot and killed Billy the Kid on the 13th of July 1881, a mere boy; for the exact age of Wm. H. Bonney was 21 years 7 months and 21 days. He was laid to rest in the Military Cemetery at Fort Sumner.

For years the mail brought by the Texas and Pacific, reached us but twice a week, coming by stage or in saddle bags from Pecos. In driving from Roswell down the Valley, a distance of sixty-five miles, in 1887, we passed but one house after leaving the Chisum Ranch, and as only a mail carrier spent an occasional night there, it was not an attractive place.

We saw the graceful antelope feeding with the cattle just below South Spring river. The carrier rat, rattle-snakes, tarantulas, centipedes and the chapparal bird were not rare in those days. I was fortunate enough to secure the rattles and fangs of the largest rattlesnake I ever saw. It touched the ground on either side when hung across the saddle on a large horse.

Two years later capitalists became interested in the lower Valley. The town of Eddy was laid out, an irrigating canal was taken from the Rio Pecos and the desolate sandy plain, was transformed. This was not so easily done as it would seem, for the high winds filled in the whirling sand almost as fast as the men could make the ditch.

In 1889 a railroad was begun which was to connect Pecos City, Texas, with Amarillo, Texas. In January 1891 the first division, 89 miles long, from Pecos City to Eddy was completed. This gave us a daily mail. The second division of 75 miles connecting Eddy with Roswell was opened for transportation with great rejoicing on the 15th of October 1894. The third division of 206 miles was completed on February 15, 1899 when Mrs. J. J. Hagerman drove the golden spike which closed the connection between the Santa Fe and the Pecos Valley railway at Amarillo.

Our population in 1890, the year before the railroad came to Eddy, was estimated at 400, in 1900 it had reached 2,000 and now it is more than 3,500 and the railroad has been completed but three years.

I have been asked to tell of the first social function I attended in the Valley.

The year was 1886, the month December. My friend was the wife of a large cattle owner here and they were giving a party to their cowboys and their friends. She thought there might be thirty present. They began coming at three in the afternoon in prairie schooners, riding horse or mule, single or double, and with a baby in arms, until there were seventy-five guests including grand-parents and babies a few weeks old. The girls were brave with ribbons and all were very decorous. The young lady's consent was obtained before a new cowboy was introduced and asked her to dance. My host, getting sleepy about one in the morning, thought he would lie down on the floor behind the bed where no one would see him, but he disturbed so many sleeping babies he beat a retreat and napped outside in a wagon. They only danced square dances. When they got sleepy they went to the dining room ate and took a cup of strong coffee. One fourteen-year old bride I felt sorry for. It was her first party since her marriage. Her husband, a foreman on one of the ranches, got to drinking and had a fight at a saloon on the way. His hand was badly cut and the blood dripped on her wedding dress. She wanted to turn back home but he was stubborn. She looked as tho she had stepped from some old painting with her big brown eyes and sweet face. Well, they danced till sunrise, then ate once more and went home.

Then, and for many years after, supplies were freighted into Roswell by oxen, slow travelers at best. If it rained they were sure to bog in the adobe mud and often there was neither meat, flour nor sugar at the stores for days at a time. Meat then, always meant pork sides.

Angel Hash Salad

2 tablespoons cornstarch
¼ cup sugar
1 cup pineapple syrup and water
2 egg yolks
1 cup heavy cream, whipped
1 can (20 ounce or 2½ cups)
    pineapple tidbits, drained
¼ cup chopped walnuts
¼ pound (15) marshmallows,
    quartered
6 bananas, sliced
leaf lettuce

Combine cornstarch, sugar, syrup and egg yolks in saucepan. Mix well. Cook over medium heat until thickened. Cool. Fold whipped cream into egg yolk mixture. Add next 4 ingredients. Chill. Serve on leaf lettuce.

Cinnamon Candy Salad

4 cups water
4 packages (3 ounce) cherry gelatin
½ cup cinnamon red hot candies
2 jars (15 ounce) applesauce
½ teaspoon lemon juice

Filling:
2 packages (8 ounce) cream cheese
1 cup mayonnaise
1 cup coarsely chopped walnuts or
    pecans

Heat water to boiling in large saucepan. Add gelatin and stir until dissolved. Reduce heat to moderately low, add candies. Continue heating and stirring until candies are dissolved. Remove from heat; stir in applesauce and lemon juice. Pour 4 cups gelatin mixture into a 2½ quart ring mold. Cover and chill mold and remaining mixture until set (4-5 hours). Beat cream cheese in small bowl; gradually add mayonnaise. Stir in nuts. Spread filling evenly over firm mixture in ring mold. Cover and chill 1 hour or longer. Heat remaining gelatin mixture slowly until dissolved, stirring constantly. Then stir over ice until it is consistency of unbeaten egg whites, about 15-25 minutes. Pour carefully over the cream cheese mixture in the ring mold. Chill until set (about 6 hours). To unmold, dip mold in warm water for a few seconds. Loosen edge of mold with a small knife. Invert onto a serving platter. Decorate with salad greens if desired.

Apple Coleslaw

3 cups shredded cabbage
2 medium unpeeled Winesap
  apples, chopped
⅓ cup salted peanuts
½ cup raisins

Combine all ingredients. Toss with your favorite dressing and sprinkle with lemon juice.

Cranberry Cream Salad

1 package (3 ounce) cherry Jello
1 cup boiling water
1 can (16 ounce) whole cranberry
  sauce, drained
½ cup chopped celery
¼ cup chopped walnuts or pecan
1 cup sour cream

Dissolve cherry Jello in 1 cup boiling water. Chill until slightly thickened. Break up cranberry sauce and stir into chilled Jello; add celery and nuts. Fold in sour cream. Chill until firm in a 4 cup mold.
Serves 6 to 8.

Cranberry Pineapple Salad

1 can (8 ounce) crushed pineapple
  and juice
1 box (3 ounce) orange Jello and 1
  cup of water
1 box (3 ounce) cherry Jello and 1
  cup of water
1 can (16 ounce) whole cranberry
  sauce
1 can (21 ounce) cherry pie filling

Drain juice from pineapple and add enough water to make 2 cups of liquid. Pour liquid in a medium size saucepan and bring to a boil. Add both packages of Jello. When Jello has completely dissolved, add 2 cups of water, cranberry sauce, pineapple and cherry pie filling. Pour into a 9 x 12 inch glass dish and chill several hours before serving.
This salad is also very good if you add ½ cup chopped nuts and/or a tablespoon grated orange rind.
Serves 6 to 8.

Hint: Never use fresh or frozen pineapple with gelatin.

Curried Fruit

1 can (1 pound 13 ounce) peach
   halves
1 can (1 pound 13 ounce) pineapple
   rings
1 can (1 pound 13 ounce) apricot
   halves
1 can (1 pound 13 ounce) pears
1 cup prunes
1 jar (4 ounce) maraschino cherries

Use any fruit you wish but do think of color such as a few maraschino cherries, a few cooked prunes, light fruits and yellow fruits. The amount depends upon the number of servings needed. Use a 9 x 13 inch glass pan with turned up edge. Drain fruit for at least 2 hours. Arrange attractively on pan or large dish to be used on the table. Dot with 3 tablespoons butter or margarine.

Curry Mixture:
1½ cups brown sugar
3 teaspoons curry powder
3 tablespoons margarine, melted

Sprinkle curry mixture over fruit. Heat in oven about 10 minutes or until the mixture has melted and fruit is reasonably hot.
Use as an auxiliary dish with meat. Can be arranged ahead of time but not heated.

Frozen Daiquiri Salad

½ cup mayonnaise
½ can (6 ounce) Daiquiri Mix
   (frozen), thawed
1 package (3 or 4½ ounce) no-bake
   vanilla custard mix
1 package (8 ounce) cream cheese,
   cubed and softened
several drops green food coloring
1 can (20 ounce) crushed pineapple,
   drained
1 bottle (4 ounce) maraschino
   cherries, drained and chopped
lettuce

In blender, mix first 4 ingredients and coloring. Fold in pineapple and cherries. Put in 5 cup ring mold. Freeze until firm. Serve on lettuce bed. *Serves 8.*

Raspberry-Cranberry Salad

2 packages (3 ounce) raspberry
  Jello
1½ cups boiling water
½ cup 7-up
¼ cup cold water
1 envelope unflavored gelatin
1 package (10 ounce) frozen
  raspberries
1 package (10 ounce) frozen
  cranberry relish or 1 can (16
  ounce) whole cranberry sauce
juice of 1 lemon
grated lemon rind

Dissolve Jello in boiling water. Add gelatin which has been dissolved in cold water. Add 7-up, raspberries and cranberries. Mix and stir thoroughly. Add juice and rind of lemon and stir again. Pour into mold. After mixture thickens in refrigerator, stir again to distribute fruit evenly. Serve with mayonnaise that has been thinned with a little skim milk. Can be prepared the day before.

Summer Fruit Salad

1 cantaloupe, cut into ¾ inch
  cubes
1 can (20 ounce) pineapple chunks
  and juice
1 unpeeled apple, cubed
2 peaches, peeled and wedged
2 bananas, ¼ inch slices
1 cup halved strawberries
1 can (6 ounce) frozen orange juice
  concentrate, thawed and
  undiluted

Layer fruits in ORDER GIVEN in large bowl (preferably glass). Spoon orange juice over. Cover and chill 6-8 hours.
Serves 8 to 10.

Southwest Mango Salad

2 packages (3 ounce) lemon Jello
1 package (3 ounce) apricot Jello
1 can (29 ounce) mangos, drained
  (reserve liquid)
3 cups boiling liquid (a combination
  of reserved liquid and water)
1 package (8 ounce) cream cheese
juice of 1 lime
sour cream
brown sugar
grated coconut

Dissolve the Jello in boiling liquid; set aside. Put drained mangos and cream cheese into blender and blend until creamy. Mix Jello mixture, mango mixture and lime juice together. Pour into ring mold, individual molds or oblong pan and chill 4-6 hours or overnight. Serve on a bed of lettuce and top with any combination of: sour cream, brown sugar and coconut.
Serves 12.

Hot Fruit

3 cans (11 ounce) mandarin oranges
1 can (16½ ounce) Bing pitted
    cherries
2 cans (20 ounce) crushed
    pineapple
1 can (29 ounce) pears
⅓ cup butter
¾ cup brown sugar, packed
3 teaspoons curry powder

Drain juice from all fruit. Melt butter in saucepan, remove from heat; stir in brown sugar and curry powder. Arrange fruit in a 9 x 12 inch pan and pour hot mixture over fruit. Bake 1 hour at 350° uncovered. Cover and refrigerate overnight. Heat ½ hour before serving.
Serves 10.

Mixed Fruit Salad

3 bananas, sliced
1 cup peaches, sliced
2 cans (15¼ ounce) pineapple
    chunks, cut into halves
¾ cup marachino cherries, cut in
    half
2 packages (3¾ ounce) instant
    vanilla pudding

Drain juice from all fruit and reserve. Put fruit in a 9 x 12 inch dish. Add ¼ cup pineapple juice to pudding powder and mix until smooth. Add 1 cup peach juice and 1 cup pineapple juice. Pour over top of fruit, cover, and chill overnight.
Serves approximately 6.

Orange-Avocado Salad

2 heads lettuce (preferably 1 red
    leaf, 1 romaine)
¼ cup vinegar
1 cup salad oil
2 teaspoons grated orange peel
½ cup orange juice
juice of one large lemon
1 purple onion, cut in rings
½ teaspoon dry mustard
½ teaspoon salt
2 avocados, diced
1 can (11 ounce) mandarin oranges,
    drained

Combine all ingredients except lettuce and marinate in refrigerator at least 5 hours. Wash lettuce, dry and tear into bite-sized pieces. Just before serving time, pour all marinated ingredients over lettuce and mix gently and thoroughly. *Shrimp may also be added, if desired.*
Serves 6 to 8.

Chicken Curry Layered Salad

6 cups shredded lettuce
2 packages (10 ounce) frozen peas, cooked, drained and chilled
3 cups chopped cooked chicken or turkey
3 cups chopped tomatoes
1 bunch green onions, chopped
2 cups seeded cucumber slices, halved
3 cups mayonnaise
1 tablespoon sugar
2½ teaspoons curry powder
2 tablespoons lemon juice
3 cups croutons

Layer lettuce, peas, chicken, tomatoes (mixed with onions) and cucumber in 5 quart salad bowl. Combine mayonnaise, sugar and curry; mix well. Spread over salad. Cover with plastic film; refrigerate overnight. Before serving, sprinkle with croutons.
Serves 12.

Curried Chicken-Pecan Salad

2 cups cooked and cubed chicken breasts
½ cup crushed pineapple, drained
1½ cups cooked long grain rice
1 tablespoon red wine vinegar
2 tablespoons salad oil
1 teaspoon salt
¾ teaspoon curry powder
¼ cup chopped green pepper
¼ cup chopped celery
¾ cup broken pecans
½ to ¾ cup mayonnaise
lettuce cups

Combine chicken, pineapple, rice, vinegar, oil, salt and curry powder. Chill 2 hours. Fold in celery, pepper, broken pecans and mayonnaise. Place on lettuce and garnish with cherry tomatoes.
Serves 6 to 8.

Easy Chicken Salad

9 split chicken breasts
1 cup water
1 teaspoon chicken bouillon
  granules
1 cup chopped celery
¼ cup chopped green onions
¾ cup mayonnaise
¼ cup chicken broth
1 cup chopped pecans

Wrap chicken breasts tightly in foil with water and bouillon. Bake 400° until done (about 1 hour). Chop chicken, add celery, onion, mayonnaise and broth sparingly. Add pecans and serve. *Serves 10 to 12.*

Exotic Chicken Salad

1 cup mayonnaise
1 tablespoon soy sauce
1 tablespoon chutney
1 cup lemon juice
1½ tablespoons curry powder
1 cup chopped celery
1 pound seedless grapes
4 cups cooked diced chicken
1 can (8 ounce) water chestnuts,
  sliced
1 package (1½ ounce) slivered
  almonds, toasted

Mix mayonnaise, soy sauce, chutney, lemon juice and curry powder. Toss all except nuts into mayonnaise mixture. Put in refrigerator overnight so flavors blend. Sprinkle with nuts. *Serves 6 to 8.*

Hot Chicken Salad

¾ cup mayonnaise
¼ cup water
1 can (10¾ ounce) cream of
  chicken soup
2 cups cooked chicken chunks
2 tablespoons grated onion
½ cup chopped almonds or water
  chestnuts
¼ cup chopped green pepper
1½ cups cooked rice
½ teaspoon salt
2 cups crushed potato chips

Mix together mayonnaise, water and soup. Stir in remaining ingredients, except chips. Place mixture in lightly greased 2 quart casserole. Top with 2 cups crushed potato chips toward the end of cooking time so that the chips do not burn. Bake at 350° for 30 to 40 minutes.

Tropical Chicken Salad

5 cups cooked diced chicken
1 can (8 ounce) sliced water
  chestnuts
2 cups pineapple tidbits, drained
½ cup sliced celery
½ cup sliced green olives

Combine ingredients and mix lightly with dressing.
This dish should be served at once.
It can be served as individual salads on a lettuce leaf or on an avocado half.
Serves 8.

Dressing:
1 cup sour cream
1 cup mayonnaise
1 teaspoon curry powder
1 tablespoon chutney

Combine all ingredients.

Buffet Egg Salad

2 envelopes unflavored gelatin
½ cup water
½ cup Dijon mustard
2 teaspoons salt
4 tablespoons lemon juice
2 teaspoons Worcestershire sauce
1 teaspoon or more cayenne pepper
1½ cups mayonnaise
3 teaspoons dehydrated onion
  flakes
1 cup finely chopped celery
1 green bell pepper, chopped
½ cup diced pimiento
8 hard-boiled eggs, chopped

Sprinkle gelatin on water, heat to dissolve. Add ingredients in order given. Pour into a greased 8 cup mold. Chill overnight; unmold.

Overnight Layered Lamb Salad

6 cups shredded lettuce
1 cup bean sprouts, fresh preferred,
    or 1 can (15 ounce), drained
½ cup chopped celery
1 can (8 ounce) water chestnuts,
    drained and sliced
½ cup chopped green olives
1 can (4 ounce) sliced ripe olives
1 medium cucumber, thinly sliced
4 cups lamb, cooked and slivered
2 packages (10 ounce) frozen peas,
    thawed, uncooked
2½ cups mayonnaise
1 teaspoon curry powder
½ teaspoon garlic salt
1 teaspoon sugar
1 cup shredded Cheddar cheese

In glass bowl place lettuce in even layer. Layer sprouts, celery, water chestnuts, onions, olives, cucumber, lamb and peas one layer at a time. In small bowl mix mayonnaise, curry powder, garlic salt and sugar. Spread evenly over salad mixture, sealing edges. Refrigerate 24 hours. Garnish with cheese. Serve by lifting out layers, making sure to scoop clear to the bottom. *Pass sesame seed bread sticks.*
Serves 10 to 12.

Shrimp-Avocado Ring in Tomato Aspic

1 cup cold water
2 tablespoons plus 1 teaspoon
    gelatin in water
1½ cups boiling water
2 cups tomato juice
1 cup catsup
1 cup chopped celery
⅓ cup minced onion
½ pound small shrimp, cooked
1 green pepper, chopped
¼ cup lemon juice
1 avocado, peeled and seeded
1 tablespoon horseradish
salt

Soften gelatin in cold water for 5 minutes. Stir in 1½ cups boiling water. Add rest of ingredients. Chill 2 hours in refrigerator until thickened but not set. Lightly grease 2 quart mold with liquid oil. Cut avocado and decoratively place in mold. Spoon mix over top. Chill 3 hours. Unmold. Serve with dill sauce.

Dill Sauce:
1½ cups sour cream
½ cup mayonnaise
¼ cup snipped dill
salt and pepper

Mix all ingredients together.

Shrimp Salad or Spread

1 can (10¾ ounce) mushroom soup
   or tomato soup
1 envelope unflavored gelatin
¼ cup cold water
8 ounces cream cheese, softened
1 cup mayonnaise
8 ounces cooked cocktail shrimp
   (canned or frozen)
¼ cup finely chopped onion
½ cup finely chopped celery

Heat soup; add gelatin which has been soaked in the water. Stir to dissolve gelatin and bring mixture to a boil. Remove from heat and add to cream cheese mixing until smooth with electric beater or wire whisk. Add rest of ingredients and pour into mold. Refrigerate until set.
Serves 40 as a spread or 8 as a salad.

Artichoke and Mushroom Salad

1 pound fresh mushrooms
1 package (9 ounce) artichoke
   hearts, or 1 jar (6 ounce)
   marinated artichoke hearts
⅓ cup chopped green onions
1 jar (2 ounce) pimiento-stuffed
   green olives, drained and sliced
1 tablespoon chopped pimiento
½ cup olive oil
½ cup white wine vinegar
3 tablespoons sherry
½ teaspoon salt
½ teaspoon garlic salt
¼ teaspoon oregano
¼ teaspoon ground pepper
lettuce

Wash and trim mushrooms, slice. Cook in boiling salted water for about 30 seconds, drain and turn into mixing bowl. Cook artichokes as directed on package until just tender, if using frozen. Drain and add to mushrooms. Add onions, olives and pimiento. Combine oil, vinegar, sherry, salt, garlic salt, oregano and mix until blended. Pour over vegetables, cover and marinate in refrigerator for at least 4 hours or overnight, stirring several times. Arrange on crisp greens and serve.
Serves 6.

Artichoke Rice Salad

1 package chicken flavored rice mix
¾ teaspoon curry powder
2 jars (6 ounce) marinated artichoke
  hearts, halved
2 tablespoons sliced pimiento-
  stuffed olives
6 green onions, sliced
½ bell pepper, chopped
½ cup mayonnaise

Cook rice as directed on package, but omit the butter. Let cool in large bowl. Add artichokes, saving oil from one jar. Add olives, pepper and onion. Mix curry powder, mayonnaise and reserved oil. Stir until smooth; mix into rice. Refrigerate before serving.
Serves 6.

Fresh Asparagus Salad

2 pounds fresh cooked asparagus
  (cooked in chicken broth to just
  tender crisp)

Dressing:
6 tablespoons olive oil
4 tablespoons white wine vinegar
2 tablespoons finely chopped green
  onion
2 tablespoons finely chopped
  pimientos
1 teaspoon hot mustard
¼ teaspoon salt
¼ teaspoon fresh ground pepper

Garnish:
2 hard cooked eggs
cherry tomatoes
anchovy filets

Pour dressing over asparagus. Cover and chill at least 4 hours. Arrange on shredded lettuce. Garnish and drizzle remaining dressing over all.

Austrian Warm Cabbage Salad

1 pound cabbage, thinly sliced
¼ cup wine vinegar diluted with ¼
   cup water
1 teaspoon horseradish
1 tablespoon sugar
1 teaspoon caraway seeds
½ teaspoon salt
¼ teaspoon pepper
8 slices bacon, diced and cooked
   (reserve fat)

Mix all ingredients except bacon together and bring to boil. Simmer 10 minutes. Add fried bacon with the fat and serve.
Tastes best freshly prepared but can be reheated. In Austria this salad is served with roast pork.
Serves 4.

Avocado Salad

1 package (6 ounce) lime Jello
3 cups boiling water
1 package (8 ounce) cream cheese
2 large avocados, mashed
½ cup mayonnaise
½ cup finely chopped green pepper
½ small onion, grated
1 teaspoon tarragon vinegar
½ cup finely chopped pecans
⅛ teaspoon salt

Dissolve Jello in boiling water, cool. Place in refrigerator until thick. Mix the cream cheese, avocado and mayonnaise. Add the last 5 ingredients. Combine with the Jello mixture. Pour into a 2 quart mold and refrigerate at least 6 hours.
Serves 8 to 10.

Blue Cheese Salad Bowl

1 small head cauliflower
½ cup sliced onion rings
¼ cup sliced pimiento-stuffed
   olives
⅔ cup clear French salad dressing
   with herbs and spices
½ cup crumbled blue cheese
1 head lettuce, torn in pieces

Separate cauliflower into flowerets. Add onion rings and olives. Marinate in dressing ½ hour in refrigerator. Add blue cheese and lettuce. Toss.
Serves 8.

Belgian Tossed Salad

1 package (10 ounce) frozen
    brussels sprouts
½ cup salad oil
¼ cup vinegar
1 garlic clove, minced
1 teaspoon dried, crushed parsley
½ teaspoon salt
¼ teaspoon dried, crushed basil
⅛ teaspoon pepper
2 quarts mixed salad greens, torn
    into bite-size pieces
½ medium red onion, sliced and
    separated into rings
6 slices bacon, crisp-cooked and
    crumbled

Cook brussels sprouts in boiling, salted water until barely tender (about 5 minutes). Drain. Meanwhile, combine oil, vinegar and seasonings. Cut brussels sprouts in half LENGTHWISE; add to marinade and chill. Arrange greens, onion rings and bacon in salad bowl. Add brussels sprouts with marinade and toss gently.
Serves 8.

Fresh Broccoli Salad

1 medium bunch fresh broccoli, cut
    flowerets into bite-size pieces
4 hard boiled eggs, sliced
½ onion, chopped
½ cup stuffed olives, sliced
1 cup mayonnaise
½ cup lemon juice
salt and pepper to taste

Combine all the dry ingredients. Combine mayonnaise, lemon juice, salt and pepper. Stir and blend with the dry ingredients. Chill to serve. Best if chilled overnight.
Serves 6 to 8.

Cabbage Salad

2 cups shredded cabbage
1 green onion, minced
⅓ cup mayonnaise
⅓ cup sour cream
1 teaspoon curry
1 teaspoon wine vinegar
1 teaspoon Dijon mustard
1 package (10 ounce) frozen peas,
   thawed
1 cup Spanish peanuts

Mix cabbage and onion. Stir together mayonnaise, sour cream, curry, vinegar, mustard and spread over cabbage. Top with peas and peanuts. Refrigerate overnight or at least 3 to 4 hours.

Hot Bean Salad

1 can (1 pound) kidney beans,
   drained
1 cup chopped celery
¼ cup sweet pickle relish
½ cup chopped onion
1 cup grated longhorn cheese
½ teaspoon salt
1 tablespoon chili powder (hot)
½ teaspoon Worcestershire sauce
½ cup mayonnaise
¼ cup grated longhorn cheese
1 cup crushed corn chips
pepper rings

Drain beans, combine with celery, pickle relish, onions and cheese. Blend seasonings with mayonnaise. Toss lightly with bean mixture. Spoon into shallow baking dish. Top with cheese and corn chips. Bake at 400° for 10 to 15 minutes. Garnish with pepper rings.
Serves 4.

Kidney Bean Salad

1 can (15 ounce) kidney beans,
   drained
¼ cup sweet pickle relish
1 tablespoon minced onion
½ teaspoon salt
½ teaspoon prepared mustard
¼ teaspoon chili powder

Place all ingredients in a small bowl and stir until well combined. Cover and refrigerate until serving time. Serve on romaine or chicory.
Serves 6.

Congealed Beet Salad

1½ cups canned Julienne beets,
    drained, save juice
beet juice plus enough water to
    make 2 cups of liquid
2 packages (3 ounce) lemon Jello
¼ teaspoon cider vinegar
¼ teaspoon celery seed
1 onion, finely diced
1 tablespoon horseradish

Heat the liquid and dissolve Jello in it. Add beets and fold in next 4 ingredients. Pour into ring mold and chill.
Serve salad on plate with greens and put a bowl of dressing inside ring.

Dressing:
1 cup sour cream
3 to 4 tablespoons of mayonnaise
horseradish to taste

Combine all ingredients.

Day Ahead Green Salad

1 small head Iceberg lettuce, bite-
    size pieces
1 bunch fresh spinach, bite-size
    pieces
1 package (10 ounce) frozen peas,
    uncooked
2 bunches green onions, chopped
8 slices bacon, cooked and
    crumbled
4 hard-boiled eggs, sliced

Dressing:
1 cup sour cream
½ cup mayonnaise
1 package Italian salad dressing
    mix (Good Seasons preferred)

In a long glass dish, layer lettuce, spinach, peas, onions, bacon and eggs. Mix dressing ingredients together and spread over top. Seal tightly with plastic wrap and refrigerate for 24 hours. Sprinkle with croutons before serving.
Serves 8 to 10.

Garbanzo Salad

2 cans (15 ounce) garbanzo beans, drained, rinsed
2 medium tomatoes, chopped
3 green onions with tops, thinly sliced
¾ cup snipped fresh parsley
¾ cup (4 ounces) finely cubed Cheddar cheese
½ cup fresh lemon juice
⅓ cup olive oil
½ teaspoon ground cumin seeds
½ teaspoon salt
¼ teaspoon freshly ground black pepper

Combine beans, tomatoes, onions, parsley and cheese in medium-size bowl. Mix remaining ingredients in jar with tight-fitting lid; pour over bean mixture. Cover and refrigerate at least 1 hour.
May be stored in refrigerator up to one week.

Layered Vegetable Salad

1 head lettuce, shredded
½ cup chopped celery
½ cup chopped green bell pepper
1 large onion, chopped
1 package (10 ounce) frozen green peas, uncooked
1 cup mayonnaise
2 tablespoons sugar
½ cup grated Cheddar cheese
8 slices bacon, fried and crumbled

Cover bottom of 9 x 13 inch pan with shredded lettuce. Layer celery, green pepper, onion and peas. Spread mayonnaise evenly over all. Sprinkle with sugar and cheese. Fry bacon until crisp. Crumble and spread over top. Cover tightly and refrigerate overnight.
Serves 10.

Molded Gazpacho Salad with Avocado Dressing

2 envelopes unflavored gelatin
¾ cup tomato juice
1½ cups tomato juice
⅓ cup red wine vinegar
1 teaspoon salt
⅛ teaspoon Tabasco
2 small tomatoes, peeled and diced (1 cup)
1 medium cucumber, pared and diced (1 cup)
½ medium green pepper, diced (½ cup)
¼ cup chopped red onion
1 tablespoon chopped chives
1 clove garlic, crushed

In medium saucepan, sprinkle gelatin over ¾ cup tomato juice to soften. Place over low heat, stir constantly until gelatin is dissolved. Remove from heat. Stir in ½ cup tomato juice, vinegar, salt, Tabasco. Set in a bowl of ice, stirring occasionally until mixture is consistency of unbeaten egg white (about 15 minutes). Fold in all remaining ingredients until well combined. Pour into 1½ quart mold that has been rinsed with cold water - or individual molds. Refrigerate until firm (at least 6 hours). Serve with avocado dressing. *Serves 10 to 12.*

Avocado Dressing

1 large ripe avocado (about 1 pound)
½ cup sour cream
½ cup light cream
1 tablespoon grated onion
1½ teaspoons salt
⅛ teaspoon cayenne pepper
1 clove garlic, crushed
1 tablespoon lemon juice

Peel and cut avocado into chunks. Place with all the above ingredients into a blender. Blend until smooth. Refrigerate covered (place plastic film directly on surface) until well chilled.
Yields 2 cups.

Marinated Tomato Salad

3 medium tomatoes, coarsely
    chopped
3 medium onions, coarsely chopped
3 green peppers, chopped
2 tablespoons snipped parsley
1 clove garlic, pressed
1 teaspoon salt
¼ teaspoon pepper
¾ cup red wine vinegar
2 tablespoons vegetable oil

Combine all ingredients in glass bowl. Toss well.
Marinate 4-5 hours.
Will keep several days.
Serves 8.

Oriental Salad

1 can (14 ounce) fancy Chinese
    vegetables
1 cup cut green beans
1 cup small English peas
1 cup water chestnuts, sliced
1 medium onion, sliced
½ cup cider vinegar
½ cup salad oil
½ cup sugar
⅛ teaspoon coarse pepper
⅛ teaspoon white pepper
salt to taste

Layer the first 5 ingredients. Thoroughly blend
the last 6 ingredients, pouring the liquid over each
layer. This should be made at least one day
ahead.
*This can be kept 3 or 4 weeks, if covered and
refrigerated.*
Serves 12.

Spinach Salad Julie

½ pound fresh spinach, chopped or
    1 package (10 ounce) frozen
    chopped spinach, thawed
2 hard-boiled eggs, sieved
2 tablespoons cottage cheese
4 tablespoons chopped Cheddar
3 tablespoons mayonnaise
1 teaspoon dry mustard
salt
1 tablespoon grated onion
1 tablespoon finely chopped celery
2 teaspoons lemon juice

If using frozen spinach, squeeze out moisture.
Mix all but eggs, let set for 2 hours. Serve on lettuce leaf with sieved egg on top and ½ teaspoon
horseradish on the side.

Oriental Spinach Salad

2 bunches spinach (1 pound)
½ pound bacon, diced and cooked
1 large onion, sliced
2 cans (8 ounce) water chestnuts,
   sliced
4 boiled eggs, sliced
1 can (14 ounce) bean sprouts,
   drained

Dressing:
1 cup salad oil
½ cup wine vinegar
⅓ cup catsup
2 teaspoons salt
¾ cup sugar

Wash spinach and dry. Mix salad ingredients. Mix together ingredients for dressing. Pour over salad just before serving.
Serves 8.

Dilly-Pickle Potato Salad

8 to 10 small whole red new
   potatoes (about 1 pound)

Dressing:
1 hard-cooked egg
½ cup mayonnaise
1 tablespoon fresh lemon juice
¼ cup half and half
½ cup minced green onions
½ cup minced sweet cucumber
   pickle slices
¼ to ⅓ cup minced green bell
   pepper or red pepper
1 tablespoon minced parsley
1 teaspoon salt
½ teaspoon marjoram
½ teaspoon summer savory
¼ teaspoon pepper

Garnish:
Chopped pimiento (optional)

In large saucepan, cook unpeeled potatoes until fork-tender, about 20 minutes. While the potatoes are cooking, mix dressing. In medium bowl chop the egg. Stir in mayonnaise and lemon juice; add cream. Stir in minced onion, pickles, green or red pepper, parsley and seasonings until well mixed. Taste for flavor (the dressing may taste salty; do not be concerned; the potatoes will absorb the salt). After potatoes are cooked, drain; plunge into cold water and drain immediately. Peel and slice into medium bowl; pour dressing over warm potatoes and toss until well coated. Cool. Then cover and refrigerate until chilled.
Serves 4 to 6.

Hot German Potato Salad

½ **pound bacon (10 to 12 slices)**
½ **cup chopped onions**
2 **tablespoons flour**
2 **tablespoons sugar**
1½ **teaspoons salt**
¹⁄₁₆ **teaspoon pepper**
1 **teaspoon celery seed**
½ **cup cider vinegar**
¾ **cup water**
6 **cups boiled, sliced potatoes**
2 **hard-boiled eggs, sliced**
2 **tablespoons chopped parsley**
1 **can (2 ounce) pimiento, chopped**
bacon curls

Cook bacon until crisp, drain and crumble. (Reserve 2 or 3 slices for garnish.) Cook onions in ¼ cup of bacon fat until tender. Blend in flour, sugar, salt, celery seed and pepper. Add vinegar and water and cook until mixture is bubbly, stirring constantly. Add potatoes, bacon and heat thoroughly, tossing lightly. Garnish with sliced eggs, parsley, pimiento and bacon curls.

Tabbouli Salad from Lebanon

1 **cup Bulghur wheat (cracked**
   wheat)
2 **cups boiling water**
¼ **cup olive oil**
¼ **cup lemon juice**
¼ **cup white wine vinegar**
2 **teaspoons salt**
1 **teaspoon pepper**
2 **cups parsley, chopped**
½ **cup fresh mint or 2 tablespoons**
   dried mint, chopped
1½ **cups chopped fresh tomatoes**
1 **cup chopped green onions, or ¾**
   cup chopped scallions
1 **cup chopped cucumber (optional)**

Combine Bulghur wheat and boiling water. Refrigerate. Let stand overnight. Add remaining ingredients. Refrigerate. Let stand overnight again or at least 4 more hours. Serve cold. *Serves 6 to 8.*

Tomato Mousse

1 tablespoon gelatin
½ cup cold water
1 can (10½ ounce) tomato soup
½ can water
1 package (8 ounce) Philadelphia
   cream cheese
½ cup mayonnaise
½ cup chopped celery
¼ cup chopped green stuffed olives
¼ cup chopped green pepper
¼ cup chopped onion
¼ cup pecans, chopped

Soak gelatin in ½ cup cold water. Heat soup and water to boiling. Take from heat and add gelatin. Then add cheese and stir to dissolve. Cool and add mayonnaise, celery, olives, pepper, onion and pecans. Place in a 4 cup greased mold. Let chill until firm. Unmold.

Tomato Slices in Roquefort Marinade

4 firm tomatoes, sliced
2 onions, sliced
1 green pepper, sliced
½ cup salad oil
¼ cup vinegar
2 tablespoons finely chopped
   parsley
1 teaspoon salt
½ teaspoon sugar
⅛ teaspoon crushed savory
1¼ ounces Roquefort cheese,
   crumbled

Alternate layers of tomato, onion and green pepper in large bowl. Blend remaining ingredients except savory and cheese and pour over vegetables. Refrigerate. Allow to marinate 2 hours. Spoon marinade over vegetables. Just before serving, garnish with savory and cheese.

Tossed Mushroom Salad

3 cups sliced fresh mushrooms
1 package (10 ounce) frozen cut
  green beans, cooked
1 medium red onion, cut into rings
½ cup olive or salad oil
⅓ cup red wine vinegar
1 teaspoon oregano
1 teaspoon salt
¼ teaspoon onion powder
¼ teaspoon garlic powder
⅛ teaspoon ground black pepper
crisp salad greens
4 slices bacon, cooked and
  crumbled
2 hard-cooked eggs, chopped

Arrange mushrooms, green beans and onion in a 3-quart shallow glass salad bowl. Combine oil, vinegar and seasonings in a screw-top jar. Shake well. Pour over vegetables. Cover and refrigerate 1 hour. Drain off marinade and save to use as additional dressing. Toss vegetables with crisp salad greens. Pass bacon and eggs as toppings. *Serves 4 to 6.*

24-Hour Slaw

1 head cabbage (3 pounds),
  chopped
2 bell peppers, chopped
1 small can pimientos, chopped
1 small onion, chopped
1 cup white sugar
½ cup brown sugar
1 cup vinegar
1 teaspoon celery seed
1 teaspoon mustard seed
¼ teaspoon turmeric

Place chopped ingredients in bowl. Boil remaining ingredients together for 5 minutes. Immediately pour the hot dressing over the chopped vegetables, refrigerate overnight. This will keep 2 or 3 weeks.
During the summer this is excellent to keep on hand for a ready salad. Good sweet-sour taste. Would be good with pork or bland meat dishes. Salt-free salad.
Serves 8.

24-Hour Vegetable Salad

10 to 15 fresh mushrooms, sliced
¼ cup chopped green onions
2 cucumbers, peeled and sliced
¼ cup chopped fresh parsley
1 large green pepper, sliced thin
3 large tomatoes, cut into wedges
6 ounces Swiss cheese, cut into
   thin strips
1 can (6 ounce) whole pitted black
   olives
garlic salt and salt
¾ cup Italian salad dressing (Good
   Seasons made with white wine
   vinegar preferred)

In a large deep glass bowl layer first 8 ingredients in order given, top with drained olives. Add ½ teaspoon garlic salt and ½ teaspoon salt to the ¾ cup salad dressing, stir and pour over top of salad. Cover and refrigerate for at least 12 hours, better if it stays 24 hours. Toss and serve.
Serves 6.

Vegetable Salad Elegante

1 can (10 ounce) small whole
   carrots, drained
1 can (8½ ounce) artichoke hearts,
   drained
1 can (16 ounce) green beans (thin,
   whole, little ones) about 2 cups
   in a can, drained
1 can (16 ounce) wax beans,
   drained
1 green pepper, cut in circles
1 small whole onion, cut in circles

Marinade:
1 teaspoon salt
1 teaspoon pepper
½ teaspoon dry mustard
1 cup sugar
½ cup salad oil
1 cup white vinegar

Combine all ingredients. Marinate overnight. Drain off dressing a couple of hours before serving.
Serves 6 to 8.

Blue Cheese Dressing or Dip

4 ounces blue cheese, crumbled
1 small garlic clove, pressed
1 cup mayonnaise
½ cup sour cream
1 teaspoon lemon juice
¼ teaspoon cayenne

Use pastry blender for crumbling cheese. Combine all ingredients. Blend well.
Best made a day or two ahead.

Boiled Salad Dressing

1 egg
1 tablespoon butter
1 teaspoon mustard
1 cup cream
½ cup sugar
¾ teaspoon salt
1 teaspoon pepper
1 cup vinegar
1 teaspoon horseradish
(As substitute for cream, 1 cup milk
  and 2 tablespoons flour)

Boil vinegar, sugar and butter over low heat or in a double boiler, stirring until thoroughly mixed. Stir beaten egg into cream until smooth. Add seasoning and stir this slowly into the hot saucepan. Keep stirring as it is slowly cooked to a creamy consistency. Place in covered jar and chill.

Bombay Salad Dressing

½ quart mayonnaise
¼ cup Worcestershire sauce
¼ cup water
2 tablespoons vinegar
1½ avocados
1½ garlic cloves
½ tablespoon MSG
½ tablespoon salt
½ tablespoon pepper
¼ bunch green onions and tops,
  diced

Put all ingredients in food processor or blender. Blend well. Chill before serving.

India Relish Dressing

1 quart Miracle Whip
1 bottle catsup
½ jar India relish
1 large onion, grated
1 clove garlic, minced
3 hard-boiled eggs, chopped

Combine all ingredients. Chill well before serving.
Yields 3 pints.

Mary's Salad Dressing

1 cup sugar
3 tablespoons grated onion
1 teaspoon salt
2 teaspoons prepared mustard
½ cup vinegar
½ cup catsup
1 cup salad oil

Mix onion and sugar. Let stand one hour. Add rest of ingredients. Beat well. Put in a jar and refrigerate. Keeps well.
Yields 1 ½ pints.

Onion Dressing

⅓ cup red wine vinegar
½ cup sugar
2 tablespoons onion (¼ of small onion)
1 teaspoon seasoned salt
1 teaspoon dry mustard
1 cup salad oil

Place vinegar and sugar in food processor or blender, mixing until sugar is dissolved. Add onion, puree. Add salt and mustard; slowly pour in oil, while processor or blender is running. This dressing keeps for weeks in the refrigerator. If it should become separated, allow to come to room temperature, and stir.

Celery Seed Dressing

½ cup brown sugar
1 teaspoon dry mustard
1 teaspoon salt
1 teaspoon paprika
1 teaspoon celery seed
1 cup salad oil (safflower preferred)
¼ cup cider vinegar
1 teaspoon onion juice

Mix dry ingredients. Add oil and vinegar alternately, using a wire whisk. Add onion juice. Beat until thick.
Great served on fruit, or avocado and lettuce salad with lamb.

Cole Slaw Dressing

1 whole egg, beaten
½ cup sugar
⅓ cup vinegar
1 tablespoon butter or margarine
½ cup mayonnaise
½ cup whipping cream

Heat skillet sizzling hot. Pour in mixture of egg, sugar and vinegar and stir until thick. Add butter. Allow to cool 20-30 minutes. Add mayonnaise and whipping cream when ready to use.

Fruit Salad Dressing

½ pint heavy whipping cream
1 cup powdered sugar
2 egg yolks
juice of ½ lemon

Whip heavy cream. Gradually add powdered sugar while beating. Beat egg yolks and blend in lemon juice. Fold into whipped cream. Mix well just before serving and pour over fresh and canned fruit combination.

Savoring Vegetables

THE GATE AND BEYOND
Artist - Peter Hurd
47" X 90"   1952
egg tempera painting
In the Permanent Collection
Roswell Museum and Art Center

Peter Hurd

Peter Hurd was born in Roswell, New Mexico, February 22, 1904 and passed away July 7, 1984. His parents were New Englanders who left Boston, where his father was a prominent lawyer, and settled in Roswell, New Mexico, because of a respiratory ailment. Peter attended New Mexico Military Institute where Paul Horgan was a fellow student who became Peter's lifelong friend. In fact, he and Paul wrote a novel as a class assignment together.

After graduation from the Institute in 1925, Peter was appointed to the United States Military Academy at West Point. General Douglas MacArthur offered the cadet the choice of graduating to become an officer or an honorable resignation to become an artist. Cadet Hurd chose to become an artist.

He studied with N.C. Wyeth and for a short time he attended Haverford College. After leaving Haverford, he became an apprentice of Wyeth for five years and attended Pennsylvania Academy of Fine Arts in Phaladelphia at the same time.

In 1927, he became engaged to the daughter of N.C. Wyeth, Henriette, who was a practicing artist. They were married and lived and worked in Chadds Ford, Pennsylvania, for some time. The Hurds moved to New Mexico and made their home on the Sentinel Ranch, San Patricio, in the Hondo Valley fifty miles west of Roswell, where they are still residing in 1983. He was commissioned to do murals in public buildings in New Mexico and Texas. His most ambitious mural was for Texas Tech University in Lubbock, Texas.

After Pearl Harbor, he was sworn in as Captain in the Army Air Corps and became an illustrator for Life Magazine with the title of War Correspondent. He sketched war scenes in Britain, India, Arabia, Italy and Africa, first in tempera and later in a faster method in watercolor.

Peter took a postwar commission for American Factors and painted ten works commemorating the Centennial of the Hawaiian Islands development. They are now installed in American Factors in Honolulu.

He did many portraits of prominent people, among them, Senator Barry Goldwater, Governor Rockefeller of Arkansas, King Faisal of Saudi Arabia and President Johnson. President Johnson rejected the painting for the White House. However, it is now hanging in the National Portrait Gallery in the Smithsonian Institution in Washington, D.C. The artist was happy with this arrangement because even more people would get to see the painting there than at the White House.

Peter Hurd's works are in the collections of: Art Institute of Chicago, Chicago, Illinois; Canajoharie Library and Art Gallery, Canajoharie, N.Y.; Carlsbad Municipal Fine Arts Museum, Carlsbad, N.M.; Amon Carter Museum of Western Art, Fort Worth, Texas; Carter Museum of Western Art, Fort Worth, Texas; Colorado Springs Fine Arts Center, Colorado Springs, Colo.; Dallas Museum of Fine Arts, Dallas, Texas; Delaware Art Museum, Wilmington, Delaware; Denver Art Museum, Denver, Colorado; El Paso Museum of Art, El Paso, Texas; Fort Worth Art Museum, Fort Worth, Texas; Indianapolis Museum of Art, Indianapolis, Indiana; Metropolitan Museum of Art, New York City, N.Y.; The Museum, Texas Tech University, Lubbock, Texas; Museum of New Mexico, Santa Fe, New Mexico; National Gallery of Scotland, Edinburgh, Scotland; National Portrait Gallery, Smithsonian Institution, Washington, D.C.; William Rockhill Nelson Gallery and Atkins Museum of Fine Art, Kansas City, Missouri; and The Roswell Museum and Art Center, Roswell, New Mexico.

THE GATE AND BEYOND was created from several locations near Roswell and looks west to the Capitan Mountain. This painting, a gift from the artist, is part of the permanent collection in the Hurd Wing at The Roswell Museum and Art Center, Roswell, New Mexico.

Baked Artichokes

2 packages (9 ounce) frozen
   artichokes
4 green onions, chopped
2 tablespoons butter
¼ pound fresh mushrooms,
   chopped
1 clove garlic, minced
1½ cups fresh bread crumbs (use
   white bread with sesame crust)
½ teaspoon salt
¼ teaspoon dried basil
½ teaspoon (or more) cracked black
   pepper
1½ cups shredded mild Cheddar
   cheese
2 eggs
½ cup sour cream (or sour ½ and
   ½)
2 tablespoons butter, melted

Thaw artichokes by running water over them until they separate. Arrange in single layer in shallow, greased 6-cup baking dish (9 inch square pan). Saute onions in 2 tablespoons butter until soft; then add mushrooms and garlic and cook 5 minutes. Remove from heat. Stir ¾ cup bread crumbs, salt, basil, pepper and 1 cup cheese into mushroom mixture. In small bowl, beat eggs and sour cream with a fork until smooth. Stir into skillet with mushroom mix until well blended. Spread mix over artichokes in baking dish. Combine remaining bread crumbs with remaining ½ cup cheese and sprinkle over top of casserole. Drizzle with 2 tablespoons melted butter. Bake at 350º for 20 minutes or until artichokes are tender when pierced with a fork. Sprinkle with bacon crumbles for optional garnish.
Dish can be prepared a day ahead and kept in refrigerator. Baking time probably should be increased if dish is placed cold in oven.
Serves 4 main dishes, or
6 side dishes

Artichoke Hearts Au Gratin

2 packages (9 ounce) frozen
   artichoke hearts
¼ cup margarine
salt and freshly ground black
   pepper
¼ teaspoon dry mustard
2 teaspoons finely chopped onion
⅓ cup flour
1½ cups milk
1 egg, slightly beaten
¾ cup grated Swiss cheese, divided
1 tablespoon fine bread crumbs
¼ teaspoon paprika

Cook artichoke hearts as directed on package. Drain well, reserving ½ cup liquid. Melt margarine in skillet. Add seasonings, onion, flour, milk and artichoke liquid. Blend and cook until thickened. Gradually stir hot sauce into egg, add ¼ cup cheese. Blend well. Put artichokes in a buttered 9 x 9 inch casserole. Pour sauce over artichokes, covering well. Sprinkle remaining ½ cup cheese, bread crumbs and paprika over top. Bake in preheated 450º oven for 12 minutes.
Serves 6.

Artichoke and Spinach Casserole

**2 packages (10 ounce) frozen
   chopped spinach
8 ounces cream cheese, softened
1 cup sliced water chestnuts
½ cup butter, softened
1 can (14 ounce) artichoke hearts,
   rinsed and drained
salt and pepper to taste
buttered bread or cracker crumbs to
   cover top**

Slightly cook spinach and drain in sieve, squeezing out excess moisture with back of large spoon. Return spinach to pan; add softened butter and cream cheese. Heat mixture enough to melt and blend, stirring constantly. Add water chestnuts, salt and pepper. Quarter artichokes, then dry with paper towel, and place in a buttered 1½ quart baking dish. Pour spinach mixture over, then sprinkle on the buttered crumbs. Bake at 350º for 15-20 minutes.
Serves 8.

Asparagus Au Gratin

**2 cans (16 ounce) whole green
   asparagus
1 tablespoon minced onion
1 tablespoon chopped green pepper
1 tablespoon finely cut celery
4 tablespoons butter (divided)
1 cup sliced water chestnuts
sliced almonds
2 tablespoons flour
½ cup milk or light cream
¼ teaspoon salt
½ cup shredded sharp Cheddar
   cheese
1 jar (2 ounce) pimientos**

Drain asparagus, and place in rows down center of an 8 x 12 inch baking dish. Set aside. Simmer onion, green pepper and celery in 2 tablespoons butter until tender. Add water chestnuts and almonds. Set aside. Mix remaining butter, flour, milk and salt; cook over low heat until thick. Add white sauce to onion mixture; pour over asparagus. Cover top with cheese and lay strips of pimiento on top of cheese. Bake in 350º oven for 20 minutes.
Serves 8.

Asparagus Casserole

**2 cans (20 ounce) asparagus
1 cup grated Cheddar cheese
1 cup slivered almonds
1 cup crumbled Ritz crackers
½ teaspoon salt
½ cup butter, melted
¾ cup milk**

Into a 1½ quart baking dish, place the above ingredients except milk in layers as listed. Use ½ of each ingredient in each of the 2 layers. Assemble 3 hours before cooking and pour milk over and let set. Bake at 350º for 1 hour.
Serves 8.

Bean Pot Casserole

4 tablespoons bacon drippings
2 or 3 medium onions, chopped
1 tablespoon seasoned salt
½ cup brown sugar
½ cup catsup
1 tablespoon prepared mustard
½ teaspoon pepper
3 tablespoons vinegar
1 can (16 ounce) pork and beans
1 can (16 ounce) kidney beans
1 can (16 ounce) chili beans

Fry chopped onion in grease until soft but not brown. Drain off half of juice from each can of beans. Mix all ingredients and pour into 2 quart baking dish or bean pot. Bake uncovered in 350⁰ oven for 60-75 minutes.
Can be prepared ahead of time. Great for picnic suppers.
Serves 6 to 8.

Green Bean Beppu

1 pound mushrooms, sliced
1 small onion, grated
½ cup butter, melted
¼ cup flour
1½ teaspoons salt
½ teaspoon white pepper
3 cups milk, scalded
1 tablespoon soy sauce
⅛ teaspoon hot pepper sauce
2 cups sharp Cheddar cheese, grated
2 pounds green beans, cut Julienne style and cooked crisp-tender
2 cans (6 ounce) water chestnuts, drained and sliced
1 jar (4 ounce) pimiento, chopped
1 can (3 ounce) french fried onions, crumbled

In large heavy skillet saute mushrooms and onion. Blend in flour, salt and pepper. Gradually add milk. Cook stirring constantly until thick and smooth. Blend in soy sauce, pepper sauce and cheese. Stir in beans, water chestnuts and pimiento. Turn into 3 quart casserole. Bake at 350⁰ for 15 minutes. Top with onions and bake 10 minutes longer.
3 packages (10 ounce) frozen green beans Julienne style thawed can be substituted for the fresh beans.
Seves 8 to 10.

Green Beans with Tomatoes

1½ pounds beans, cut into 1½ inch
  pieces
salt
1 cup heavy cream
½ cup red wine vinegar
2 tomatoes, peeled and cubed

Bring water to boil. Add salt and beans. Cook 7 minutes. Immediately rinse in cold water to stop cooking. In serving bowl beat cream, add vinegar, fold in beans and tomatoes.
Serves 6.

Sweet and Sour Beets

1½ pounds beets
¼ cup plus 1 tablespoon vegetable
  oil
¼ cup frozen orange juice
  concentrate
¼ cup cider vinegar
1 tablespoon Dijon mustard
1 tablespoon soy sauce
¼ teaspoon salt
freshly ground pepper

Cover beets with water in a 2-quart saucepan and bring to boil over high heat. Reduce heat and simmer until beets are fork tender. Remove from pan, cool and peel. Slice beets and transfer to large mixing bowl. Combine oil, concentrate, vinegar, mustard, soy sauce, salt and pepper in small saucepan and bring to boil over medium high heat. Pour over beets and mix gently. Serve warm or cover and refrigerate and serve chilled. Spoon into lettuce cups if desired.
Best when prepared a day ahead. May be heated gently if desired.
Serves 8.

Baked Broccoli

½ pound mushrooms, sliced
¼ cup butter
¼ cup flour
1 teaspoon salt
3 packages (10 ounce) frozen
  broccoli spears
1 can (6 ounce) tomato paste
1 chicken bouillon cube
2 tablespoons grated Cheddar
  cheese

Saute mushrooms in butter about 5 minutes. Blend in flour and salt. Set aside. Cook broccoli until about half done. Drain and save liquid. Mix tomato paste with 1½ cups broccoli liquid and gradually blend into the butter and flour mixture, stirring constantly and cooking until smooth and thickened. Add bouillon cube and stir until dissolved. Stir in cheese. Place broccoli spears in large greased baking dish and cover with sauce. Bake in 350º oven for about 30 minutes.
Serves 8.

Creamed Cabbage - Fit for a King

4 cups shredded cabbage
½ cup minced onion
2 tablespoons butter or margarine
3 ounces cream cheese, softened
    and diced
2 tablespoons snipped fresh dill
salt and white pepper

Blanch cabbage in boiling water for 3 minutes. Drain well, refresh under running cold water, then drain well. In sauce pan saute onions in butter until onions are softened. Add cabbage and toss well. Add the cream cheese, cook the mixture over low heat, stirring, until the cheese is melted. Add the dill, salt and pepper to taste, and simmer the cabbage 2 minutes.
Serves 4.

Chinese Stirred Cabbage

2 pounds Chinese cabbage
¼ cup oil
salt
½ cup water

Cut cabbage in half lengthwise and remove stems. Slice cabbage crosswise into ½ inch strips. Chop stem. Fry stem in oil for 1 minute. Add salt and ½ cup water. Cover and cook for 3 minutes. Add the sliced cabbage leaves, cover and cook over medium heat for 3 minutes. Serve cabbage with any juice that remains. New American cabbage may be substituted for the Chinese. Quarter cabbage. Discard center stalk, then cut cabbage crosswise into ½ inch strips. Heat oil in skillet, add cabbage, cook for 1 minute. Add salt and water. Cook covered for 3 minutes.
Serves 6.

THE ROSWELL REGISTER   MARCH 7, 1902

Young Ladies Entertained

Mrs. Jno. W. Poe's party for the young ladies, in honor of Miss Ramer and Miss Lucy Lea, was one of the most delightful affairs the young ladies of Roswell have been treated to. Each young lady carried an Irish potato and displayed her acquaintance with the vegetable by the way she peeled it, and it was also used in various other ways to furnish amusement. Cake and coffee were the refreshments.

German Red Cabbage

½ cup shortening
1 onion, diced
1 apple, peeled and diced
1 medium head of red cabbage,
  shredded
1 cup sugar
3 bay leaves
dash cinnamon
1 tablespoon salt
1 teaspoon pepper
dash cloves
½ cup white vinegar
2 cups bouillon or beef stock

In large saucepan or kettle melt shortening and saute apples and onions over medium heat for 3 minutes. Add rest of ingredients and simmer 40 minutes, turning ingredients 2 or 3 times during cooking period.
Serves 6 to 8.

Glazed Carrots

6 or 7 carrots, peeled and sliced
3 tablespoons butter, melted
3 tablespoons lemon juice
¼ cup honey
1 ounce Drambuie
mint leaves

Cook carrots until nearly tender in salted water. Drain. While hot, place in baking dish with butter and lemon juice. Pour honey and Drambuie over carrots, then sprinkle with mint leaves. Cover dish and bake in 325º oven, turning carrots now and then until carrots are glazed and sauce is almost absorbed, 15-20 minutes.
Serves 4.

Carrot Pudding

1 pound fresh carrots (enough to
  make 2 cups when mashed)
1 small onion, chopped
1 cup Ritz cracker crumbs
1 cup Colby or mild cheese, grated
2 eggs
1¼ cups milk
1 teaspoon salt
¼ teaspoon pepper

Cook carrots and onions, mash the carrots. Beat eggs and milk together. Add all ingredients and pour into lightly greased 1½ quart baking dish; set in a pan of water. Bake in 400º oven for 30 to 40 minutes, or until set.
Serves 6 to 8.

Calcutta Carrots

1 can (20 ounce) pineapple chunks
water
8 medium carrots, cut into strips
½ teaspoon curry powder, or more
   to taste
½ teaspoon salt
¼ teaspoon pepper

Drain pineapple syrup into measuring cup and add enough water to make 1 cup. Pour into 10 inch skillet and add carrots, curry, salt and pepper. Over medium heat, heat to boiling; then cover and cook 10 minutes (until carrots are tender). Stir in pineapple chunks; heat.
Serves 4 to 6.

Carrot Charlotte

6 large eggs
¼ teaspoon salt
1 cup sugar
⅓ cup matza meal
1½ cups grated carrots
½ cup blanched almonds, finely
   ground
2 tablespoons wine

Separate the eggs. Beat egg whites with salt, until stiff but not dry. Beat the egg yolks until thick and lemon colored; add the sugar gradually, continuing to beat as you add. Fold in matza meal, grated carrots, almonds, and wine. Fold in the beaten egg whites. Pour into a greased 2½ quart baking dish. Bake in a moderate oven (350º) for 50 to 60 minutes. Serve with wine sauce.

Wine Sauce:
4 egg yolks
⅓ cup sugar
¼ teaspoon cinnamon
1 cup sweet wine

Place the egg yolks in a deep bowl that will fit over a pan of water. Beat until yolks are thick; then gradually beat in the sugar mixed with the cinnamon. Place the bowl over hot, not boiling, water and beat as the wine is slowly poured in. Continue to beat until the sauce stands up high and fluffy. Serve at once over the Charlotte.

Cauliflower En Casserole

1 large head cauliflower
3 tablespoons butter
3 tablespoons flour
2 cups milk
1 cup grated Swiss cheese
1 tablespoon lemon juice
½ teaspoon pepper
¼ teaspoon nutmeg
1 teaspoon paprika
2 egg yolks, beaten
1 cup grated Monterey Jack
  cheese
½ cup cracker crumbs

Break cauliflower into flowerets. Cook in salted water 10 to 15 minutes just to crisp stage. Make a sauce by melting the butter, gradually adding the flour, blending until smooth. Slowly add milk, stirring constantly until smooth and thickened. Add the Swiss cheese, stirring until smooth, add lemon juice and spices. Add several spoonfuls of sauce to the egg yolks. Combine sauce, egg mixture and cauliflower (drained). Turn into a buttered 2 quart casserole. Add Monterey Jack cheese and top with cracker crumbs. Bake in a 350° oven for 30 minutes.

Cauliflower with Topping

1 large head cauliflower
1 cup olive oil
3 cloves garlic, minced
1 tablespoon chopped parsley
1 tablespoon sesame seeds,
  toasted
salt and pepper to taste

Cook cauliflower in salted water until just tender. While cooking make the topping. Cook the garlic and parsley in the olive oil until crisp. Drain the cauliflower, top with the garlic and parsley mixture and then top with the sesame seeds. The topping may be used on broccoli.

Corn Casserole

⅓ cup margarine
¼ cup sugar
1 teaspoon flour
½ teaspoon salt
½ cup evaporated milk
2 eggs, beaten
2 tablespoons chopped parsley
1½ teaspoons baking powder
2 cans (16 ounce) whole kernel
  corn, drained

Melt margarine. Add sugar, mixing well. Stir in flour and salt until well-blended. Remove from heat. Gradually add milk and stir in eggs, blending well. Add parsley and baking powder, mixing quickly. Fold in corn. Pour into buttered 1½ quart dish. Bake in 350° oven for 35 to 40 minutes. *Serves 6 to 8.*

Corn Custard

3 eggs, well beaten
1 cup milk
1 teaspoon flour
1 tablespoon (heaping) sugar
1 tablespoon melted butter or
  margarine
1 can (16 ounce) creamed corn
salt to taste

Mix all ingredients together. Pour into buttered 1½ quart casserole; set in pan of water. Bake at 375°, covered, for 40 minutes. Remove cover for last 20 minutes. This is a light custard type dish. Cannot be made ahead.
Serves 6.

Shoe Peg Corn Casserole

½ cup butter
8 ounces cream cheese
3 cans (12 ounce) shoe peg corn,
  drained
1 can (4 ounce) chopped green
  chiles

Melt butter, stir in cream cheese; stir until well-blended. Add corn and chiles. Bake in 350° oven for 20 minutes.
Serves 8.

Eggplant Supreme

1 large eggplant, peeled and thinly
  sliced
3 tablespoons butter
1 can (8 ounce) minced clams (save
  juice)
2 cups cracker crumbs
½ cup milk
salt

Boil in salted water until tender. Drain and then mix in 2 tablespoons butter. In buttered casserole place layer of eggplant, layer of clams, layer of cracker crumbs. Dot with butter. Blend milk, clam juice and salt and pour over mixture. Bake at 350° for 30 minutes.
Serves 4 to 6.

To remove bitterness in an eggplant, soak slices in cold, salted water for 20 minutes. Rinse and drain well.

Eggplant Etc.

1 cup olive oil
1 eggplant (1 pound), peeled and
   cut in ½ inch cubes
3 cups vegetables, such as onions,
   green peppers, zucchini, celery,
   cut in ½ inch cubes
2 cloves garlic, minced
1 can (28 ounce) solid pack
   tomatoes, undrained
⅓ cup red wine vinegar
2 tablespoons sugar
2 tablespoons capers (optional)
2 tablespoons tomato paste
salt
½ cup chopped parsley
½ cup large manzanillo olives,
   rinsed and thickly sliced
2 teaspoons crumbled dried basil
½ cup salted sunflower seeds, or
   ½ cup raw skinned Spanish
   peanuts

In a large, heavy saucepan combine the first 5 ingredients, and cook for about 30 minutes. Add the rest of the ingredients except nuts, cover, and simmer for 15 minutes. Add nuts and serve warm, not hot, at room temperature.
Should not be frozen, but keeps well in refrigerator for up to 3 weeks.
Serves 10 to 12.

Gingered Peas with Water Chestnuts

2 packages (10 ounce) frozen peas
2 tablespoons butter or margarine
1 can (6 ounce) button mushrooms,
   drained
1 can (8½ ounce) water chestnuts,
   drained, thinly sliced
1 cup green onions, cut in 1 inch
   lengths
¾ teaspoon ground ginger
¼ teaspoon nutmeg
1 can (13¾ ounce) chicken broth
2 tablespoons cornstarch
1 teaspoon salt
⅛ teaspoon garlic salt
⅛ teaspoon pepper

In saucepan, break up frozen peas. Add butter, mushrooms, water chestnuts, green onions, ginger, nutmeg and all but ¼ cup chicken broth. Cover and simmer over low heat for 6 to 8 minutes. In cup, blend cornstarch and reserved chicken broth until smooth. Stir in peas. Cook slowly, stirring constantly, until liquid thickens and boils. Add salt, garlic salt and pepper; simmer 2 to 3 minutes longer
Serves 6 to 8.

Delicious Potatoes

1 large clove garlic, minced
1 large onion, sliced
3 tablespoons butter or margarine
1 large or 2 medium potatoes,
   peeled and sliced
¾ cup heavy cream
½ cup milk
1 teaspoon salt
⅛ teaspoon nutmeg
pepper

In medium size pan, cook garlic and onion in butter over slow heat until tender, about 5 minutes. Add sliced potatoes and cream, milk, salt, nutmeg and pepper. Cook over very low heat about 25 minutes, stirring occasionally to prevent scorch, or until potatoes are tender.
Double or triple according to number of servings needed. Can be covered with shredded cheese then placed under broiler until cheese is melted. Serves 2.

Gourmet Potato Casserole

6 large potatoes, sliced
2 onions, sliced
2 to 4 tomatoes, sliced
2 carrots, grated
½ bell pepper, sliced thin
2 cups chicken broth, heated
2 garlic cloves, minced
4 teaspoons chopped parsley
salt and freshly ground pepper
¼ cup olive oil

Put sliced potatoes, layered with onions in 9 x 12 inch glass casserole. Layer tomatoes, carrots, green pepper on top. Pour hot chicken broth, garlic, parsley and seasonings over casserole. Cook covered in 325° oven for 30 minutes. Add olive oil. Cook uncovered for 15 more minutes.
Good hot or cold.
Serves 6 to 8.

Hash Brown Potato Bake

2 pounds frozen hash brown
   potatoes
1 cup chopped onion
1 can (10½ ounce) cream of
   chicken soup
1 cup sour cream
½ cup butter or margarine
8 ounces sharp cheese, shredded
1 cup crushed potato chips

Thaw potatoes for 30 minutes. Mix all ingredients except potato chips together in 9 x 13 inch baking pan. Spread crushed potato chips on top. Bake in 375° oven for 1 hour.
Serves 10 to 12.

Potato Dumpling

2 medium potatoes, cooked,
    mashed and seasoned with salt,
    or leftover potatoes to equal that
    amount
4 eggs, unbeaten
1 cup flour
chicken broth for poaching
½ cup evaporated milk
2 tablespoons flour

Combine potatoes and eggs. Stir in flour and beat until well mixed. Drop by tablespoon into boiling chicken broth, cooking until they rise to top when done. Lift from broth with slotted spoon into bowl until all are cooked. Combine milk with 2 tablespoons flour; pour into boiling broth. When thickened, pour over dumplings in bowl.
Serves 6.

Savory Potatoes

6 large potatoes
¾ pound sharp Cheddar cheese
1½ pints commercial sour cream
3-4 tablespoons milk
salt and pepper
Parmesan cheese
paprika

Parboil potatoes in jackets. Refrigerate for 24 hours, then remove skins. Grate potatoes and cheese. Dilute sour cream with milk. Lightly toss potatoes with sour cream, salt, pepper and grated cheese. Mixture should be very moist and mushy. Add more sour cream if necessary. Place in large buttered casserole. Top generously with Parmesan cheese. Dust with paprika. Bake uncovered in 350° oven for 1 hour.
May be prepared ahead of time and reheated. Do not freeze.
Serves 12.

Sweet Potato Fluff

3 eggs, separated
3 cups sweet potatoes, mashed
4 tablespoons brown sugar
½ cup butter, melted
1 teaspoon vanilla
2 tablespoons cooking wine, rum or
    brandy
½ teaspoon cinnamon
½ teaspoon nutmeg
salt and pepper to taste

Beat egg yolks well. Add rest of ingredients except egg whites. Beat egg whites and fold in. Bake in buttered 1 quart casserole in 350° oven for 20-25 minutes.
Serves 6 to 8.

Southern Sweet Potatoes

4 large sweet potatoes, baked
½ teaspoon dry mustard
salt and pepper to taste
1 cup bourbon
4 tablespoons butter
tiny marshmallows

Mash sweet potatoes, place in a shallow baking dish. Mix potatoes, dry mustard, salt and pepper and bourbon. Generously dot the top with butter and cover with the marshmallows. Bake in 350° oven for 30 to 45 minutes until the marshmallows are brown.
Keeps well in refrigerator and also freezes well. Can be prepared ahead and baked just before serving.
Serves 8.

Spinach Casserole

1 package (10 ounce) frozen
   chopped spinach
1 tablespoon grated onion
2 eggs, beaten
½ cup sour cream
1 tablespoon flour
2 tablespoons butter, melted
½ cup freshly grated Parmesan
   cheese

Cook spinach and drain well. Mix all other ingredients and add to spinach. Put in casserole. Bake in 350° oven for 30 to 40 minutes.
Serves 4.

Spinach with Rosemary

2 pounds fresh spinach
¼ teaspoon minced fresh rosemary
1 teaspoon chopped parsley
1 tablespoon chopped green onion
2 tablespoons butter
salt and pepper to taste

Wash the spinach 3 or 4 times. Chop rather fine and place in a heavy iron pot or skillet. Add herbs and butter and cover well; let simmer in its own juice until tender (about 15 minutes). Remove cover and add salt and pepper. Serve very hot.
Serves 4.

Spinach Souffle

½ cup butter
¼ cup flour
1 cup milk
⅓ cup grated Cheddar cheese
3 eggs, separated
salt and white pepper
⅛ teaspoon nutmeg
1 package (10 ounce) frozen
   chopped spinach, cooked,
   drained well
1 package (10 ounce) frozen
   chopped spinach, defrosted,
   drained well

Melt butter. Blend in flour, then milk. Stir constantly until thick. Mix in cheese until smooth. Remove from heat. Blend 1 tablespoon of hot mixture into beaten egg yolks, then blend yolk mixture back into sauce. Fold in salt, pepper, nutmeg and spinach cooked and uncooked. Beat egg whites until stiff but not dry, and fold into spinach mixture. Pour all into ungreased 1½ quart baking dish. Place dish in the middle of the oven over a pan of hot water on a shelf below. Bake in 375⁰ oven for 40 minutes.
Serves 8 to 10.

Scalloped Squash

6 yellow squash (about 3 pounds),
   sliced
½ cup minced onion
3 eggs, well beaten
1 tablespoon sugar
salt and pepper
½ cup butter or margarine, divided
1 cup crushed crackers, divided

Boil squash until soft, about 20 minutes. Drain well, and set aside. Combine onion, eggs, sugar, salt and pepper and ½ the butter and crackers. Mix with squash. Place in greased casserole dish. Cover top with remaining butter and crackers. Bake in 350⁰ oven for 25-30 minutes.
Serves 4 to 6.

Squash Supreme

2 pounds yellow squash (frozen can
   be used)
1 onion, chopped, divided
1 cup water chestnuts, sliced
1 carton (8 ounce) sour cream
1 can cream of chicken soup
½ cup margarine
salt and pepper to taste
1 package (8 ounce) Pepperidge
   Farm cornbread dressing

Cook squash with half of onion. Drain well, then add the chestnuts, sour cream and soup. Mix the dressing with the other half onion and melted margarine. Layer in a casserole, reserving some of the dressing for the top. Bake in 350⁰ oven for 30 minutes.
This can be mixed and frozen.
Serves 8 to 10.

Yellow Squash St. Tammany

1 pound yellow squash, sliced
salt and pepper to taste
1 can (10¾ ounce) cream of
  chicken soup, undiluted
1 jar (2 ounce) pimientos, drained,
  diced
2 carrots, grated
1 small onion, chopped (more if you
  wish)
1 carton (8 ounce) commercial sour
  cream
¼ cup butter or margarine, melted
1½ cups seasoned bread crumbs

Cook squash in small amount of boiling water until tender. Drain well. Add salt and pepper. Combine soup, pimiento, carrots, onion, sour cream, and butter. Blend well. Add squash, stirring gently. Alternate layers of squash mixture and bread crumbs in a lightly greased 2 quart casserole. Bake in 350º oven for 30 minutes, or until bubbly.
Freezes well.
Serves 6 to 8.

Tamal

Onions, thinly sliced
Potatoes, thinly sliced
Goose neck squash, sliced
Fresh tomatoes, sliced
Salt and Pepper
Butter

In a buttered glass baking dish, put a layer of onions, a layer of potatoes, a layer of squash and a layer of tomatoes. Sprinkle generously with salt and pepper and dot with lots of butter. Cover and bake in a slow oven, 225 to 250º, for 3 hours. Do not lift the lid during cooking. This dish is better made in advance and reheated.

Tomatoes Nicoise

¼ cup olive oil, divided
2 garlic cloves, minced
2 cups finely chopped onion
6 to 8 large ripe tomatoes, sliced
¼ cup chopped fresh parsley
¼ cup chopped fresh basil leaves
2 tablespoons snipped chives
¾ cup herb stuffing
salt and freshly ground pepper

Heat 2 tablespoons oil in large skillet. Add garlic and onion, stirring frequently, about 5 minutes. Spread this mixture evenly in 9 x 13 inch glass baking dish. Top with sliced tomatoes. Mix remaining ingredients and sprinkle on top. Drizzle with 2 tablespoons oil and bake in preheated 350º oven for 25 minutes until lightly browned.
Serves 8 to 10.

Tomato Timbale

4 pounds ripe tomatoes, peeled
4 eggs, beaten
1 cup milk
½ cup sugar
½ teaspoon salt
⅛ teaspoon nutmeg

Stew tomatoes in own juice. Puree in blender or food processor. Cool, then add rest of ingredients. Bake in buttered custard cups in 325⁰ oven about 1 hour, until a knife inserted midway between center and rim comes out clean. *Serves 6.*

Braised Turnips

2 pounds turnips, peeled and cubed
¼ pound bacon, diced
½ cup minced onion
2 tablespoons butter or margarine
½ cup chicken stock
¾ teaspoon sugar
¾ teaspoon salt
2 tablespoons fresh minced parsley
2 tablespoons lemon juice
salt and pepper to taste

Blanch turnips in boiling salted water for 1 minute. Drain, refresh under running, cold water and pat dry. Set aside. In skillet saute bacon until crisp; remove and drain. Add onion and butter to skillet and cook over moderate heat, stirring, until onion is softened. Add turnips, chicken stock, sugar and salt, and braise, covered, over low heat for 15 minutes or until turnips are tender. Cook mixture, uncovered, stirring, until all liquid is evaporated. Add bacon, parsley, lemon juice, and salt and pepper.
This can be cooked ahead of time, refrigerated, and then put in the microwave for reheating. When this is done, do not add the parsley leaves until after the reheating.
Serves 8.

Zucchini Rice Bake

1 large onion, chopped
1 green pepper, chopped
3 tablespoons butter
2 pounds zucchini, sliced
1 cup cooked rice
2 eggs, beaten
1 cup grated Cheddar cheese
salt to taste

Saute onion and pepper in butter. Set aside. Cook zucchini until nearly tender. Drain. Mix rice, eggs, onion and pepper. In greased 1 quart casserole put layer of rice mixture, then layer of zucchini. Top with cheese. Bake in 350⁰ oven for 30 minutes.
Serves 4 to 6.

Southwest Zucchini

4 cups sliced zucchini squash
1 medium bell pepper
1 small white onion
1 stalk celery
2 tablespoons butter
2 eggs
1 cup mayonnaise
²/₃ cup grated Cheddar cheese
²/₃ cup cracker crumbs

Cook squash for a few minutes in 3 or 4 table-spoons water (until partially tender). Saute pepper, onion and celery in butter until tender. Mix eggs into mayonnaise. Combine mayonnaise mixture with all vegetables. Pour into casserole. Sprinkle cheese, then cracker crumbs over all. Bake at 350⁰ for 30 mintues.

2 cups zucchini and 2 cups of summer squash can be used. Also, Monterey Jack or Parmesan cheese can be used. ¼ teaspoon pepper can be added to egg and mayonnaise. One can (4 ounce) chopped green chiles may be added.
Serves 8.

Zesty Sandwich

1½ tablespoons red wine vinegar
¼ teaspoon salt
¼ teaspoon pepper
¼ teaspoon Dijon mustard
¼ cup olive oil
1 loaf French bread
1 clove garlic
2 tomatoes, thinly sliced
2 tablespoons chopped green
   onions
garlic salt
10-12 ripe black olives, sliced
½ cup sliced, cooked green beans
½ medium green pepper, thinly
   sliced
6-8 fresh mushrooms, thinly sliced
2 tablespoons fresh minced parsley

In a bowl whisk together the vinegar, salt, pepper and mustard. Add olive oil in a stream, whisking, and continue to whisk until all ingredients are well blended. Cut the French bread in half horizontally. Cut the garlic clove in half and rub on cut sides of the bread. Drizzle half the dressing on bottom half of the bread. Cover bottom of bread with tomatoes, sprinkle with garlic salt. Now add the green onions, olives, green beans, green pepper, mushrooms and parsley in that order. Top with remaining dressing and place the top part of bread on the vegetables. Tie with string 6 to 8 times at equal intervals. Wrap tightly in foil. Weight the loaf with a heavy board in the refrigerator for at least 2 hours. Unwrap, remove strings and slice into 3 inch pieces.
Serves 4 to 6.

Vegetable Curry on Rice

2 tablespoons salad oil
2 cups fresh or frozen chopped
   onions
1 cup chopped celery
2 garlic cloves, minced
1 medium head cauliflower
1 can (16 ounce) tomatoes
1 package (16 ounce) frozen peas
1 large potato, peeled and cut into
   ¾ inch cubes
2 tablespoons curry powder
1 tablespoon salt
1 tablespoon sugar
¼ teaspoon ground ginger
⅛ teaspoon cayenne pepper
4 cups hot cooked rice
2 tablespoons sesame seed

In 12 inch skillet over medium heat, in hot salad oil, cook onions, celery and garlic until tender, about 10 minutes, stirring occasionally. Meanwhile, break cauliflower into small flowerets. To skillet add cauliflower, tomatoes and their liquid and remaining ingredients except rice and sesame seed. With spoon, break tomatoes into pieces; heat mixture to boiling. Reduce heat to low; cover and simmer 30 minutes or until vegetables are tender, stirring occasionally. To serve, spoon mixture onto rice; sprinkle with sesame seed.
Serves 5.

Zucchini Tomato Medley

2 medium zucchini, sliced
   diagonally
1 medium onion, thinly sliced
1 teaspoon oregano or other herbs,
   divided
salt and freshly ground pepper
2 tablespoons butter, diced
2 medium tomatoes, sliced
½ green pepper, cut into ½ inch
   strips
½ cup grated Cheddar or Parmesan
   cheese

Arrange zucchini slices in bottom of 2 quart casserole. Top with onion rings, sprinkle with oregano, salt and pepper. Dot with some of the butter. Top with tomatoes and green pepper. Dot with remaining butter, and sprinkle with remaining oregano. Cover and cook 7 minutes at high in microwave. If cooking in oven, parboil the zucchini for 5 minutes only. Drain and continue as previously given. Bake in 350⁰ oven for 25 minutes. Top with cheese.
Serves 4 to 6.

Savoring Eggs & Cheese

"STRUGGLE FOR STATEHOOD"
BY MRS. J. J. HAGERMAN

The Mexican war was virtually ended by the taking of the City of Mexico by Gen. Scott, on September 1st, 1847. The treaty of Guadalupe Hidalgo, was concluded on March 2nd, 1848. By this treaty Mexico ceded to the United States territory which now forms California, Nevada, Utah, most of Arizona, a large part of New Mexico and parts of Colorado and Wyoming. The treaty was ratified on May 30th, 1848, and proclaimed at Santa Fe, in August.

Four months after the signing of the treaty of Guadalupe Hidalgo, a convention was held at Santa Fe, at which a memorial to Congress was framed, asking for a "speedy organization by law of a territorial government."

In September 1849, another convention was held at Santa Fe, attended by nineteen delegates. This body elected a delegate to Congress and adopted a plan of government which he was instructed to present to that body. This delegate was refused a seat in Congress. Thus began a struggle over the government of New Mexico which was to last for more than sixty years.

In May, 1850, a convention met at Santa Fe, and after sessions lasting ten days, framed a constitution for the State of New Mexico. This constitution was modeled on those of the newer states and, among other things, contained a clause prohibiting slavery......and states officers were elected. The legislature assembled in July and two senators were chosen. Trouble began almost at once between the newly elected officers and the old ones, but meantime, one of the senators-elect, Weightman, went to Washington to present the constitution of New Mexico, ask for admittance and claim his seat. What was his surprise and indignation to find on his arrival that a compromise bill, organizing a territorial government for New Mexico had just passed Congress. A governor for the new territory was appointed and sworn in and so the state government of New Mexico "so soon was done for that it wondered what it was begun for." It was believed that it was the clause in this constitution prohibiting slavery that was the cause of its rejection........for nearly a quarter of a century, session after session of the Congress, whatever its political complexion, continued to oppose the demands of the people of New Mexico, which remained a territory.

At one time, "it was proposed to admit Colorado and New Mexico to the Union at the same time and bills for that purpose were introduced in Congress." However, that relating to New Mexico was defeated by what Thomas M. Patterson, who happened to be in Washington at the time promoting the Colorado bill, calls a thoughtless act. So it came about that, instead of two centennial states, we have only one.

For a time, the question of joint statehood for New Mexico and Arizona was the vital one. Mr. Roosevelt, then President, was strongly in favor of it and used all of his great influence to bring about jointure. It was always bitterly opposed by the people of Arizona and by many it was thought that its support in New Mexico was only half-hearted and given in order to better the conditions for future work along the old lines.

When the bill was presented to the people of the two territories for their vote on it, New Mexico voted for it by a substantial majority while Arizona rejected it by about five against for one in favor of it, so the measure was lost.

However, the struggle for statehood by these two territories was not again to be laid aside or even abated.

On February 3, 1909, Hon. E. L. Hamilton, of Michigan, chairman of the House Committee, who had been always friendly to the territories, introduced a bill which was an enabling act for New Mexico and one for Arizona. (continued on page 176)

Sherried Eggs

1½ pounds hot sausage (cooked)
2 dozen eggs
1½ cups milk
1 can (10¾ ounce) undiluted cream
　of mushroom soup
1 pound fresh mushrooms, sauteed
　and chopped
½ cup dry sherry
½ pound Cheddar cheese, grated

In 9 x 13 inch buttered casserole layer sausage, then the eggs and milk scrambled *very soft,* soup and mushrooms, sherry and cheese. Cover and refrigerate for 24 hours. Bake at 350⁰ for 30 minutes. Scramble the eggs in three batches because there are so many and they should be soft (underdone). Can be reheated.
Serves 10 to 12.

Eggs in Spanish Sauce

1 can (29 ounce) tomatoes
1 sliced onion
1 tablespoon sugar
¾ teaspoon Tabasco
¾ teaspoon salt
⅛ teaspoon ground cloves
½ bay leaf
2 tablespoons butter or margarine
2 tablespoons flour
3 cups cooled rice
6 eggs
¼ cup grated Cheddar cheese

Simmer tomatoes, onion, sugar, Tabasco, salt, cloves and bay leaf in saucepan about 10 minutes. Remove bay leaf. Blend butter and flour together and add to tomato mixture. Cook, stirring constantly, until thickened. Spread rice in greased shallow 2½ quart casserole, making 6 hollows in it with a tablespoon. Break an egg into each nest. Carefully pour sauce over all. Sprinkle with cheese. Bake in 350⁰ oven 20 minutes or until eggs are firm.
Serves 6.

Brunch Casserole

1 dozen eggs
1 pound mild cheese, grated
1 can (16 ounce) tomato wedges,
　drained
1 cup melted butter
8 ounces sour cream
1 pound ham, cubed
1 green pepper, diced

Mix all ingredients together. Bake at 350⁰ for ¾ to 1 hour. May be prepared the night before, but do not bake in advance.

Zucchini-Spinach Frittata

6 eggs
½ teaspoon salt
¼ teaspoon ground black pepper
dash Tabasco sauce
4 small zucchini, sliced
1 large onion, sliced
1 clove garlic, crushed
2 cups chopped fresh spinach or
   Swiss chard
1 tablespoon chopped parsley
½ teaspoon oregano leaves or 1
   teaspoon snipped fresh oregano
   leaves
½ teaspoon basil leaves or 1
   tablespoon snipped fresh basil
   leaves
6 tablespoons butter or margarine
½ cup grated Parmesan, Romano,
   Swiss or Jarlsberg cheese

Beat eggs with salt, pepper and Tabasco. Prepare vegetables and herbs. In medium size ovenproof skillet melt 3 tablespoons butter or margarine. Add zucchini, onion and garlic and saute until limp. Add spinach (or Swiss chard), parsley, oregano and basil. Heat; stir until just wilted. Combine vegetable-herb mixture with eggs in bowl. Add remaining 3 tablespoons butter to skillet and heat until hot and a drop of water bounces in pan. Add vegetable-egg mixture all at once. Turn heat down. Cook without stirring until set and top is just moist. Sprinkle with cheese and place under broiler about 4 inches from source of heat and broil until top is golden brown. Cut into wedges to serve.
Serves 4 to 6.

Breakfast Casserole

3 tablespoons butter
3 tablespoons flour
2 cups milk
1 cup grated medium Cheddar
   cheese
½ teaspoon salt
¼ teaspoon pepper
1 cup cubed cooked ham
3 tablespoons butter
12 eggs, beaten
1 can (4 ounce) mushrooms, drained
½ cup melted butter
4 cups soft bread crumbs

Make sauce, melt butter, stir in flour, slowly add milk and blend until smooth. Stir in cheese, salt and pepper. Stir constantly until smooth. Saute ham in 3 tablespoons butter. Add eggs that are beaten. Cook until large soft curds form. Add mushrooms and cheese sauce. Pour into greased 13 x 9 x 2 inch pan. Combine butter and bread crumbs and sprinkle on top. Place covered casserole in refrigerator overnight. When ready to bake, uncover and bake at 350º for 30 minutes or until heated thoroughly. Can be frozen instead of placing in refrigerator. Thaw and bake as above instructions.
Serves 12.

Broccoli Cheese Pie

1 ½ pounds fresh broccoli
1 cup thinly sliced leeks or ⅔ cup
    minced onion
4 eggs, slightly beaten
1 ¼ cups milk
1 teaspoon salt
freshly ground pepper to taste
few drops hot pepper sauce
1 tablespoon minced parsley
⅛ teaspoon nutmeg
⅔ cup shredded Swiss cheese
⅓ cup grated Parmesan cheese

Cut flowerets from broccoli in thin slices. Peel tender stems and cut coarsely. Place broccoli and leeks in saucepan with 2 tablespoons water. Cover and cook over medium-low heat for 4 to 5 minutes. Drain. Combine eggs, milk, salt, pepper, pepper sauce, nutmeg, minced parsley and Swiss cheese; stir in vegetables. Turn into well-buttered 10 inch pie pan. Sprinkle top with Parmesan cheese. Bake in center of preheated 350⁰ oven for 30 to 35 minutes. Let cool 10 minutes.
This is nice served in wedges with sliced tomatoes and hot biscuits.
Serves 4 to 6.

Canadian Bacon and Egg Pie

10 slices Canadian bacon
½ pound Swiss cheese, shredded
6 to 8 eggs
salt and pepper
2 tablespoons grated Parmesan
    cheese
¾ cup cream

Fit bacon around edge and bottom of a 10 inch pie plate. Sprinkle Swiss cheese on top of bacon. Mix eggs, cream, Parmesan cheese, salt and pepper and pour over bacon. Bake at 350⁰ for 40 minutes or until eggs are set and top is light brown. Serve with English muffins.

Cheese Pit

5 slices buttered bread
¾ pound sharp Cheddar cheese,
    grated
4 eggs, slightly beaten
2 cups milk
½ teaspoon dry mustard
½ teaspoon salt
red pepper

Cut bread in small cubes. Alternate layers of bread and cheese in buttered glass dish. Mix remaining ingredients and pour over cheese and bread. Let stand overnight in refrigerator. Bake 1 hour at 350⁰. You can add ham, chicken or sausage.
Great for brunch with fruit juice or compote and sweet rolls.
Serves 6.

Egg and Ham Squares

2 cups cooked ground ham
1 small onion, minced
2 cups grated Cheddar cheese
3 eggs, well beaten
1½ cups milk
15 double soda crackers, finely
  crushed
1 to 2 cans (4 ounce) chopped
  green chiles

Mix all ingredients together. Pour into greased 9 x 13 inch baking pan. Bake in preheated 300° oven for 45 minutes. Cut in small squares for serving.
This is an unusual dish to carry to a coffee or brunch, different than a cookie or coffee cake.

Eggs Pirouette

10 hard-boiled eggs
½ teaspoon Worcestershire sauce
1 tablespoon grated onion
¼ cup butter or margarine,
  softened
¼ teaspoon prepared mustard
⅓ cup boiled chopped ham

Peel and cut eggs in half. Set whites aside. In bowl mash egg yolks; add remaining ingredients and mix well. Stuff cooked whites with mixture and arrange in greased baking dish.

Sauce:
3 tablespoons butter or margarine
3 tablespoons flour
1 cup milk
salt and pepper to taste
¾ cup mayonnaise
1 cup grated cheese

Melt butter in skillet; blend in the flour; add milk, mayonnaise, salt and pepper. Cook until thick and smooth. Pour over eggs. Sprinkle with grated cheese and bake in 325° oven, covered, about 25 minutes.
Can prepare eggs the day before and add sauce just before baking. Chopped bacon may be substituted for ham.
Serves 8 to 10.

Egg-Sausage Delight

1 pound roll sausage
6 eggs, beaten
2 cups milk
6 slices bread, cubed 1 inch
1 teaspoon dry mustard
1 teaspoon salt
1 cup grated Cheddar cheese
⅛ teaspoon oregano (more, if you like)

Brown and crumble meat. Drain. Mix with cheese and bread. Blend remaining ingredients in blender or with mixer. Pour over the sausage mixture and stir; then put into a greased 9 x 13 inch glass baking dish. Refrigerate overnight. Bake at 350° for 1 hour. Cut into squares and serve hot. *This can be frozen and re-heated or frozen and then cooked.*
Serves 12.

Garlic Cheese Grits

1 cup grits, uncooked
4 cups water
1 teaspoon salt
1 roll garlic cheese
½ cup butter
2 eggs, well-beaten
¼ cup milk
salt and pepper to taste

Cook grits in water according to package directions, add salt. Add garlic cheese, broken into pieces. Add butter, eggs, salt and pepper and milk. Pour into greased 1½ quart casserole. Bake in 350° oven for 1 hour.
Serves 6.

Savory Eggs

¾ cup chopped onions
1 tablespoon butter
1 teaspoon dry mustard
½ teaspoon savory
2 cans (10½ ounce) condensed cream of mushroom soup
1 cup milk
3 cups shredded Cheddar cheese
6 hard-cooked eggs, sliced
Rusks or toast

Saute onion in butter in a saucepan until lightly browned. Mix in mustard, savory, and soup. Gradually stir in milk and cheese. Cook over medium heat, stirring constantly until the cheese is melted. Gently mix in egg slices. Serve over Rusks or toast.
Serves 8.

Eggs and Cheese / 169

Hetty's Enchanted Egg Brunch

Sauce:
4 slices bacon, diced
½ pound chipped beef, coarsely
  shredded
¼ cup butter
8 ounces canned, sliced
  mushrooms

In large pan saute bacon; remove pan from heat. Add chipped beef, butter and three-fourths of the mushrooms. (Reserve remaining mushrooms for garnish.) Mix well.

½ cup flour
Pepper to taste
1 quart milk

Sprinkle flour and pepper over bacon-mushroom mixture. Gradually stir in milk. Cook until sauce is thickened and smooth, stirring constantly. Set aside.

16 eggs
½ teaspoon salt
1 cup evaporated milk
½ cup butter, melted
Reserved mushrooms

Combine eggs with salt and milk and scramble in butter in LARGE skillet.
In 12 x 9½ x 2 inch baking dish, alternate four layers - two of scrambled eggs and two of sauce, ending with sauce. Garnish with reserved mushrooms. Cover and bake at 275 degrees for one hour.
This may be fixed the day before and refrigerated - then baked according to directions. Allow extra time to heat through. After it is cooked, it can be frozen and kept for several weeks.
Recipe can be "halved" satisfactorily.
Serves 12.

Salmon Quiche

1 can (15½ ounce) salmon
½ lemon
2 tablespoons butter
1 large onion, diced
1 clove garlic, minced
½ pound mushrooms, sliced
1 (16 ounce) carton dairy sour cream
4 eggs
1½ cups grated Gruyere cheese (6 ounces)
1 teaspoon crushed dill seed
¼ teaspoon salt

Drain salmon, squeeze lemon on it, then break into bite-size pieces. Saute onion, garlic and mushrooms in butter until onion is soft. Beat sour cream and eggs together. Stir fish into sour cream mixture with sauteed vegetables, 1 cup of Gruyere cheese, dill weed and salt. Pour into cooked Parmesan crust and top with remaining cheese. Bake in 375° oven 60-70 minutes. Cool in pan 15 minutes and cut into wedges.

Parmesan Crust:
1½ cups flour
½ cup grated Parmesan cheese
¾ cup vegetable shortening
3-4 tablespoons water

Mix flour and cheese. Cut in shortening until mixture is size of peas. Sprinkle with 2 tablespoons of water and form into dough with hands adding more water if necessary. Press dough into bottom and high on sides of 8 or 8½ inch spring form pan. Bake at 375° for 10 minutes before filling.

Shrimp and Spinach Quiche

(A crustless Quiche)

12 medium shrimp, sliced
½ cup torn spinach leaves
1 tablespoon diced onion
1 cup grated Swiss cheese
5 eggs, beaten
2 cups skim milk
½ teaspoon vegetable salt
a pinch of paprika

Place shrimp, spinach, and onion in lightly oiled 8 inch quiche casserole or pie tin. Sprinkle cheese over top. Combine eggs, milk, and seasonings, and pour over cheese. Bake at 325° for 30-40 minutes or until set.
Serves 4 to 6.

Strata

1 pound sliced bread, trim crusts
1 package (8 ounce) cream cheese, softened
¼ pound Muenster cheese, sliced
1 package (10 ounce) chopped broccoli, drained
1 pound hot pork sausage
1 cup milk
1½ cups water
1 can (13 ounce) evaporated milk
6 eggs
2 tablespoons chopped onion
1¾ teaspoons salt
½ tablespoon pepper
1 teaspoon grated lemon rind
melted butter
½ to 1 cup grated sharp Cheddar cheese

Grease 13 x 9 inch glass casserole. Place bread in casserole, stacking slices. Spread top layer with cream cheese. Add Muenster cheese slices. Add layer of broccoli. Add sausage by patting flat in your hand to make layer. Beat milk, water, evaporated milk, eggs, onion, salt, pepper and lemon rind. Pour slowly over casserole. Drizzle melted butter, cover. Place in refrigerator 24 hours or freeze. Thaw before baking. Bake at 350º uncovered for 60-90 minutes. Remove from oven. Top with grated cheese. Let stand 5 minutes before serving.
Serves 10 to 12.

Swiss Cheese Souffle

2 tablespoons whipped margarine
3 tablespoons flour
¾ cup skim milk, hot
¼ teaspoon white pepper
½ teaspoon prepared mustard
a pinch of cayenne pepper
4 drops of hot pepper sauce
1 teaspoon vegetable salt
1 cup grated Swiss cheese
4 egg yolks, beaten
6 egg whites, beaten stiff

Melt margarine, stir in flour, and cook until bubbly. Add milk and seasonings. Boil for 1 minute, stirring constantly. Remove from heat and stir in cheese. Add beaten egg yolks. Let mixture cool. Stir ⅓ of beaten egg whites into mixture, and fold in the rest. Pour mixture into 1½ quart souffle dish, lightly greased. Bake at 375º for 30 minutes, or until puffed and brown.
Serves 4.

Super Quiche

½ cup mayonnaise
2 tablespoons flour
2 beaten eggs
¼ teaspoon salt
½ cup milk
1 box frozen crabmeat or 1 cup
    cooked shrimp or 1 can bits of
    bacon
1 bunch green onion, chopped
8 ounces or less Swiss cheese,
    grated
unbaked pie shell (9 inch)

Beat together first 5 ingredients, then stir in crabmeat, onion and cheese. Pour into pie shell. Bake at 350⁰ for 45 minutes. Let stand 10 minutes.
For vegetable quiche: 1 bunch green onion, chopped, 1 cup Monterey Jack cheese, 1 box (10 ounce) cooked and drained broccoli or spinach.
Serves 6 to 8.

Eggs—Texas Style

1 dozen eggs
½ teaspoon garlic salt
4 cans (4 ounce) chopped green
    chiles
1½ pounds Cheddar cheese, grated

Beat eggs well. Add garlic salt. Stir in green chiles and cheese. Pour into greased 9 x 12 inch pan. Bake at 350⁰ for 35 minutes. Cool slightly and cut into squares.
Serves 12.

Tomato Quiche

1 9 inch pie crust
½ pound cheese, grated
3 tablespoons butter
3 large tomatoes, peeled, seeded,
    and chopped
1 medium onion, chopped
salt
¼ teaspoon thyme
3 eggs, beaten well
1 cup half and half

Bake pie crust in preheated 450⁰ oven for 10 minutes. Sprinkle cheese over crust. Mix next 5 ingredients, and boil until reduced to half, then pour into crust. Pour eggs and cream over mixture. Bake in 425⁰ oven for 10 minutes. Reduce heat to 350⁰ and bake for 35 minutes more. Allow to set before slicing.
Freezes well.
Serves 6 to 8.

Stuffed Eggs New Mexico

6 eggs, hard boiled
1 small onion, minced
½ teaspoon salt
2 tablespoons mayonnaise
4 drops Tabasco
jalapeno jelly (see index)

Cut eggs lengthwise and remove yolks. Mash yolks with onion, salt, mayonnaise and Tabasco. Fill egg whites with yolk mixture. Top with jalapeno jelly.
Serves 6.

Sizzling Cheese

1 egg, separated
4 slices salami, cut into strips
1 cup grated Cheddar cheese
¼ cup stuffed olives, sliced
2 tablespoons chopped green onion
dash cayenne pepper
salt and pepper, to taste
1 tablespoon butter, melted
1 clove garlic, minced
4 slices white bread
olives for garnish

Beat egg white until stiff. Beat in egg yolk. Fold in salami, cheese, olives, green onions and seasonings.

Add garlic to melted butter. Toast bread on one side and brush the untoasted side with garlic-butter. Spoon the cheese mixture over bread and place under broiler for 3-5 minutes, or until golden brown. Serve immediately, garnished with olives.
Serves 4.

Zia Rarebit

2½ cups grated Cheddar cheese
1 tablespoon butter, melted
½ cup milk
1 teaspoon Worcestershire sauce
1 teaspoon dry mustard
½ teaspoon salt
1 can (4 ounce) chopped green chili
1 egg, lightly beaten
toast points

Combine cheese, butter and milk in saucepan. Over low heat stir until cheese is melted. Add seasonings and green chili. Remove from heat and stir in beaten egg. Pour over toast points.
Serves 4.

Savoring Crepes, Pasta & Rice

(continued from page 164)

The bill was passed by the House without opposition, but when it went to the Senate the following day, it was referred to the Committee on Territories. Because of the committee chairman's opposition, it was postponed. On June 15, 1910, the Statehood bill was announced and, as the hour was late, by general agreement, it was made "unfinished business," which meant that it must be brought up each day at two o'clock p.m. until it was finally disposed of.

Shortly after two o'clock on the afternoon of Saturday, June 18, 1910, Speaker Cannon laid the bill, as amended by the Senate before the House. Shouts of "vote" were heard on all sides. There was no demand for a roll call; the question was put viva voce, and the House concurred by a unanimous vote. Thus ended the long conflict of sixty years. The news was flashed over the wires to the people most concerned and the rejoicing was great.

During all these years there had been frequent discussions of the desirability of changing the name of New Mexico when it should come into the Union as a state. The chief reason for this was the fact that people, not only foreigners, but many in other sections of our country,---were constantly associating and confusing NEW Mexico with the old country bearing that same name, of which it was once a part.

At one time the name "Acoma" was proposed by the delegates in Congress, but that most frequently and most warmly advocated was "Lincoln." However, the native population was opposed to any change, and among Americans were many who were attached to the historical associations of the old name. Hence, all advocacy of the change was ineffective.

Has the change (from Territory to State) brought, thus far, all the benefits that was confidently expected by its ardent advocates?

It rests with the law makers and the people who elect them and are obliged to live under the laws which they enact to determine whether or not the hopes of those who struggled so long for self-government are to be realized.

THE ZIA SUN SYMBOL
(AS SHOWN ON THE COVER)

New Mexico's distinctive insignia is the Zia Sun Symbol which originated with the Indians of Zia Pueblo in ancient times. Its design reflects their tribal philosophy, with its wealth of pantheistic spiritualism teaching the basic harmony of all things in the universe.

Four is the sacred number of the Zia, and the figure is composed of a circle from which four points radiate signifying the earth with its four main directions; in the year, with its four seasons; in the day, with sunrise, noon, evening and night; in life, with its four divisions, childhood, youth, manhood and old age. Everything is bound together in a circle of life and love, without beginning, without end.

The Zia believe, too, that man has four sacred obligations; he must develop a strong body, a clear mind, a pure spirit, and a devotion to the welfare of his people. The sun is the emissary of the Great Spirit without which all life on earth would perish.

The symbol's proportions are fixed by legislative act, with the four groups of rays set at right angles.

Basic Crepes

4 eggs
1½ cups flour
½ teaspoon salt
1 cup milk
1 cup water
1 tablespoon melted butter
½ cup butter clarified; note below

In blender or food processor, mix all ingredients until smooth. Allow batter to stand, at room temperature, for 30 minutes. Heat a small skillet until it is very hot. Brush with clarified butter. Pour in a scant ¼ cup batter, tilting the skillet to distribute batter evenly. Cook the crepe until it is lightly browned. Lift one edge with spatula, flip the crepe over, and brown the other side. Stack crepes to keep moist. Crepes may be made ahead and refrigerated (will keep 1 week), or frozen (will keep 30 days). Wrap in plastic to prevent drying.

To clarify butter: Place butter in small saucepan. Slowly bring butter to boil and skim milk particles as they rise to surface. The remaining butter is clarified. Save milk particles to season vegetables.
Serves 18 to 20.

Crepes a la Bolognese

2 cups small curd cottage cheese
1 cup grated mozzarella or
   Monterey Jack cheese
1 package (8 ounce) cream cheese,
   softened
4 tablespoons butter, softened
4 tablespoons chopped parsley
2 tablespoons minced green onions,
   including tops
2 large eggs
½ cup grated farmers cheese or dry
   curd cheese
1 can (15 ounce) Marinara sauce
½ teaspoon salt
¼ teaspoon pepper
crepes (see index)
Parmesan cheese, grated

Combine first 8 ingredients thoroughly. Use ⅓ cup for each cooked crepe. Roll loosely; place in shallow baking pan, seam side down. Pour Marinara sauce or spaghetti sauce over them. Sprinkle with grated Parmesan cheese. Bake 20 to 30 minutes in 350º oven.
Crepes may be prepared ahead of time. Also filling; but do not fill crepes more than 12 hours ahead of time.
Serves 6.

Rich Pastry - For Tarts or Turnovers

1 cup cottage cheese, drained
1 pound margarine, room
  temperature
4 cups flour

Put cottage cheese and margarine in blender. Mix thoroughly. Remove to mixing bowl and add flour, more if possible. Mold into walnut size balls, cover and let stand in refrigerator overnight. Roll into circles. Put desired amount of filling on one side of circle.
Filling: (About 1 tablespoon preserves, chopped chicken, etc.) Fold over and seal. Bake at 375º for about 12 minutes.

Blintzes

Crepes, see Index

Filling:
1 egg yolk
2 tablespoons sugar
8 ounces cream cheese, softened
2 cups cottage cheese, drained
¼ teaspoon vanilla
2 tablespoons butter for sauteing

Topping:
powdered sugar
1 cup sour cream
1 cup strawberry or cherry
  preserves

Combine egg yolk and sugar and beat until thick and yellow. Add cheeses and vanilla; stir until well combined. Spread 3 level tablespoons filling on browned side of each crepe, making rectangle 4 inches long. Fold two opposite sides over filling; then overlap ends, covering filling completely. Melt 1 tablespoon butter in large skillet over medium heat. Add half of blintzes, not touching, seam side down. Saute until golden brown on under side; turn; saute other side. Keep warm in a low oven while cooking rest. Serve hot, sprinkled with powdered sugar, with sour cream and preserves.
Yields 16.

Garden Fettuccine

2 tablespoons olive oil or salad oil
1 clove garlic, minced or pressed
1 small green pepper, seeded and chopped
4 green onions, including tops, thinly sliced
3 medium size tomatoes, peeled, seeded and chopped
¼ cup chopped parsley
10 ounces fresh fettuccine
3 quarts boiling water
¼ cup butter or margarine
⅔ cup whipping cream
salt and pepper
Parmesan cheese, freshly grated

Heat oil in a 10-12 inch frying pan on medium high heat; add garlic and green pepper and cook, stirring occasionally until pepper is limp. Add onions and stir 1-2 minutes longer, then mix in tomatoes and parsley and cook until tomatoes are heated through. Keep warm on lowest heat, uncovered. As vegetables are cooking, cook the fettuccine in boiling water in a 5-6 quart pan on high heat just until tender to bite (about 2 minutes). Pour pasta into a colander and drain well. At once return kettle to high heat, add butter and cream, and heat thoroughly until butter melts. Remove kettle from heat and add pasta and vegetables. Mix, lifting with fork, to blend; season to taste with salt and pepper. Pour onto a warm serving platter and sprinkle generously with Parmesan cheese.
Serves 4.

Southwest Fettuccine

¼ cup butter
1 cup sliced Canadian bacon or 8 ounces ham
1 jar (8 ounce) roasted sweet red peppers, drained and diced
1 package (10 ounce) frozen green peas
1 cup heavy cream
½ teaspoon salt
¼ teaspoon pepper
homemade egg noodles or 1 pound fettuccine package
1 cup grated Parmesan cheese

Melt butter in large skillet. Add bacon; cook and stir 1 minute. Add peppers and peas; cook 1 minute, stirring to coat with butter. Stir in cream, salt and pepper. Bring to boiling; lower heat; simmer, stirring occasionally, until sauce thickens slightly, about 3 minutes. Remove sauce from heat; reserve while cooking pasta. Cook and drain pasta; return to kettle. Add sauce and cheese; toss over low heat until mixture is well blended and heated thoroughly. Serve on heated plates.

Eggplant Lasagne

1 pound ground beef
2 medium onions, chopped
½ teaspoon salt
½ teaspoon oregano
1 can (8 ounce) tomato sauce
1 package (12 ounce) frozen
　 chopped spinach
1 large eggplant, cut in lengthwise
　 slices ⅜ inch thick
¼ teaspoon salt
2 eggs, beaten
¼ cup salad oil
¼ pound Mozzarella cheese, thinly
　 sliced

Brown beef and onions. Stir in salt, oregano and tomato sauce. Simmer for 10 minutes. Skim fat if necessary. Slightly cook spinach. Drain well. Add to beef mixture. Simmer 10 minutes. While meat is simmering, salt eggplant slices and dip in egg. Brown eggplant slices on both sides in salad oil. Make a layer of ⅓ eggplant slices in deep 2-quart casserole. Spoon in ⅓ of meat sauce. Top with 2 more alternating layers of eggplant and sauce. Finish with sauce. Cover with sliced cheese. Bake at 375º for 30 minutes.
Serves 6.
Can be frozen.

Three-Cheese Lasagna Rolls

6 wide lasagna noodles
1 container (15 or 16 ounces) ricotta
　 cheese
½ package (8 ounces) mozzarella
　 cheese, shredded
¼ cup grated Parmesan cheese
1 egg
¼ teaspoon salt
¼ teaspoon oregano leaves
1 jar (15½ ounce) spaghetti sauce

In boiling, salted water, cook lasagna noodles as label directs; drain and cool. Meanwhile, in medium bowl, thoroughly mix ricotta and next five ingredients. Cut lasagna noodles in half crosswise. On each half, evenly spread ¼ cup cheese mixture. Roll up each noodle, jelly-roll fashion. Into 13 x 9 inch baking pan, spoon 1 cup spaghetti sauce. Arrange rolls on sauce; top with remaining sauce. Bake in 350º oven for 45 minutes or until hot and bubbly.
Serves 4.

Linguini and Eggplant

1 large eggplant peeled and cut
   into 1 inch cubes
olive oil
½ cup chopped onion
1 garlic clove, crushed
1 can (29 ounce) Italian plum
   tomatoes, undrained
1 can (8 ounce) tomato sauce
1 cup chopped celery
¼ cup fresh chopped parsley
1½ teaspoons salt
1 teaspoon basil, crushed
¼ teaspoon pepper
⅔ cup sliced Italian green olives
2 tablespoons capers
1 pound linguini
freshly grated Romano or Parmesan
   cheese

Brown eggplant ⅓ at a time in hot olive oil; set aside. Saute onion and garlic in oil until tender, but not brown. Add tomatoes, tomato sauce, celery, parsley, salt, basil and pepper; simmer uncovered about 15 minutes. Stir in eggplant, olives and capers; cover and simmer 25 minutes. Cook linguini in boiling salted water (1 gallon water plus 2 tablespoons salt) until tender, yet firm, 10 to 12 minutes; drain. Serve sauce over hot linguini. Sprinkle generously with grated cheese.
Serves 8 to 10.

Saucy Chicken Manicotti

6 manicotti shells
2 tablespoons minced onion
1 package (3 ounce) cream cheese
1 cup sour cream
¼ cup milk
3 ounces chopped mushrooms
1 tablespoon parsley
2 cups cooked diced chicken
1 envelope cheese sauce mix
¼ cup Parmesan cheese

Cook manicotti shells according to directions on package. Mix onions, cream cheese, sour cream, milk, mushrooms, parsley, chicken and salt and pepper to taste. Spoon in shells. Prepare cheese sauce. Pour over single layer of shells in baking pan. Sprinkle Parmesan cheese on top. Cover and bake 40 minutes at 350⁰.

Spaghetti a la Carbonara

6 large purple onions, sliced thin
½ cup butter
1 pound bacon

Saute onions in butter until soft. Fry bacon until crisp, drain and crumble.

1 cup butter, softened
3 eggs
3 to 5 cloves garlic, minced
½ cup chopped parsley
1½ cups fresh grated Parmesan or
   Romano cheese
1½ pound spaghetti

Beat 1 cup of butter, add eggs, garlic, parsley, cheese and salt and pepper to taste. Cook spaghetti according to package directions, drain. Mix onions and bacon together, add to spaghetti. Add butter mixture, serve immediately. *Serves 6 to 8.*

Magic Pasta

1 cup loosely packed basil
½ cup pine nuts or shelled walnuts
2 cloves garlic, peeled
¾ cup freshly grated Parmesan
   cheese
½ cup olive oil
1 pound spaghetti, cooked
3 tablespoons butter

Place basil in blender and add pine nuts and garlic. Blend, stirring down carefully. Add cheese when well blended. Gradually add the olive oil while blending on low speed. When spaghetti is cooked, drain and pour into hot serving dish. Toss with butter. Serve immediately. Pass sauce separately.

ROSWELL REGISTER   **MARCH 7, 1902**

Protestant Episcopal Church

Services Sunday at 11 a.m. and 7:30 p.m. Holy communion at the morning service. Subject of discourses, morning, "Earnestness in Work." Evening, "The Living Christ". Sunday School at 9:30 a.m. Being Mid-Lent-Communion, the members are particularly and offectionately requested to be present at the morning service. A cordial invitation is extended to all the citizens and visitors of Roswell.
George Hinson, Rector

Noodles Romanoff

1 package (8 ounce) noodles
½ pint sour cream
1 clove garlic, mashed
4 scallions, chopped
2 tablespoons Worcestershire sauce
¾ cup freshly grated Parmesan cheese

Cook noodles according to package direction and drain. Combine noodles and all ingredients, except Parmesan cheese. Turn into a well buttered 2 quart casserole. Sprinkle with cheese on top and bake in a 350⁰ oven for 35 minutes.

Coe Ranch Rice

3 tablespoons margarine
2 large onions, chopped
1 cup rice
1 teaspoon savory salt
1½ teaspoons marjoram
4 cups chicken broth

Melt margarine in electric frypan. Saute onions. Add rice and brown slightly. Add salt, marjoram and chicken broth. Simmer until rice is tender and liquid is absorbed.

Company Rice

1 cup raw rice
2 tablespoons oil
¾ cup chopped green onions
½ cup chopped green pepper
½ cup chopped fresh parsley
1 can (14 ounce) chicken broth or 10½ ounce can plus 3 ounces water or white wine
1 teaspoon salt
¼ teaspoon pepper

Saute rice in oil until lightly brown. Stir in green onion, cook until soft. Mix in green pepper, parsley, broth, salt and pepper. Pour into 1½ or 2 quart casserole. Bake covered in 375⁰ oven for 30 to 40 minutes until liquid is absorbed. Toss lightly before serving.
Can be made in advance. Cook 30 minutes. When ready to serve, reheat in 350° oven for 15 minutes. Can substitute beef consomme for chicken broth to serve with beef dishes. Serves 6.

Rice a la Barbara

1 cup rice
4 tablespoons butter or margarine
1 can (10½ ounce) onion soup
1 can (4 ounce) mushrooms -
    optional

Brown rice slightly in butter. Add soup, undiluted. Bake in 350º oven for 1 hour. Stir after 45 minutes and add water if dry at this point. Add optional mushrooms the last 10-15 minutes.
Serves 4.

Rice Monterey

1 cup rice
¾ pound Monterey Jack cheese,
    grated
2 cans (4 ounce) chopped green
    chiles
1 pint sour cream
salt and pepper

Cook rice as directed, drain. Add sour cream, salt and pepper. In a well-buttered casserole place a layer of rice, layer of grated cheese, layer of chiles. Repeat layers. End with cheese on top. Cook 30 minutes uncovered at 350º.
Serves 6 to 8.

Saffron Rice with Avocados

3 tablespoons butter
1 small yellow onion, peeled and
    chopped
1 small clove garlic, crushed,
    peeled, and minced
½ cup water
1 cup long grain rice
½ teaspoon saffron threads
2½ cups condensed chicken broth
Salt to taste
4 medium, ripe avocados, peeled
    and diced

Heat the butter in a heavy saucepan. Add onion, garlic, and water. Cook over a medium heat until all the water has evaporated. Onion should be soft and transparent. Add the rice and continue to cook, stirring constantly, until the rice becomes slightly opaque. Add the saffron and chicken broth. Bring to a boil. Cover, reduce heat to simmer, and cook until the rice is tender and all the liquid has been absorbed - about 20 minutes. Taste for seasoning. Just before serving, fold in the diced avocado.
Serves 4.

Pasta Pesto

1 pound ricotta cheese
1½ cups freshly grated Parmesan
   cheese
1 cup minced mozzarella
½ cup minced fresh parsley
½ cup minced green onion
1 egg yolk
½ teaspoon marjoram
½ teaspoon minced garlic
½ teaspoon dried basil
¼ teaspoon oregano
salt and pepper
9 ounces lasagne noodles, cooked
   al dente and cooled

Generously grease a shallow 2½ quart baking dish. Combine ingredients except noodles and blend well. Spread portion of cheese filling over each noodle. Roll up individually and stand vertically in single layer in baking dish. Pour pesto sauce over, cover and bake in preheated 350⁰ oven for 30-40 minutes or until sauce is bubbly and heated through.

Pesto Sauce:
2 cups tightly packed fresh basil
   leaves OR
1½ cups parsley and 2 tablespoons
   dry basil
¼ cup freshly grated Parmesan
   cheese
2 garlic cloves, halved
1 tablespoon toasted pine nuts
salt and pepper
⅔ to 1 cup olive oil

Combine in blender, or processor, adding enough olive oil to make thick smooth sauce.
May be stored in refrigerator for 3 to 4 months.
May be assembled one day ahead.
Serves 6.

Wild Rice with Sausage

2 cups uncooked wild rice
2 pounds bulk sausage broken into
   pieces
1 quart canned tomatoes and juice
5 medium onions, sliced
salt to taste
Ritz crackers, crushed

Layer ingredients into 2 large casserole dishes. Cook 1 hour at 350⁰, then crumble Ritz crackers on top and bake 45 minutes more. Be sure the rice is covered by the liquid at all times.

Festive Parsley Rice

1 cup rice
2 cups boiling water
2 chicken bouillon cubes
1 teaspoon salt
2 tablespoons butter
¼ cup chopped onions
½ cup chopped green pepper
½ cup chopped cashew nuts
½ cup fresh minced parsley

In a pot combine water, rice, chicken bouillon cubes and salt. Bring to a boil, cover and simmer 14 to 20 minutes. In a skillet heat butter, add onions and peppers. Cook 1 minute and add to rice. Add nuts and parsley, toss lightly.

Zucchini Sauce on Green Noodles

1 large onion, chopped
1 bell pepper, chopped
1 clove garlic, minced
3 tablespoons olive oil
1 can (16 ounce) Italian-style
   tomatoes
¼ cup chopped parsley
1 teaspoon basil
½ teaspoon marjoram
½ teaspoon salt
½ teaspoon pepper
½ cup dry red wine
3 medium size zucchini, grated
1 package (8 ounce) medium-wide
   green noodles
grated Parmesan cheese

In saucepan over medium high heat, saute onions, peppers, and garlic in olive oil. Add tomatoes, including liquid, parsley, basil, marjoram, salt, pepper and wine. Mix well; bring to a boil. Reduce heat, cover, and simmer 30-35 minutes.

Cook noodles according to directions on package. Drain. Pour into serving dish.

Add grated zucchini to tomato sauce, stirring to combine. Pour over noodles. Sprinkle with Parmesan cheese.
Serves 4.

THE ROSWELL REGISTER-TRIBUNE   TUESDAY, OCTOBER 12, 1909

The Pecos Valley HONORS ITS GREATEST FRIEND
In Memory of Mr. J. J. Hagerman

The first volume of the History of the Pecos Valley has been closed. We may add a few chapters, by way of explanation or emphasis, but the great "doer of the Word" has laid down the burden and is at rest. He has solved the mystery of life and has entered the realms of immortality.

It is proper that we should assemble to pay a tribute of respect and admiration to the memory of the man who made it possible for many of us to be here today.

After the storm, the mountain peaks pierce the sky in clearer outline-so after the strife and struggles of life are over, we can see with clearer vision the characteristics which elevate few above the many. In the cool, clear, impersonal atmosphere that surrounds the departed, we can estimate those great qualities which enable the gifted and the fortunate to write their names in the story of their times.

Let us remember that in paying this tribute of appreciation to the memory of Mr. Hagerman we are simply acknowledging our obligations to the man whose energy, indomitable will and vigor, irrepressible, opened for us the door of opportunity.

Savoring Entrees

NEW MEXICO MILITARY INSTITUTE

Military Heights, the northern suburb of Roswell, is situated on a beautiful mesa some thirty feet above the main part of the city. Forty acres of this mesa is owned and occupied by the New Mexico Military Institute, the only strictly military school in the Southwest. The location of the school is all that could be desired; at an elevation of 3,700 feet above sea level, where the air is light and pure; in an arid country where the sun shines almost continually day after day throughout the entire year, in the artesian belt where an abundance of water can be had for irrigating purposes and in a mild climate where outdoor sports and field work can be indulged in and enjoyed throughout the entire school session.

The buildings consist of seven large well built structures. The main barracks and the mess hall are of brick. They are heated with steam, lighted by gas and have hot and cold water on all floors. The arrangement of the building is suited to the needs of the school and they are so grouped that with the additions to be made during the next year or two, the whole will present the general appearance of an army post.

The gymnasium is a large roomy building and well furnished for physical culture, but on account of the delightful weather enjoyed in this locality, especially during the winter months, it is very little used. Cadets do not care for, or need, indoor exercise when they can get outside to indulge in field sports.

The hospital consists of a five-room cottage neatly furnished and supplied with a bath. On account of the wonderfully good health which has always prevailed among the cadets, this building is seldom used. Yet in a boarding school of this size, it is necessary that an emergency hospital be maintained.

The Institute was created by an act of the legislature of the Territory of New Mexico in the year 1895, but the first building was not completed until the summer of 1898. On September the 6th, 1898, the school was formally opened to students and regular military and academic departments established. The Institute has flourished from the very first, and is today the leading military school in the Southwest. Cadets are matriculated from every county and town throughout the Territory, and quite a number come from the states. For the past two years the school has been full to its utmost capacity, applicants being refused admission early in the session on account of limited quarters.

At present there are over one hundred cadets enrolled for the session, and for the most part they are large manly fellows. They come from all parts of the West, true sons of the bold manly spirits who braved the hardships of the frontier and established homes in this country. Their bodies are muscular, full of life and vigor, which naturally gives them a strong, active brain. The Institute boasts of a higher percentage of athletes among her students than any other school in the United States. Her baseball team has never been defeated, although she has met all comers and played against every school and town within a radius of 400 miles, still her colors have never drooped in defeat.

The school is ably managed by the Superintendent, Col. Jas. W. Willson, who has been connected with the Institute ever since it was first opened in 1898.

He is assisted by six vigorous, cultured young men who are specialists in the lines they teach.

Never were the prospects of any school brighter than those of the New Mexico Military Institute. With an able and efficient corps of instructors, backed by the hearty support of the Territory, intrenched in the good will of the people and with a large and increasing patronage, it is no wonder that the New Mexico Military Institute is the pride of the Territory and deserves the full confidence of the parents who may decide to send their sons to this school.

Anchovy Pie

2 medium onions, sliced very thin
3 tablespoons butter (divided)
3 medium potatoes, peeled and grated
18 anchovy filets
4 ounces ripe olives, sliced
pepper
1 cup heavy cream

Saute onions in 2 tablespoons butter until light brown. In greased pie pan, arrange thin layer of potatoes, then the onions, the anchovies, the olives, then a final layer of potatoes. Dot with 1 tablespoon of butter and sprinkle pepper over top. Bake in preheated oven at 300° for a total of 55 minutes*. After first 10 minutes, pour ½ cup of the cream over the top. Ten minutes later, pour on the rest.
*May be refrigerated overnight after cooking 50 minutes, then reheat in preheated 300° oven for 10-15 minutes.

Capered Cod

1½ pounds cod fillets
2 tablespoons fresh lemon juice
salt and pepper
4 tablespoons butter
½ cup flour
1 teaspoon minced shallot
½ cup dry white wine
½ tablespoon capers, drained
1½ teaspoons Dijon mustard
½ cup heavy cream
dill weed

Sprinkle both sides of the fillets with the lemon juice. Season with salt and pepper, then coat with flour. Melt the butter in a heavy skillet. Cook the fillets until brown, about 1½ minutes a side. Remove and keep warm. Add the shallot to the skillet and cook until soft but not brown. Add the wine, capers and mustard, stirring the bottom of the skillet. Boil for 2 or 3 minutes. Add the cream and stir, cooking over moderate heat until the sauce is reduced and thickened. Spoon over the cod fillets and serve. Garnish with dill weed. Serves 4.

ROSWELL REGISTER   FEBRUARY 14, 1902

For the Institute Y.M.C.A.

Dr. Lukens will give a phonograph entertainment at the Presbyterian church next Monday night, the proceeds to go into a fund to be used for buying an organ for the Military Institute Y.M.C.A. organization. This is a worthy object and should draw a good audience. The cadets who are members of the association should receive every possible encouragement in the work they have undertaken.

Cantonese Shrimp & Snow Peas

1 pound medium shrimp, shelled
2 tablespoons vegetable oil
1 clove garlic, minced
¼ cup finely sliced green onion
½ teaspoon ginger or small amount
  ginger root
½ teaspoon salt
¼ teaspoon pepper
1 can (10½ ounce) chicken broth or
  bouillon
1 package (6 ounce) frozen snow
  peas or fresh pea pods
1 tablespoon cornstarch mixed with
  1 tablespoon water

Heat oil in skillet and saute shrimp, garlic and green onion 5 minutes; stir in ginger, salt, pepper, chicken broth and pea pods; simmer 6 minutes. Stir cornstarch mixture into shrimp mixture; simmer for 1 minute longer and serve over rice.
Serves 6.

Crab and Artichoke Casserole

3 tablespoons butter
3 tablespoons flour
1½ cups milk
1 teaspoon salt
⅛ teaspoon pepper
1 teaspoon Worcestershire sauce
⅓ cup grated Parmesan or Romano
  cheese
mustard and Tabasco to taste
4 hard-boiled eggs, quartered
1 can (16 ounce) artichoke hearts,
  drained and quartered
2 cups crab meat
¼ cup grated Parmesan or Romano
  cheese
paprika

Melt butter in saucepan. Stir in flour to make a roux. Add milk, salt, pepper and Worcestershire sauce, mustard and Tabasco, stirring constantly, until sauce thickens. Add ⅓ cup grated cheese. Mix together eggs, artichokes, and crab meat. Put into buttered casserole, cover with sauce, sprinkle with ¼ cup cheese and paprika for color. Bake in 350° oven for 30 minutes.

Fish Fillets in Mustard Sauce

1 pound frozen fish fillets partially
   thawed and separated
½ cup mayonnaise (do not use
   salad dressing)
2 tablespoons Dijon mustard
¼ cup chopped onion
⅓ cup chopped parsley
¼ teaspoon thyme
dash of paprika for color

Put fish in greased glass dish; set aside. Mix together remaining ingredients except paprika, until sauce is smooth. Pour mixture over fish. Bake in preheated 400º oven for 20-25 minutes or until fish flakes when touched with a fork. *Serves 4.*

Grilled and Smoked Freshwater Trout

trout
salt and pepper
lemon
butter
apple tree twigs or hickory chips
parsley
lemon wedges

Equipment needed:
hooded outdoor charcoal grill

The trout range from 7½ to 11 inches long. Ideal is 8 inches. Season the trout with salt, pepper and lemon butter, made with the proportions of ½ cup butter to juice of ½ lemon. Clean grill well, then grease well. Broil the trout over moderately hot coals until the skin begins to blister and turn brown, 4½ to 6 minutes a side, depending on the trout size and heat of coals. Do not overcook! Remove fish to one side of the grill, and the coals to the opposite side. It may be necessary to remove some of the coals. Place two handfuls of apple tree twigs and leaves (or, if not available, wet hickory chips) directly on coals. This will immediately create a lot of smoke. Close hood and smoke about 12 minutes, adding more twigs or chips if necessary to keep the smoke level high. Garnish with sprigs of parsley and serve with lemon wedges.

Jane Davisson

Jane is a descendant of early settlers who came to this area in 1905. Although she lived in West Texas and first studied art there, she graduated from Roswell High School.

She received a Bachelor of Arts degree from the University of Arizona, Tucson. She did her post-graduate work in painting, commercial art and design at the University of California at Berkeley and The Corcoran Gallery School of Art in Washington, D.C. She earned her Master of Arts degree from the University of Denver, in both painting and ceramics.

Her first one artist show was held at The Roswell Museum and Art Center. More recently, her work was presented in a one artist show in North Dallas.

For the last few years, she has been busy painting commissions in Texas and New Mexico. Her paintings may be seen in The Featherstone Gallery and the New Mexico Military Institute Chapel. Examples of her calligraphy and illumination may be seen in the repositories at the First Presbyterian Church and the Chapel at New Mexico Military Institute, Roswell, New Mexico.

LAS FLORES
Artist - Jane Davisson
30" X 40"   1972
oil on linen
Private collection

Panfried Freshwater Trout

8 (8 inch) trout
salt and pepper
flour
3 ounces almonds, slivered
½ cup butter
juice of ½ lemon
parsley sprigs and lemon wedges

Season trout with salt and pepper, then lightly with flour. Brown almonds slightly over moderate heat in heavy skillet. When almonds are brown, remove with slotted spoon and keep warm. To skillet, add lemon juice. Add trout, and cook trout over moderate heat until skin begins to brown and blister, 3½-4½ minutes to each side. Do not overcook! Remove trout, pour remaining butter in skillet over trout, sprinkle with almonds, and garnish with parsley sprigs and lemon wedges. The trout are exceptional smothered with freshly ground pepper.
Serves 4.

Red Snapper Veracruz

1 large red snapper (3 pounds),
    fileted
salt and pepper
½ cup lemon juice
1 onion, thinly sliced
1 cup white wine
1 teaspoon basil
1 teaspoon oregano
1 teaspoon rosemary

Sauce:
1 garlic clove, minced
1 tablespoon olive oil
1 onion, diced
3 tomatoes, pureed and strained
¼ cup chopped jalapeno peppers
½ cup sliced green olives
¼ cup capers (optional)

Rinse fish, rub with salt and pepper and place in a large shallow, well-greased baking dish. Add lemon juice, onion, wine, and spices. Bake at 325° for 20-35 minutes. Pour sauce over fish, and serve at once. To prepare sauce, fry garlic in olive oil, add onion, tomatoes, chiles, olives and capers. Simmer until sauce thickens.

Sour Cream Pastry:
2 ¼ cups flour
½ teaspoon salt
12 tablespoons butter, cut in small
  pieces
1 egg, slightly beaten
½ cup sour cream

Salmon Filling:
2 cans (7 ¾ ounce) salmon
½ cup sour cream
3 tablespoons snipped fresh dill
¼ cup butter
¼ cup chopped parsley
¼ cup chopped onion
½ pound fresh mushrooms, sliced
  lengthwise
2 tablespoons fresh lemon juice
5 hard-cooked eggs, sliced ¼ inch
  thick
salt and pepper

For Pastry Top;
1 egg yolk, beaten with 1
  tablespoon water

Sauce:
2 cups sour cream
3 tablespoons snipped fresh dill
2 tablespoons fresh lemon juice

Pastry: Into large bowl, sift flour with salt. Drop in small pieces of chilled butter. Using fingertips, rub the flour mixture and the butter together until it feels like coarse cornmeal. In small bowl, mix egg with sour cream. Stir into flour mixture; work with hands to make a soft dough. Refrigerate 1 hour, wrapped in wax paper.

Salmon Filling: Drain salmon, removing bones and skin. Mix with sour cream, dill and parsley. In ¼ cup hot butter in small saucepan, saute onion. Add mushrooms and lemon juice; cook 2 minutes longer. Remove from heat; stir in salt and pepper.

Cut dough in half. On lightly floured surface, roll each half to form a 12 x 6 inch rectangle. Place one rectangle on lightly greased baking pan. On top, layer the sliced egg, then the mushroom mixture and last, the salmon mixture. Place second layer of pastry over top, pinching edges together. Brush with egg yolk mixture. Prick the loaf with fork in several places. Bake at 375º for 45 minutes, or until golden brown. Combine sauce ingredients, and serve cold with hot salmon. *Serves 6 to 8.*

Super Shrimp

1 bottle low calorie Italian salad dressing
¼ pound butter
juice of 1 lemon
2 tablespoons crushed black pepper
4 pounds shrimp, in shell, no heads
cocktail sauce

Melt butter in heavy pot and add all other ingredients. Cook in 450° oven up to 40 minutes, depending on size of shrimp, stirring every 10 minutes. Test for doneness after 20 minutes and frequently thereafter. Serve with any good cocktail sauce.

This is the best shrimp ever! Can be stored in the refrigerator if you have any leftovers (there is NEVER any left over). Serve with green salad, hard rolls and lots of paper napkins.
Serves 8.

The Best Shrimp Creole

½ cup chopped onion
½ cup chopped celery
1 clove garlic, minced
3 tablespoons oil
1 can (16 ounce) tomatoes, chopped
1 can (8 ounce) tomato sauce
1½ teaspoons salt
¼ teaspoon sugar
½ to 1 teaspoon chili powder (increase chili powder if you like it spicier)
1 tablespoon Worcestershire sauce
½ teaspoon Tabasco
1 tablespoon cornstarch
2 tablespoons cold water
12 ounces shrimp (shrimp need not be cooked but must be thawed if frozen)
½ cup chopped green pepper

Cook onion, celery, garlic in hot oil until tender, not brown. Add tomatoes, tomato sauce and seasonings. Simmer uncovered for 45 minutes. Mix cornstarch and water. Add to sauce and stir until smooth and thickened. Add shrimp and green pepper. Simmer covered about 10 minutes. Serve with rice.
Serves 6 to 8.

Angel Wings

3 whole chicken breasts, split and skinned
3 tablespoons butter or margarine
salt and pepper
1¼ cups chicken broth
1 onion, chopped
2 cans (4 ounce) diced green chiles
1 clove garlic, minced
1 tablespoon flour
½ cup cream
½ cup shredded Cheddar cheese

Brown chicken lightly in half the butter in skillet and season with salt and pepper. Lay in single layer in greased shallow baking dish (9 x 12 inch). Splash with ¼ cup chicken broth. Cover tightly and bake in preheated 350º oven for 20 minutes. While chicken bakes, saute onion gently in remaining butter until soft. Add chiles to pan with garlic and flour. Stir and cook a minute or so. Stir in the remaining 1 cup of broth and simmer until smooth and slightly thickened. Pour into blender or food processor and whirl until pureed. Put back into skillet and stir in the cream. Heat just to simmering and pour over chicken. Sprinkle with cheese. Bake in 350º oven an additional 30 minutes, or until chicken is baked and the cheese is glazed.
Serves 6.

Baked Chicken Breasts

4 cups chicken breasts, cooked and cut up
2 cans (10¾ ounce) creamed chicken soup
1½ cups real mayonnaise
2 cups diced celery
1 cup raw rice (cooked)
2 tablespoons lemon juice
2 tablespoons chopped onion
salt
pepper

Topping:
2 cups crushed corn flakes
2 tablespoons butter
1 package (4 ounce) slivered almonds
paprika, if desired

Mix all ingredients together. Put in a 9 x 13 inch baking dish. Top with 2 cups buttered, crushed cornflakes. Add slivered almonds if desired and paprika. Bake 30-40 minutes at 350º.
Prepare chicken day before or entire casserole. May be prepared ahead and refrigerated or frozen except for the topping which should be put on at time of baking.
Serves 8 to 12.

Chicken Au Gratin

4 chicken breasts
½ cup butter
½ cup flour
1 cup milk
1 can (10¾ ounce) chicken broth
1 cup shredded Cheddar cheese
½ teaspoon salt
1 teaspoon thyme
1 teaspoon instant onion
1 can (6 ounce) mushrooms, drained
1 cup sour cream
biscuits - recipe below

Simmer chicken in broth 20 minutes. Cut in bite-sized pieces. Melt butter, add flour. Add milk and chicken broth. Cook, stirring constantly until thick and smooth. Add cheese and seasonings. Add chicken, mushrooms and sour cream. Turn into baking dish (2½ quart) and top with biscuits. Bake at 350° for 20 to 25 minutes or until biscuits are golden brown.

Biscuits:
1½ cups sifted flour
½ teaspoon salt
3 teaspoons baking powder
¼ cup butter
⅔ cup milk

Sift flour with salt and baking powder. Cut in butter until crumbly. Add milk; knead until smooth. Roll out ½ inch thick. Cut with floured biscuit cutter, about 2 inches in diameter. Place on casserole.
Serves 6 to 8.

Chicken Baccigaluppi

4 whole chicken breasts or 8 pieces
  (boned and skinned)
3 tablespoons flour
½ teaspoon seasoned salt
¼ teaspoon pepper
¼ teaspoon oregano leaves,
  crushed
6 tablespoons margarine
1 cup Marsala or dry sherry
juice of ½ lemon

Pound breasts slightly and dredge in flour with seasonings. Melt margarine in skillet, brown chicken on both sides. Add Marsala, cover and simmer ½ hour or until tender. Serve with risotto or thin spaghetti. Add ¼ cup more sherry before serving, plus juice of ½ lemon.
Half pound fresh, sliced mushrooms added while chicken is cooking is a nice addition.
Serves 4.

THE ROSWELL RECORD   APRIL 3, 1896

Some people say that Sandhill cranes are not good eating. This is a mistake. Rob Hayes killed one last week and we ate it. It was first class and better than the average turkey gobbler.

Chicken Broccoli Casserole with Spaghetti

1 large frying chicken
½ cup butter or margarine
½ cup flour
2½ cups light cream or milk (may substitute 1½ cups milk and 1 cup sherry)
2½ cups chicken broth
¾ cup grated sharp cheese
½ cup Parmesan cheese
juice of 1 lemon
1 tablespoon prepared mustard
1 tablespoon chopped parsley
1½ tablespoons grated onion
2½ teaspoons salt
⅛ teaspoon rosemary
¾ cup mayonnaise
2 boxes (10 ounce) frozen broccoli spears
½ pound spaghetti or noodles

Boil chicken; reserve broth. Bone chicken. Melt ½ cup butter in double boiler, blend in flour. Slowly add cream and broth, stirring constantly. Add grated cheese, Parmesan cheese and lemon juice. Season with mustard, parsley, onion, salt, pepper and rosemary. Cook, stirring until thickened. Remove from heat and add mayonnaise. Cool. Add broccoli (cooked just until crisp). Prepare spaghetti; drain and rinse. In large casserole arrange layers of spaghetti, chicken, sauce and broccoli. Be sure to end up with sauce on top. Bake uncovered in 350º oven until bubbly. *You may cook the chicken the day before if desired. This can be prepared in the morning and not cooked until just before serving time. Serves 10.*

Chicken Casserole

3 pounds chicken, cut into pieces
½ cup flour
½ cup olive oil
½ cup chopped red pepper
¼ cup chopped onion
½ cup chopped carrots
½ cup peas
2 cups tomato juice
1 cup sliced mushrooms
¼ cup sliced green olives
¼ cup sliced black olives
¼ cup water
1 tablespoon flour

Sprinkle chicken with salt and pepper. Dredge with ½ cup flour. Heat olive oil in skillet, being careful it does not burn. Brown chicken in oil. Place in deep casserole. Saute peppers, onions, carrots, peas; add 2 cups tomato juice. Pour over chicken. Bake in 325º oven for 1 hour covered or until chicken is tender. Add mushrooms, olives and ¼ cup water in which the tablespoon of flour has been dissolved. Stir until thickened. *Serve with cooked egg noodles. Serves 6 to 8.*

Chicken-Ham-Shrimp Casserole

¾ cup butter
¾ cup flour
1 teaspoon salt
¼ teaspoon pepper
3 cups milk
4 cups grated Cheddar cheese
⅓ cup sherry
4 cups cooked diced chicken
2 cups cooked diced ham
1 package (24 ounce) frozen shrimp
   (cooked)
1 package (8 ounce) wide noodles
   cooked according to package
   directions for noodles used in
   casseroles. (Al dente)

Make white sauce of butter, flour, salt, pepper and milk. Add cheese, stirring until melted. Remove from heat and stir in sherry. Add chicken, ham, shrimp and noodles. Pour into greased baking dish or casserole (9 x 13 inch or 5 quart) and bake, covered, 35 minutes in 350° oven.
May be frozen before baking. If frozen before baking, sprinkle a tablespoon of sherry on top before baking, and an additional ½ cup of cheese. Serves 12.

Chicken Paprikas

1 onion, chopped
4 tablespoons shortening
paprika
10-12 pieces chicken
2 to 3 pints sour cream
salt and pepper
1½ cups water

Brown onions in shortening in dutch oven on top of stove. Add one layer of chicken pieces; sprinkle salt, pepper and paprika on chicken; then make another layer of chicken and sprinkle seasonings. Repeat until all chicken is used. Add enough water to cover bottom of the pan (about 1½ cups). Cover and simmer slowly until tender (about 2 hours). Remove chicken to a platter. Add 2 pints sour cream to the drippings in the pan and mix well. (If not consistency of thick gravy, add a little flour or more sour cream.) Pour some of this gravy on chicken pieces. Cover with foil and keep warm in oven until dumplings are finished.

Dumplings:

3 eggs, beaten
3 cups flour
1 tablespoon salt
½ cup water
6 to 8 cups boiling water

Mix first 4 ingredients together and beat with a spoon. Drop batter by teaspoonful into boiling salted water. Cook until dumplings rise to the top, then drain and put into gravy. Serve with chicken.

1¾ **pounds chicken breasts, split,**
   or 2 pounds cut-up fryer parts
½ **cup sliced onion**
1 **cup chopped green pepper**
1 **cup quartered fresh mushrooms**

Sauce:
1 **cup orange juice**
3 **tablespoons sherry wine**
½ **cup water**
1 **tablespoon brown sugar**
1 **teaspoon salt**
¼ **teaspoon freshly ground pepper**
1 **teaspoon grated orange rind**
1 **tablespoon flour**
1½ **tablespoons chopped fresh**
   parsley

Garnish:
paprika
orange slices

Place the chicken pieces, skin side up, in a shallow baking dish. Add the onions, pepper, and mushrooms. Combine the sauce ingredients in a shallow saucepan. Cook, stirring, over moderate heat until the mixture thickens and bubbles. Pour over the chicken. Bake in a preheated 375° oven for 1 hour or more, basting occasionally, until tender. Sprinkle with paprika and garnish with fresh orange slices.
Serves 6.

ROSWELL REGISTER-TRIBUNE   SEPTEMBER 17, 1909

Population, 10,000
Altitude, 3,600 feet
National Banks, 3; Deposits $2,100,000
New Sewer and Water Works, Cost $200,000
New Federal Building, Cost $130,000
Territorial Military School, Accomodates 350 students
Roswell and Vicinity Shipments
   Apples, 12,000,000 pounds
   Wool, 2,000,000 pounds
   Cattle, about 10,000 cars
   Alfalfa Hay, 28,800,000 pounds
   Sheep 50,000 head
   Acme Cement 86,400,000 pounds
   Bearing Orchards 15,000 acres
   Young Orchards 8,000 acres
   Alfalfa 23,500 acres
   Other Crops, 16,000 acres

Chicken Hawaiian

1 bell pepper, diced
1 or 2 garlic cloves, chopped
2 tablespoons salad oil
2 cans (10¾ ounce) cream of
  chicken soup
1 can (13 ounce) pineapple tidbits
  and juice
2 cups cooked and chopped
  chicken
2 tablespoons soy sauce
3 cups cooked rice
¼ cup slivered almonds

Cook green pepper and garlic in the oil until tender. Blend in soup and the pineapple juice. Add chicken, pineapple and soy sauce. Stir and heat thoroughly. Serve over rice. Top with almonds.
Serves 6.

Chicken Rosemary

1 medium onion, chopped
1 garlic clove, crushed
¼ cup butter
2 teaspoons rosemary, crushed
1 teaspoon lemon-pepper
1 cup flour
1 teaspoon salt
4 chicken breasts, split
1 cup Chablis wine
1 cup half and half

Lightly brown onion and garlic in butter. Mix rosemary, lemon-pepper, flour and salt in bowl. Dredge chicken in dry ingredients and brown with onion and garlic. Sprinkle 2 tablespoons of flour mixture on chicken as it is browning. Add wine and cook covered over low heat about 1 hour. Add cream; heat through. Remove chicken to platter.
Serves 4.

Chicken Savory

8 Chicken breasts, boned and
  skinned
8 slices bacon, slightly cooked, not
  crisp (limp)
10 to 12 slices dried beef, blanched
  to reduce salt
1 can (10¾ ounce) cream of
  mushroom soup
1 cup sour cream
1 teaspoon savory

Wrap chicken with bacon strips, secure with a toothpick. Place beef over chicken in a 9X13½ baking dish. Mix soup with sour cream. Add savory and pour this mixture over the top. Cover and bake for 1 hour at 350°. This is nice served with rice.
Serves 8.

Chicken Shimona

1 cup flour
1 teaspoon salt
½ teaspoon paprika
¼ teaspoon garlic powder
oil
8 chicken breasts, halves or 8
   pieces of chicken
1 onion, sliced
¼ pound mushrooms, sliced
1½ cups chicken broth
½ cup vermouth
¼ cup brandy
½ cup canned peach slices,
   drained (reserve syrup)
½ cup peach syrup

Mix flour, salt, paprika and garlic powder. Dust each chicken piece with flour mixture. Brown chicken in oil until golden. Remove chicken to plate. In remainder of oil, saute onion and mushrooms; add broth. Then add vermouth, brandy and syrup. Return chicken to pan and cook over low heat until tender (30 minutes). 10 minutes before dish is done, add peach slices. Serve with rice and sauce.
Serves 8.

Chicken N' Stuffing Scallop

1 package herb stuffing, 3½ cups
4 cups cooked and cubed chicken
½ cup margarine
½ cup flour
¼ teaspoon salt
¼ teaspoon pepper
3½ to 4 cups chicken broth
6 eggs, slightly beaten

Prepare package stuffing according to directions on package. Spread in 13 x 9 x 2 inch baking dish. Top with layer of chicken. Melt margarine and blend in seasonings and add broth. Cook and stir until thick. Stir small amount of broth mixture over beaten eggs and add to mixture. Pour over chicken and stuffing. Bake at 325° for 40 minutes. Let stand 5 minutes; cut into squares. Serve with pimiento sauce.

Sauce:
1 can condensed mushroom soup
¼ cup milk
1 cup sour cream
¼ cup chopped pimientos

Heat and stir until hot.

Chicken with Tarragon

3 whole chicken breasts
1 onion, thinly sliced
1 carrot, thinly sliced
¼ teaspoon dried tarragon
½ cup white wine
3 tablespoons butter or margarine
3 tablespoons flour
½ teaspoon salt
⅛ teaspoon pepper
2 tablespoons butter or margarine
1 egg yolk, slightly beaten
3 tablespoons heavy cream
parsley flakes

With poultry shears cut breasts in halves along the backbone. Pull off the skin. Place chicken, onion, carrots, tarragon and wine in a large saucepan. Add just enough water to cover chicken, about 4 cups. Cover and bring to a boil over moderate heat. Lower heat and simmer gently about 25 minutes, until fork tender. Remove chicken and keep warm. Strain liquid, then cook over high heat until it is reduced to 2 cups. In a heavy saucepan melt the 3 tablespoons butter; stir in flour salt and pepper. Gradually add the 2 cups chicken broth; cook and stir over moderate heat until thickened and smooth. Add the 2 tablespoons butter; simmer gently 5 minutes, stirring occasionally. Combine egg yolk and cream. Stir into hot sauce. Arrange chicken breasts on a warm serving platter and pour the hot sauce over them. Sprinkle parsley flakes over the chicken or garnish with sprigs of fresh parsley.
Has a white appearance so serve with colorful vegetables.
Serves 6.

Chicken Tetrazzini

½ pound fresh mushrooms, sliced
5 tablespoons butter, divided
1 tablespoon lemon juice
2 tablespoons flour
¼ teaspoon paprika
1½ teaspoons salt
¼ teaspoon white pepper
⅛ teaspoon nutmeg
2½ cups chicken broth
¼ cup sherry wine
8 ounces spaghetti, cooked
4 cups cooked and diced chicken
Parmesan cheese

Saute mushrooms in 2 tablespoons butter, add lemon juice; set aside. Melt the rest of butter, stir in flour, paprika, salt, white pepper and nutmeg. Add chicken broth. After sauce thickens add sherry wine. In 12 x 8 x 2 inch dish, layer one half of the spaghetti, then one half of the chicken, then one half of the mushrooms. Pour on half of sauce and repeat layering once more, finishing with the sauce. Sprinkle heavily with the Parmesan cheese and paprika. Bake in 400° oven for 25 minutes until hot and bubbly.

Country Captain

3½ to 4 pounds chicken (breasts or
    mixed pieces)
flour, salt, and pepper
shortening
2 onions, finely chopped
2 green peppers, chopped
1 clove garlic, minced
3 heaping tablespoons currants
3 teaspoons curry powder
3 cans (16 ounce) whole tomatoes
½ teaspoon thyme
½ teaspoon parsley
¼ pound blanched, roasted
    almonds
3 cups cooked rice

Roll chicken pieces in flour, salt, and pepper. Brown and remove chicken from pan (keep warm). Put onions, pepper, and garlic into the shortening and cook slowly, stirring frequently. Season with salt, pepper, and curry powder. Add tomatoes, parsley, and thyme. Put chicken into pan (15 x 10 inch) and pour sauce over it. If it does not cover chicken, rinse out the skillet in which the sauce was cooking and pour over to cover chicken (about ½ cup water). Bake at 350° for 1 hour, covered, or until tender. Place chicken on serving platter. Sprinkle currants and almonds over. Serve sauce with cooked rice.
Serves 6 to 8.

Easy Baked Chicken

6 pieces chicken (large pieces or 10
    assorted small pieces)
½ cup flour
1 teaspoon salt
2 tablespoons paprika
1 tablespoon onion powder
1 teaspoon pepper
2 teaspoons fines herbs or bouquet
    garni
4 tablespoons margarine

Put flour and spices in a bag. Shake chicken in bag until well coated. Melt margarine in baking pan. Add coated chicken skin side down. Bake in 425° oven for 35-40 minutes. Turn and bake 15-20 minutes, until chicken is tender.
Serves 6 to 8.

The General's Chicken

4 whole chicken breasts, split (8
    pieces)
4 tablespoons butter, melted
    (unsalted if possible)
1 to 1½ cups sherry
2 cups water
Lawry's Seasoned salt
lemon-pepper (Lawry's is best)
garlic powder (not garlic salt)

Melt butter. Place chicken on rack in baking or roasting pan. Pour the melted butter and sherry over chicken and pour the water in bottom of pan. Sprinkle seasonings on chicken and bake at 350° for 1 hour or until skin is browned. Baste frequently in last ½ hour.
Serves 8.

Hawaiian Chicken

2 to 3 pounds chicken parts
salt
1 egg, beaten
⅓ cup frozen pineapple-orange
   juice concentrate, thawed
⅔ cup bread crumbs
⅔ cup flaked coconut
1 teaspoon curry powder

Sprinkle chicken pieces with salt. Mix egg and thawed concentrate. Mix crumbs, coconut and curry powder. Dip chicken pieces into juice mixture, then into crumb mixture. Place chicken in shallow baking pan, skin side up. Drizzle melted butter over top, cover and bake at 350⁰ for 30 minutes. Remove cover and bake 30 minutes longer.
Can be prepared ahead of time, refrigerated, then baked when needed.
Serves 6 to 8.

Hot Chicken Casserole

2 cups diced, cooked chicken
2 cups chopped celery
1 cup toasted slivered almonds
½ teaspoon salt
2 teaspoons lemon juice
2 teaspoons onion juice
1 cup mayonnaise
1 can (10¾ ounce) cream of
   mushroom soup
2 cups bread stuffing (plain)

For chicken layer - mix together chicken, celery, almonds, and salt. For soup layer - mix together lemon and onion juice, mayonnaise, and soup. In casserole, alternate layers, beginning with chicken and ending with soup mixture. Top with bread stuffing. Bake uncovered in 350⁰ oven for 45 minutes.
Can be made early in day and refrigerated. Can be frozen. Recipe can be doubled or tripled.
Serves 6.

Lemony Barbecued Chicken

½ cup melted butter
juice of 2 lemons
1 teaspoon garlic salt
1 tablespoon paprika
1 tablespoon oregano
salt and pepper to taste (white
   pepper)
2 small chickens, cut into halves or
   pieces

Combine first 6 ingredients. Marinate chicken for 3 to 4 hours in the sauce. Barbecue, basting often with remainder of sauce, or bake in the oven at 325⁰ for 45 minutes, basting often.
Serves 4 to 6.

4 cups cooked chicken
¼ cup butter
¼ cup flour
1 cup milk
1 cup chicken stock
1 pint sour cream
⅓ to ½ cup lemon juice
1 can (6 ounce) mushroom pieces
  and juice
2 teaspoons seasoned salt
1 teaspoon MSG
½ teaspoon nutmeg
1 teaspoon paprika
2 teaspoons pepper
½ teaspoon cayenne pepper
  (optional)
1 tablespoon parsley flakes
1 package (8 ounce) green spinach
  noodles
½ cup toasted bread crumbs
Parmesan cheese

Cook noodles; drain. Melt butter in a large saucepan. Stir in flour. Add milk and chicken stock. Cook over low heat, stirring constantly until sauce thickens. To the cream sauce add sour cream, lemon juice, mushrooms, seasoned salt, MSG, nutmeg, paprika, pepper and parsley flakes. Mix well. Cut chicken into large bite-size pieces (4 cups). Butter a 3 quart casserole. Place drained noodles in casserole. Add layer of chicken. Pour some sauce over chicken. Sprinkle with bread crumbs and Parmesan cheese. Repeat layers, ending with cheese on top. Heat in 350⁰ oven until bubbly, about 25 minutes. *Can be made the night before and refrigerated. Then bake at 325° for 1 hour. Serves 8 to 10.*

Swiss Chicken Cutlets

5 chicken breasts, skinned, boned
  and split, pounded until ¼ inch
  thick (10 pieces)
2 eggs, beaten
1 cup dry bread crumbs
¼ cup cooking oil
3 tablespoons margarine
avocado and tomato slices
¼ cup flour
½ teaspoon salt
2½ cups milk
½ cup dry white wine
1 cup Swiss cheese, shredded

Prepare chicken (boned, pounded). Sprinkle cutlets with salt, dip in beaten eggs, then in bread crumbs. Heat skillet; add 2 tablespoons oil; brown cutlets on both sides, adding oil as needed. In saucepan, melt margarine, blend in flour, salt and pepper. Add milk, cook and stir until thickened. Remove from heat and stir in wine. Pour half the sauce into bottom of 9 x 12 inch baking dish. Place cutlets on top; top with remaining sauce, then chill several hours or overnight. Bake (covered) in 350⁰ oven about 1 hour. Sprinkle with cheese. Place tomato and avocado wedges on top, bake 2 minutes more, or until cheese melts. *Serves 6 to 8.*

Turkey Casserole Supreme

4 cups cooked rice
3 packages (10 ounce) frozen
   spinach, chopped
¾ pound sharp Cheddar cheese,
   grated
3 cups cooked turkey or chicken,
   cut in large pieces
3 tablespoons onion juice
3 tablespoons lemon juice
3 cans (10¾ ounce) cream of
   chicken soup
1½ pints sour cream
nutmeg

Place all rice in bottom of a large pan, 10 x 15 inch (larger than a regular lasagne pan). Add one third of the grated cheese and all of the spinach. Add one third more cheese. Sprinkle lightly with nutmeg, cover with turkey or chicken. Pour lemon and onion juices over turkey. Add more nutmeg and the last one third of cheese. Mix soup with sour cream, spread on top. Bake at 350° for 30 minutes until bottom bubbles. Make the day before or early in the morning. Can be topped with sliced almonds.

Glen's Quail

8 quail or 12 dove
Flour
⅓ cup oil
1 can (10¾ ounce) cream of
   mushroom soup
1 can (10½ ounce) cream of
   chicken soup
½ pint sour cream
Salt and pepper to taste
1 cup vermouth

Season quail or dove with salt (dressed birds). Sprinkle lightly with flour. In a heavy 10 inch skillet heat oil. Brown dove or quail. Drain, discard oil. Mix together the soups and sour cream, salt, pepper and vermouth. Pour soup mixture over the birds. Cover and cook in a 325° oven for 1½ hours or until breasts are tender.

THE ROSWELL REGISTER   **FEBRUARY 14, 1902**

A duck does not "dump around" like a hen or turkey when sick. It is to all outward appearances well, or it is dead. There is small opportunity for doctoring.

Michael Hurd

Michael Hurd was born February 16, 1946, in Roswell, New Mexico. He lived with his parents, Peter Hurd and Henriette Wyeth, on the Sentinel Ranch in San Patricio, New Mexico.

He attended Stanford University and received his Bachelor of Arts degree in 1969. He now paints in San Patricio where he has his home-studio.

Michael's works are in the permanent collection of The Roswell Museum and Art Center, Roswell, New Mexico, and in numerous private collections.

His latest exhibit was in the "Four Generations of Hurd-Wyeth Painters" exhibition in 1981 at The Roswell Museum and Art Center. This exhibition traveled around the states of New Mexico and Texas.

THE GREY is a painting of a scene near Michael's home. The work is owned by Helen Hayes.

THE GREY
Artist - Michael Hurd
30" X 36"   1978
oil on canvas
Courtesy of Helen Hayes

Beef Brisket #1 (Smoked)

6 to 8 pound brisket
½ bottle (4 ounce) liquid smoke
1 clove garlic, minced
1 teaspoon onion salt
1 teaspoon celery salt
2 cups barbecue sauce

Marinate the brisket overnight in the liquid smoke. Add the garlic and salts. Cook covered for 4 hours at 200º, fat side up. Pour off liquid, trim fat, pour barbecue sauce over meat, and bake one more hour, basting at least once. *Serves 8.*

Beef Brisket #2 (Lemon)

6 to 8 pound brisket
1 to 2 lemons, thinly sliced
1 to 2 onions, thinly sliced
salt and pepper

Sauce:
¼ cup Worcestershire sauce
½ teaspoon sage
¼ cup sugar
1 teaspoon celery salt
½ teaspoon Tabasco sauce
1½ cups catsup

Salt and pepper brisket. Cover with lemon slices, then onion slices. Wrap very tightly in aluminum foil and put in baking pan. Bake at 275º for 4½ hours, or until fork-tender. Remove from foil and pan. Cool and slice. Meanwhile, combine ingredients for sauce. Pour part of sauce over sliced brisket. Pass extra sauce along with brisket. *Serves 8.*

ROSWELL REGISTER   APRIL 17, 1903

The question of taxing the bachelors has recently been agitated in a number of states and seems to meet with considerable favor. It has been argued that a bachelor is not fulfilling his duty to society and the world in general by remaining single, and that he should be compelled to pay for his selfishness. In Argentine such a law now exists but it provides that those who can show that they have made one proposal and have been rejected are exempt from the tax. Some of the bachelors there have tried to evade the law by proposing to maiden ladies whom they felt certain would reject them. In some cases this worked well, but in others it is sad to relate, the poor bachelors were snapped up so quickly that they were married before they knew it. As a result the poor bachelors are between the old maids and the tax law.

Flank Steak #1 (Korean)

1½ pounds flank steak
3 tablespoons salad oil
¼ cup chopped green onions
¼ teaspoon pepper
1½ teaspoons sugar
3 tablespoons sesame seeds
¼ cup soy sauce
1 clove garlic, minced
1 slice fresh ginger, slivered

Cube meat and marinate in remaining combined ingredients at room temperature for 1 hour. Skewer and broil for 5 minutes on both sides for medium rare. Mushrooms, zucchini, cherry tomatoes, small onions and potatoes are good additions.
Serves 4.

Flank Steak #2 (Stuffed)

1½ pounds flank steak
¼ teaspoon paprika
4 tablespoons butter
2 tablespoons chopped onion
¾ cup fine bread crumbs
2 tablespoons chopped parsley
salt
3 tablespoons chopped celery
1 egg, slightly beaten
2 tablespoons salad oil
2 tablespoons flour
½ cup water or beef stock
½ cup dry white wine

Season the steak with salt and half the paprika. Melt the butter, then add the onion and saute until brown. Add and heat briefly the bread crumbs, salt, the other half of the paprika, parsley, celery, and egg. Spread this stuffing over the steak, roll it, then tie. Heat the oil in a skillet, and sear the steak on all sides. Place the steak in an oven-proof dish. Stir the flour into the fat in the skillet. Add the water or stock, wine and salt. Pour this sauce over the steak. Bake covered in 250⁰ oven for 1½ hours.
Serves 4.

Flank Steak #3 (Red Wine)

1½ pounds flank steak
¾ cup dry red wine
1½ tablespoons Worcestershire
 sauce
black pepper, freshly ground

Marinate the steak in the other ingredients at room temperature for 1-2 hours, turning frequently. Broil 6 minutes on each side. Slice diagonally ¼ inch thick. Serve with remaining marinade as sauce.
This simple marinade also works as a tenderizer for a thick top round steak so that it can be broiled on a grill.
Serves 4.

Fletcher Minute Steaks

6 (5 ounce) tenderized top round steaks
1 large egg, beaten
2 tablespoons lemon juice
1 cup fine bread crumbs
¼ cup grated Parmesan cheese
1 tablespoon toasted wheat germ
½ teaspoon salt
¼ teaspoon white pepper
¼ teaspoon powdered thyme
¼ teaspoon onion powder
¼ teaspoon garlic powder
¼ teaspoon paprika
3 tablespoons butter or vegetable oil
6 lemon wedges
6 parsley sprigs

On sheet of waxed paper, combine bread crumbs, cheese, wheat germ, and seasonings. Beat egg with lemon juice. Dip steaks in egg and then in bread crumb mixture, coating evenly. Place meat on a cookie sheet in one layer, and refrigerate, covered with wax paper, for at least 1 hour to help keep coating intact when cooking. Saute steaks until lightly browned on both sides, about 3 minutes each side, in butter or oil. Serve immediately, garnished with lemon wedges and parsley sprigs.

Green Pepper Steak

1 pound beef top round steak, cut into ¼ inch strips
¼ cup soy sauce
1 clove garlic, minced
1½ teaspoons fresh ginger, grated or ½ teaspoon ground ginger
¼ cup salad oil
1 cup thinly sliced green onions
1 cup green peppers, cut in 1 inch squares
2 stalks celery, thinly sliced
1 teaspoon cornstarch
1 cup water

Pour over the meat the combination of the soy sauce, garlic, and ginger. Marinate for 1 hour. Heat oil in large skillet. Add beef and brown. If not tender, cover and simmer for a few minutes over low heat. Turn heat up, add vegetables and toss until tender, about 10 minutes. Mix cornstarch with water and add to pan. Stir and cook until thickened.
Serves 4.

ROSWELL REGISTER-TRIBUNE   OCTOBER 12, 1909

The Bloom Cattle Company is having a commodious stone residence building erected at the old Diamond A headquarters.

Beef Liver Creole

1 pound thinly sliced beef liver,
  lightly dusted with flour
3 tablespoons butter
1½ cups sliced onions
1½ cups heated canned tomatoes
½ cup diced celery
1 cup thinly sliced green pepper
½ teaspoon salt
⅛ teaspoon cayenne pepper
2 tablespoons flour

Brown liver in butter. Add next 6 ingredients. Cover and simmer about 20 minutes. Drain and thicken the liquid with approximately 2 tablespoons flour. Add liver and vegetables. Simmer 2 more minutes. Serve with rice or noodles.
1 pound chicken livers can be substituted for beef liver.
Serves 4.

Marinated Beef Tenderloin

3 to 4 pounds beef tenderloin

Wine Marinade:
1½ cups vegetable oil
¾ cup soy sauce
2 tablespoons Worcestershire sauce
2 tablespoons dry mustard
salt and freshly ground pepper
1 cup dry red wine
4 tablespoons chopped parsley
⅓ cup fresh lemon juice

Combine all marinade ingredients in quart jar. Shake vigorously. (Dry mustard will be hard to dissolve.) This mixture can be frozen and reused many times. Two days before serving, marinate beef overnight in wine marinade. Day before, remove from marinade and bake in 450° oven for 45 minutes. Meat will be rare. Cover and refrigerate overnight. Since this is served cold, remove from refrigerator just before serving and slice very thin diagonally with electric knife.
Delicious with homemade horseradish sauce or green chili strips marinated in a little olive oil with crushed garlic and salt.
Serves 10 to 12.

THE ROSWELL RECORD   APRIL 3, 1896

My fine Jersey bull will be permitted to serve cows at my place, 1½ miles south of town. Terms, $5.00 for each heifer or calf dropped, payable at birth of calf. No charge for bull cows dropped.

G. H. McDowell

Mediterranean Steak

1 (4 pound) top round or sirloin
  steak, cut 8 inches across and 3
  inches thick
1 clove garlic, crushed
1 tablespoon instant coffee
2 ounces Roquefort cheese
½ cup olive oil
1 tablespoon soy sauce
1 teaspoon Worcestershire sauce
salt
freshly ground black pepper

Blend all ingredients, except the steak, together for a marinade. Place steak in pan, and pour marinade over it. Marinate at room temperature for several hours. Broil for 40 minutes, turning every 10 minutes, brushing with marinade. *Serves 6 to 8.*

Maderia Tenderloin

3 pound tenderloin, trimmed
salt
2 tablespoons butter
½ pound mushrooms, minced
2 shallots, minced
1 package (16 ounce) phyllo leaves
½ cup melted butter
Madiera Sauce (see page 241)

Rub tenderloin with salt. Sear the meat in the butter in a heavy skillet. Set aside. In the same pan, saute mushrooms and shallots for 2 to 3 minutes or until soft. Set aside. Layer 12 pieces of phyllo together, brushing each layer with melted butter. Spread about half of the mushroom mixture on the pastry and place the seared beef on top. Then place remaining mushrooms on top of tenderloin and fold the dough around the fillet. Prepare an additional 5 to 6 layers of pastry, each brushed with butter. Seal all the edges by overlapping them with this additional pastry and brush with butter. Place beef in a buttered baking pan and bake in 450° oven for about 25 to 30 minutes or until pastry is browned and flaky. Serve with Madeira Sauce.
Delicious also served cold for a picnic or buffet.
Serves 6.

ROSWELL REGISTER   APRIL 17, 1903

PERSONAL

J.J. Hagerman was in the city last Friday.
Judge Frank Lea is under the weather this week.
C.H. Hon went out to his ranch last week.
Miss Annie Bell, an accomplished young lady of Dallas, Texas is visiting Roswell friends.
Mrs. Hart, manager of the Western Union telegraph office, is slightly indisposed at her boarding house on North Main Street.

Pot Roast #1 (Savory)

3 to 4 pound blade bone pot roast
¼ cup wine vinegar
¼ cup vegetable oil
¼ cup catsup
2 tablespoons soy sauce
2 tablespoons Worcestershire sauce
1 teaspoon dried rosemary, crushed
1 clove garlic, minced
½ teaspoon dry mustard

In a skillet, brown meat slowly in a small amount of oil. Sprinkle meat with a little salt. Combine vinegar, oil, catsup, soy sauce, Worcestershire, rosemary, garlic and mustard. Pour over meat. Cover and simmer slowly until tender, about 2 hours. Skim fat.
Serves 6 to 8.

Pot Roast #2 (Beer)

4 to 5 pound chuck roast
1 tablespoon salad oil
4 medium onions, sliced
6 carrots, sliced
4 tablespoons butter
2 tablespoons flour
1 can (12 ounce) beer
1 tablespoon brown sugar
1 tablespoon vinegar
1 bay leaf, crushed
2 cloves garlic, minced
salt
2 tablespoons chopped parsley

Brown meat in oil on both sides in a heavy Dutch oven. In a separate skillet, saute onions and carrots in butter, sprinkle with flour and cook 2 minutes. Pour in beer and bring to a boil, stirring. Pour over meat. Add brown sugar, vinegar, bay leaf, garlic, and salt. Cover and simmer 2 hours, or until meat is tender. Lift meat onto hot platter, sprinkle with parsley, keep warm. Cook down pan juices with vegetables until slightly thickened. Pour sauce over meat.
Serves 6 to 8.

Pot Roast #3 (Autumn)

1½ cups burgundy wine
1½ cups apple juice
3 beef bouillon cubes
2 large onions, chopped
2 cloves garlic, minced
½ teaspoon ground pepper
¼ teaspoon thyme
¼ teaspoon celery seed
5 pound pot roast
2 tablespoons olive oil

Mix first eight ingredients. Let stand until bouillon cubes soften, then stir to blend. Pour over meat. Cover and refrigerate overnight. Remove meat and drain, reserving marinade. Brown meat in olive oil. Add marinade. Bring to boil, cover, reduce heat and simmer until tender, about 2½ hours. Thicken drippings and pour over meat. Or after meat is browned, add marinade to roasting pan. Cover and bake in 325° oven for 2½ hours.
Serves 6 to 8.

Ranch Steak

⅓ cup flour
salt and pepper
2 to 2½ pounds top round steak
3 tablespoons vegetable oil
1½ cups beef bouillon
½ cup barbecue sauce
1 teaspoon chili pepper
1 bell pepper, chopped
½ cup sliced stuffed olives

Mix flour, salt and pepper. Pound well into each side of steak. Heat oil in heavy casserole and brown meat. Mix bouillon, barbecue sauce, and chili pepper. Pour over meat. Cover and simmer 1 hour. Add green pepper and olives and simmer until meat is nearly tender, about 1½ hours. Add small potatoes and carrots. Cook again for about 45 minutes.
Serves 8.

Romanian Rouladen

6 (5 ounce) tenderized top round
   steaks
salt and pepper
3 medium onions, sliced
3 teaspoons Dijon mustard
6 strips bacon, cut in 1 inch pieces
3 dill pickles, cut lengthwise into
   sticks
½ cup vegetable oil
1 cup chopped onion
½ cup chopped carrots
½ cup chopped celery
1 tablespoon tomato puree
2 tablespoons flour
4 cups beefstock

Sprinkle the round steaks lightly with salt and pepper. Saute the onions. Spread ½ teaspoon mustard on each steak. Distribute the onions on top of the mustard. Place the bacon strips across the steak, then place the pickles between them. Roll the steaks tightly and secure with toothpicks. Heat oil in casserole and sear the roulades. Remove to warm platter. Add the remaining vegetables to the oil and saute until browned lightly. Add tomato, mix well, cook about 5 minutes more. Add the flour and cook another 2 to 4 minutes. Finally add stock, stir gently, and bring to a boil. Return the meat to the sauce, and simmer gently for an hour. Remove the meat again to a warmed platter, pull out toothpicks. Adjust seasoning and thickness of sauce. Strain through sieve. Pour some of the sauce over the roulades and serve the rest in a bowl.
Serves 6.

ROSWELL RECORD   APRIL 3, 1896

Corn-fed beef is considered by epicures the best article of diet to appease the carniverous appetite of man. It can be found at the Pecos Valley meat market.

Steak Flambe

1 thick sirloin steak (about 2½ pounds)
1¼ cups bourbon (divided)
¼ cup fresh lime juice
2 tablespoon brown sugar
3 tablespoons butter, melted
salt and coarse pepper

In shallow dish, marinate steak in one cup bourbon, lime juice, and brown sugar. Cover for one hour. Then add melted butter to marinade and cook steak on grill, basting frequently. When cooked, season with salt and pepper. Pour ¼ cup bourbon over steak and ignite for serving. *Serves 4.*

Teriyaki Steak

4 small ¾ inch thick N.Y. Strip steaks or 1 (1 to 2 pound) flank steak
¼ cup honey
1 cup soy sauce
1½ inch piece fresh ginger, peeled and grated
1 clove garlic, crushed
⅛ teaspoon sesame oil

Arrange steak in shallow dish. Combine honey, soy sauce, ginger, garlic and sesame oil and blend well. Pour over steak. Cover and marinate in refrigerator at least 3 hours or overnight, turning occasionally. Broil.
Serves 4.

Scotch Beef Roulades

6 (5 ounce) tenderized top round steaks
4 ounces Roquefort cheese, crumbled
1 can (4 ounce) mushroom pieces
1 tablespoon finely chopped onion
2 tablespoons flour
2 tablespoons butter
10 ounces spicy vegetable juice
¼ cup Scotch
1 tablespoon Worcestershire sauce
salt and pepper

Sprinkle steaks with salt and pepper and half the Roquefort. Drain mushrooms, reserving juice. Combine mushrooms and onion. Sprinkle mixture over Roquefort on steaks. Roll up steaks and fasten securely with toothpicks. Dredge in flour. Heat butter in large skillet with cover. Brown roulades on all sides. Combine juice drained from mushrooms, vegetable juice, Scotch and Worcestershire. Pour mixture over beef. Cover tightly and simmer for about 40 minutes, or until tender. Remove roulades to serving platter, and keep warm. Stir remaining Roquefort into sauce in pan. Cook, stirring constantly, until sauce is blended. Pour over roulades and serve with buttered noodles or rice.
Serves 6.

Beef Pastries

1 can crescent rolls
½ pound ground beef
3 tablespoons catsup
2 tablespoons chopped green
   pepper
1½ teaspoons instant onion
salt and pepper
⅛ teaspoon oregano
1 can (8 ounce) tomato sauce
1 can (4 ounce) green chiles,
   chopped
6 ounces Monterey Jack cheese,
   grated

Unroll and separate crescent dough into 8 triangles. Combine ground beef, catsup, green pepper, onion and seasonings. Spread ¼ mixture on each of the 4 triangles. Top with remaining triangles, press edges together with tines of fork to seal. Place on ungreased cookie sheet. Bake at 375⁰ for 20 minutes or until brown. Heat tomato sauce with green chiles. Spoon over hot pastries. Sprinkle with cheese and place under broiler, for a minute or two.
Serves 4.

Beef Salami

5 pounds lean hamburger
5 teaspoons Morton Tender Quick
   salt
2½ teaspoons mustard seed
2½ teaspoons black pepper, ground
2½ teaspoons onion salt
2½ teaspoon garlic salt
1 teaspoon Schilling Hickory Smoke
   salt
1 teaspoon Cayenne pepper
(Increase last 6 items, if you like it
   spicier.)

Mix all ingredients together with your hands. Cover and refrigerate three days, working with your hands each day. On the 4th day, make into 5 rolls and cook in 200⁰ oven on a rack over a pan for 6 hours. Drain on paper towels.
Can be frozen.

ROSWELL REGISTER   MARCH 14, 1902

The Vice of Nagging

Clouds the happiness of the home, but a nagging woman often needs help. She may be so nervous and run-down in health that trifles annoy her. If she is melancholy, excitable, troubled with loss of appetite, headache and sleeplessness, or fainting and dizzy spells, she needs Electric Bitters, the most wonderful remedy for ailing women. Thousands of sufferers from female troubles, nervous troubles, backache and weak kidneys have used it, and become healthy and happy. Try it. Only 50¢ at Pecos Valley Drug Co. and Jno. R. Hodges.' Guaranteed satisfaction.

Hamburger Pie

1 cup chopped onions
1 pound ground round/chuck
2 tablespoons butter or margarine
1 teaspoon salt
¼ teaspoon pepper
1 tablespoon Worcestershire sauce
2 tablespoons catsup or chili sauce
2 tablespoons flour
1 9 or 10 inch unbaked pie shell
1 cup cottage cheese
½ cup sour cream
2 eggs, slightly beaten
paprika
chopped parsley or chives

Cook onions and beef in butter about 5 minutes, breaking up meat with a fork. Stir in next five ingredients. Turn meat into pie shell. Blend together cottage cheese, sour cream and eggs; pour over meat. Bake at 350º for 30-40 minutes. Remove from oven, sprinkle with paprika and either parsley or chives.
Serves 6.

Imitation Mignon

1 pound ground beef
1 cup bread crumbs
3 tablespoons milk
1 teaspoon salt
½ cup finely ground raw carrots
1 egg
½ teaspoon pepper
1 tablespoon onion juice
4 slices bacon

Mix ingredients, except bacon and shape into 4 patties. Wrap each patty with slice of bacon, and secure with toothpick. Place on broiler rack 3 inches from unit. Cook 6 to 8 minutes on each side. Can be made ahead and frozen. Can use ground lamb.
Serves 2 to 4.

ROSWELL REGISTER   MARCH 1, 1901

While trying to separate a couple of dogs engaged in a fierce fight, Elmer Richey, Superintendent of Chisholm's & Lee ranch was severely bitten by the outraged canines. Had he not worn a pair of heavy buckskin gloves his hand would in all probability have been "chawed" off. Drs. Kinsinger and Bradley attended to the injured member and Mr. Richey will suffer no serious consequences should blood poisoning not set in.

Moussaka

3 pounds eggplant
2 pounds ground beef
3 small onions, minced
4 ounces dry white wine
2 tablespoons tomato paste
4 ounces water
3 tablespoons chopped parsley
¼ teaspoon nutmeg
salt and pepper
2 egg whites
1 cup bread crumbs
1 cup Parmesan cheese

White Sauce:
4 cups milk
8 tablespoons butter
8 tablespoons flour
¼ teaspoon nutmeg
salt and pepper
2 egg yolks

Peel eggplants, cut into ¼ inch slices. Soak in salted water while preparing beef and white sauce.

In large frying pan brown beef and onions. Add wine, and tomato paste dissolved in water, parsley, nutmeg, salt and pepper. Cover and simmer one hour and 15 minutes or until liquid is absorbed.

Heat milk and keep hot. Melt butter in large saucepan; add flour gradually—stirring constantly, add milk gradually. Keep stirring until it comes to a boil and thickens (about 25 minutes). Add nutmeg, salt and pepper.

Drain eggplants. Brush with butter and broil on both sides until light brown.

Butter a 9 x 13 inch baking pan. Spread ¼ cup breadcrumbs on bottom. Arrange half of eggplant slices on crumbs.

Put the slightly beaten egg whites into cooked beef mixture with 4 tablespoons of bread crumbs, stirring well. Spread half of beef on eggplant. Arrange second layer of remaining eggplant. Spread balance of beef on eggplant.

Add the 2 slightly beaten egg yolks to white sauce. Stir well and spread on top of beef. Mix ½ cup Parmesan cheese with ¼ cup bread crumbs and sprinkle on top of white sauce. Dot with butter.

Bake in 350° oven for 45 mintues or until slightly browned. Remove from oven and allow to cool ½ hour before serving. Cut into squares.

Moussaka is much tastier when served the following day. When cool, cover with foil and refrigerate. Reheat uncovered. Cut and serve. This can be frozen and keeps well for a month.
Serves 10.

Terrific Double Crust Pizza

2 loaves frozen bread dough
2 tablespoons corn meal (divided)
1 cup grated Parmesan cheese
   (divided)
1½ pounds lean ground beef
1 medium onion, thinly sliced
1 pound mushrooms, sliced,
   sauteed
1 green bell pepper, thinly sliced
8 ounces mozzarella cheese, sliced
1 jar (14 ounce) extra thick pizza
   sauce
1½ teaspoons Italian seasoning or
   1 teaspoon dried thyme and 1
   teaspoon fennel seed, crushed

Thaw bread, let rise until double, punch down. While waiting, prepare filling. Brown meat with onion. Saute mushrooms. Grease 13 inch round pizza pan, sprinkle with 1 tablespoon corn meal. Roll 1 loaf to fit pan and put in pan. Sprinkle dough with ½ cup Parmesan, layer with meat mixture, mushrooms, mozzarella, green pepper, pizza sauce, seasoning, and remaining ½ cup Parmesan. Roll second loaf to fit top, place on top. Stretch bottom crust up and over top crust, then pinch edges to seal. Cut 3 slits for steam. Bake at 400º for 15 minutes. Brush top with milk, sprinkle with remaining corn meal, bake additional 15 minutes. Let rest 10 to 15 minutes before slicing.
Serves 6 to 8.

Beef Bourguignonne

3 pounds lean beef chuck, cut into
   1 inch cubes
1 can (10½ ounces) beef consomme
1 cup vegetable juice
1 cup dry red wine
¼ cup brown sugar, firmly packed
1 can (10½ ounces) condensed
   onion soup
½ teaspoon garlic powder
1 teaspoon oregano
½ teaspoon celery salt
2 bay leaves
2 tablespoons cornstarch
¼ cup water

Combine all ingredients except cornstarch and water in a large saucepan. Cover and simmer slowly until meat is tender, about 2 hours. Stir occasionally. Remove bay leaves. Combine cornstarch and water and stir mixture into hot stew. Cook until thickened. Serve with hot rice.
Serves 6 to 8.

Savory Stew

¼ cup fresh lemon juice
¼ cup light rum
3 tablespoons brown sugar
3 medium onions, quartered
4 carrots, sliced
2 tablespoons vegetable oil
2 pounds lean beef stew
2 garlic cloves, minced
salt and pepper
1 cup beef stock or water
3 tablespoons tomato paste
1 sweet red pepper, cut into ⅛ inch
   strips

Combine lemon juice, rum, and brown sugar. In a large skillet heat the oil. Add onions and carrots and cook, stirring, until the vegetables are lightly browned. Remove the vegetables. Add the beef to the skillet, adding more oil if necessary, and brown for about 5 minutes. Add the garlic, salt and pepper, and stir. Stir in the lemon juice mixture and vegetables. Cover and simmer for 15 minutes. Stir the water and tomato paste together and add to the skillet. Stir in the pepper strips and simmer until the meat is cooked and the sauce has thickened, about 30 minutes. *Serves 6.*

Sophisticated Stew

3 pounds lean beef stew meat
½ cup flour
salt and pepper
6 pieces bacon
2 cloves garlic, minced
1 ounce brandy, warmed
12 small whole mushrooms
1 cup condensed beef bouillon
1½ cups dry red wine
12 small whole onions
12 small carrots, sliced
6 peppercorns, slightly bruised
4 whole cloves
1 bay leaf, crumbled
2 tablespoons chopped fresh
   parsley
¼ teaspoon dried marjoram
¼ teaspoon thyme

Shake beef in paper bag with salt, pepper and flour a few at a time. In large iron skillet fry bacon until it browns but is not crisp. Cut bacon in 1 inch pieces after cooking. Place bacon in heavy earthenware baking dish. Cook the garlic in bacon fat. Then add beef cubes and brown quickly on all sides. Pour brandy into skillet, light it; when flame dies out, remove the meat and garlic and put them into casserole. Put mushrooms in skillet, brown lightly; add them to casserole. Put bouillon and 1 cup of red wine in skillet. Bring to a boil and stir bottom to loosen particles. Pour liquid into casserole. Add onions, carrots, peppercorns, cloves, bay leaf, parsley, marjoram and thyme to casserole. Now pour over casserole remaining ½ cup red wine. Cover casserole and bake at 300⁰ for 2 hours. Cool and place in refrigerator covered. When ready to use next day, spoon liquid from bottom of casserole over meat and cook in 300⁰ oven covered for 1 hour or until piping hot.
Serves 8 to 10.

Basque Leg of Lamb

5½ pound leg of lamb
2 tablespoons powdered ginger (or
  freshly grated)
juice of ½ to 1 lemon
salt
pepper

Let lamb stand at room temperature for 30 minutes. Combine ginger and lemon juice. Brush half of mixture lightly on lamb. Salt and pepper. Place lamb fat side up on rack in uncovered pan. Put in 450º preheated oven. Immediately reduce heat to 350º. Roast 2 hours for medium rare. Baste last 15 minutes with remaining ginger mixture.
Serves 8-10.

Brazilian Leg of Lamb

5 to 6 pound leg of lamb
garlic cloves, slivered
1 tablespoon salt
1 teaspoon dry mustard

Preheat oven to 325º. Place garlic slivers into lamb skin. Blend salt and dry mustard and rub over lamb. Bake 1½ hours.

1 cup strong coffee
2 teaspoons sugar
2 teaspoons cream
½ cup brandy
2 tablespoons water

Blend ingredients and baste lamb frequently, cooking one more hour.

1 tablespoon flour
5 tablespoons cream
2 tablespoons currant jelly

Mix flour and cream to a smooth paste. Stir into pan juices. Cook over low heat stirring until thickened. Add jelly, simmer 2 minutes and serve over lamb.
Serves 8.

ROSWELL REGISTER   APRIL 17, 1903

Elza White, the genial proprietor of the Shelby hotel, is out inspecting his sheep on Bitter Creek.

French Leg of Lamb

5½ pound leg of lamb
garlic cloves, slivered
dry white wine
hot French mustard
salt
pepper

Rinse the lamb. Cut deep slashes every two or so inches. Stuff the slits with slivers of garlic. Salt and pepper and place in a pan, covering the bottom with white wine. Roast at 325°, for 30 minutes per pound, less for slightly rare. Add additional wine if it evaporates. To serve, pass hot mustard.
Serves 8 to 10.

Grilled Lamb Patties

2 pounds ground lamb
1 small onion, minced
garlic salt and pepper to taste
1 cup soft bread crumbs
¼ cup orange juice, fresh preferred
¼ teaspoon marjoram
¼ teaspoon allspice
1 egg, beaten
½ cup currant jelly
1 teaspoon grated orange rind

Combine lamb with all but the currant jelly and orange rind. Shape into 8 patties, ¾ inch thick. Over low heat in a small saucepan, melt the currant jelly with the orange rind. Broil patties slowly, basting with the jelly mixture.
Serves 4 to 6.

Lamb a la Romanoff

5 to 5½ pound bone-in leg of lamb
½ cup orange juice
¼ cup lemon juice
¼ cup brown sugar, firmly packed
1 teaspoon Dijon mustard
salt and pepper
⅛ teaspoon allspice
1 tablespoon cornstarch
1 tablespoon water
1 can (16 ounce) Bing cherries,
    pitted and drained

Place lamb on a rack in a roasting pan, fat side up. Roast at 325° for about 2 hours, until the center is pink. Remove to warm platter; skim fat from pan drippings and discard fat.
In saucepan heat orange juice, lemon juice, sugar, mustard, allspice, and pan drippings. Blend cornstarch with water and stir in. Cook, stirring until thickened. Add cherries, season with salt and pepper. Cook 1 minute. Serve with lamb. Garnish with parsley and orange slices.
Serves 6 to 8.

Carol Hurd

Carol was born in Philadelphia, Pennsylvania, in 1935. She moved to San Patricio, New Mexico, in 1941 with her parents, Peter Hurd and Henriette Wyeth.

She attended Shipley School, Bryn Mawr, Pennsylvania, and Sarah Lawrence College, Bronxville, New York. She studied under sculptor-painter, Ezio Martinelli. She also studied with poet, Horace Gregory.

From 1958 to 1963, she lived in Spain. While living there, she met the English painter, Peter Rogers. In 1963, she returned to the United States and married Peter. They lived in San Patricio, with their three children.

In 1976, she moved to Santa Fe and studied life drawing under painter, Ely Levin. From 1978 to 1983, she has been producing work on paper in acrylic, pen and ink.

Her work has been shown at Blair Gallery and Little Plaza Gallery in Santa Fe. She has exhibited in the family group show: "Four Generations of Hurd-Wyeth Painters" which has traveled to Albuquerque, Las Cruces, Santa Fe and El Paso, Texas.

Her painting, THE JOKER, (1980) shows a head of a harlequin in the background with imaginary horses in the foreground. It is owned by the Wiggins Gallery of Art in Roswell, New Mexico.

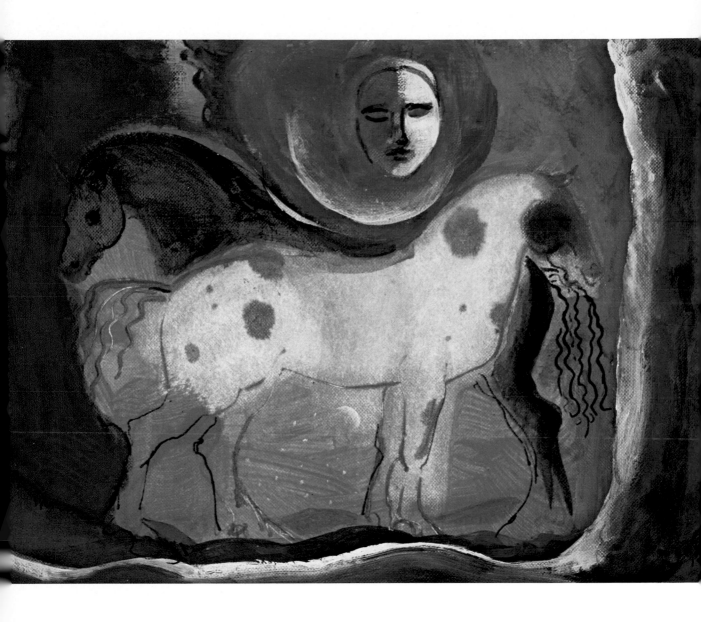

THE JOKER
Artist - Carol Hurd
18" X 24"   1980
acrylic, pen and ink
Courtesy of Wiggins Gallery
of Art, Roswell, N.M.

Lamb Curry

1 large green apple, cored, peeled and sliced
1 large onion, sliced
2 garlic cloves, peeled and halved
1 tablespoon butter
1 tablespoon flour
2 teaspoons curry powder (more or less according to taste)
juice and rind of ½ lemon
1⅓ cup bouillon
1 teaspoon Kitchen Bouquet
½ cup yellow raisins
2 whole cloves
2 cups cubed cooked lamb
salt and pepper to taste

Saute apple, onion and garlic in butter until golden brown. Remove garlic, add flour mixed with the curry powder, blending well. Combine lemon juice, Kitchen Bouquet and bouillon. Add slowly to pan stirring until smooth. Add grated lemon rind, raisins and cloves. Cover and simmer 25 minutes over low heat. Add lamb, cover and simmer 10 minutes or until lamb is well heated in sauce. Serve with rice.
Serve leg of lamb one meal, cut off leftovers and freeze until ready to make the lamb curry.

Lamb Pilaf with Apricots

6 tablespoons butter
2 pounds lean lamb - leg or shoulder, cut in 1½ inch cubes
2 onions, chopped
1 clove garlic
½ teaspoon cinnamon or 1 stick
¼ teaspoon allspice
¼ teaspoon nutmeg, freshly grated
2 tablespoons raisins or currants
salt and pepper to taste
1 cup apricots
1 cup rice
2 cups water

Remove fat from lamb cubes and brown meat in butter. Add chopped onion, garlic, cinnamon, allspice, nutmeg, raisins or currants. Cover with water 1 inch above meat. Simmer 1½ hours. Add dried apricots and cook ½ hour more. Cook rice until tender and drain. Combine rice with meat to serve.

THE ROSWELL REGISTER   APRIL 17, 1903

PECOS VALLEY SHEEP

The following clipping from the Denver Telegram shows that Pecos Valley sheep are in high demand in the Kansas City markets:

"Another sheep record was smashed today. George H. Webster of Carlsbad, N.M. brought in 2,260 lambs weighing 88 pounds that sold for $7.00 straight, the highest price ever reached here for a big string of clipped lambs. These sheep were bred by Mr. Webster, and were from Mexican Ewes and by Shropshire rams. They had been fed 105 days on Kaffir corn and alfalfa. The bunch is part of a band of 10,000 head fed by Mr. Webster this winter."

Lamb Shish Ka-Bob

½ cup oil
¼ cup dry vermouth
¼ cup soy sauce
½ teaspoon powdered ginger
1 clove garlic, crushed
1½ pounds lean lamb stew
2 zucchini
2 potatoes
2 onions
2 carrots

Combine oil, vermouth, soy sauce, ginger, and garlic to make a marinade. Marinate lamb for 1 hour. Cube vegetables, and marinate with lamb for 30 minutes. Thread meat and vegetables on skewers. Broil, turning frequently and basting with marinade until just cooked, about 20 minutes.
Serves 4.

Syrian Lamb Rolls

2 pounds boneless rolled and tied
   leg of lamb (about ½ a small leg)
Wine Marinade (recipe follows)
12 large flour tortillas
3 tablespoons soft butter
3 tablespoons lemon juice
1 cup unflavored yogurt
2 medium-sized tomatoes, chopped
½ cup chopped green onions
⅓ pound feta cheese, crumbled, or
   Monterey Jack, shredded

Wine Marinade
½ cup dry white wine
3 tablespoons olive oil
3 tablespoons lemon juice
⅓ cup chopped parsley
⅓ cup chopped onion
2 cloves garlic, minced
1 tablespoon oregano
salt and pepper

Mix together marinade ingredients and pour over the meat. Cover and refrigerate 4 to 8 hours, turning several times. Bake at 325º for 1½ hours, basting frequently with the marinade.

Butter tortillas and warm in oven. Slice meat thinly and sprinkle with lemon juice. Fill each tortilla with meat, yogurt, tomatoes, onions, and cheese, then roll. Serve with chopped mild green chiles or picante sauce.
Yields 12 tortillas.

THE ROSWELL REGISTER   APRIL 25, 1902

On Wednesday evening late, Mrs. J. W. Sansom fell in such a manner as to break her leg, the neck of the femure fractured in the hip joint. This is a very serious matter as Mrs. Sansom is very frail besides being of such an age that a union of the bones will be almost impossible.

Barbara's Pork Chops

8 pork chops
1 to 1½ cups crushed graham
cracker crumbs
½ teaspoon garlic salt
½ teaspoon onion salt

Season pork chops on both sides with onion and garlic salt. Coat pork chops well with crushed graham cracker crumbs. Lay on a cookie sheet (or pan with sides) covered with foil. Place in 350° oven for 35 minutes. Deliciously moist!

Pork Chops Stuffed with Cranberries

3 tablespoons sugar
¼ cup water
½ cup raw cranberries
6 thick pork chops with pockets cut
for stuffing
¼ cup butter
1 teaspoon rosemary
¼ teaspoon sage
¼ teaspoon tarragon
¼ teaspoon salt
⅛ teaspoon pepper
5 slices bread, cubed

Bring sugar and water to a boil, add cranberries, cook over high heat until cranberries pop. Remove from heat. Let stand 10 minutes, drain and reserve 2 tablespoons syrup. Melt butter, add seasonings, add reserved syrup. Mix well. Toss together bread cubes, cranberries and butter. Fill pocket of each chop with about ½ cup stuffing. Secure opening with toothpicks. Brown chops on both sides in skillet. Put into baking dish and bake at 325° for 1½ hours or until pork is done. *Serves 6.*

Pork Chops Grilled

4 boneless pork chops, about ¾
inch thick (butterfly cut)
garlic powder
lemon pepper

Sprinkle chops with garlic powder and lemon pepper. Grill on charcoal grill about 15 minutes a side or until well done. A charcoal grill with a lid is preferred.
Serves 4.

Pork Chops

4 pork chops, each ¾ inch thick, about 2 pounds
1 tablespoon shortening
salt and pepper

Brown pork chops in shortening in heavy skillet. Salt and pepper to taste.
Serves 4.

Pork Chops #1 (Apple Kraut)

1 can (16 ounce) sauerkraut
1 teaspoon caraway seed
⅓ cup brown sugar
3 tablespoons chopped onion
2 apples, sliced

Remove pork chops to warm platter, and pour off fat. Add the rest of the ingredients and mix thoroughly. Lay the pork chops on top of kraut mixture. Cover skillet and cook over low heat for 1 hour, basting often with juices in the pan.

Pork Chops #2 (Mustard Sauce)

12 mushrooms, sliced
2 small shallots, sliced
¾ cup dry sherry
2 tablespoons Dijon mustard
½ cup whipping cream
2 tablespoons chopped parsley

Remove pork chops to warm platter. Add mushrooms and shallots to pan. Saute about 5 minutes. Stir in sherry and mustard. Return chops to pan, cover, and simmer for 45 minutes. Transfer chops to a warm serving dish. Add cream to pan drippings and stir over high heat until sauce is reduced to 1 cup. Pour over meat. Garnish with parsley.

Pork Chops #3 (Grand Marnier)

¼ cup dry white wine
½ cup chicken broth
1 tablespoon butter
⅛ cup lemon juice
½ cup fresh orange juice
1½ teaspoons lemon rind
½ teaspoon orange rind
1 tablespoon Grand Marnier
1½ teaspoons cornstarch
½ teaspoon water

Add wine and chicken broth to chops in skillet. Cover and simmer 45 minutes. Remove to warm serving dish. While pork chops are cooking, prepare sauce. Melt butter in saucepan. Add lemon juice and cook until reduced by half. Add orange juice and cornstarch dissolved in water. Stir until smooth. Blanch and drain orange and lemon rinds and add to sauce. Stir in Grand Marnier and simmer for 10 minutes. Pour over meat.

Medallions of Pork

1 piece pork tenderloin, sliced ½
  inch thick
2 tablespoons peanut oil
salt and pepper
⅛ teaspoon allspice
⅛ teaspoon thyme
¼ cup minced green onion
1 garlic clove, minced
1 cup white wine
1 cup heavy cream

Saute pork in hot oil 2 minutes per side. Add seasonings. Add onion and garlic. Cover pan and cook slowly for 5 to 6 minutes. Remove pork, keep warm while making sauce. Pour wine in saute pan. Bring to boil, reduce to half. Pour in cream. Boil to thicken. Return pork to pan. Baste. Serve over rice. Sauteed mushrooms are a delicious addition to the sauce.
Serves 4.

Pork Ragout

3 tablespoons oil
2 pounds boneless pork shoulder,
  cut into 1½ inch cubes
6 slices bacon, cut in small pieces
1 cup chopped onion
1 clove garlic, crushed
3 tablespoons flour
3 tablespoons water
1⅓ cups condensed chicken broth
1¼ cups dry white wine, divided
1 bay leaf
½ teaspoon rosemary leaves
¼ teaspoon thyme leaves
½ teaspoon salt
¼ teaspoon ground black pepper
2 cups carrots, cut in ¼ inch slices
2 tablespoons butter or margarine
1 pound fresh mushrooms, sliced

Heat oil in a large heavy pot. Brown half of the pork at a time; remove and set aside. Add remaining pork and bacon. Add onions and garlic to drippings in saucepot; saute until golden. Add flour, then water; cook and stir for 1 minute. Stir in chicken broth, 1 cup of the wine, bay leaf, rosemary, thyme, salt and black pepper. Stir in browned pork. Simmer, covered, for 1 hour, stirring once. Stir in carrots. Simmer, covered, 30 minutes longer, adding water if needed. Meanwhile, in a large skillet, melt butter. Add mushrooms, saute until golden. Add to saucepot with remaining ¼ cup wine; stir gently. Simmer, covered, 3 minutes longer. Sprinkle with a little chopped parsley, if desired.
Serves 6.

Savory Stuffed Pork Chops

4 rib pork chops, cut 2 inches thick
  with a pocket

Savory Stuffing:
2 tablespoons butter
⅓ cup finely chopped onion
½ cup chopped celery
1½ cups soft bread cubes
¼ cup dark raisins
2 tablespoons chopped parsley
½ teaspoon marjoram
3 tablespoons apple juice
seasoned salt and pepper

Wipe pork chops with damp paper towel. Make savory stuffing. In hot butter in skillet cook onion and celery. Add bread cubes, and brown slightly. Remove from heat. Add raisins, parsley, salt, marjoram, pepper and apple juice. Fill pockets in chops with stuffing. Stand chops on rib bones on rack in a shallow roasting pan. Sprinkle with seasoned salt. Pour water to ½ inch depth in roasting pan. Water should not touch the rack. Cover chops and roasting pan with foil. Bake chops 45 minutes at 350°. Remove foil and bake, uncovered, 45 to 55 minutes longer.
Serves 4.

Tenderloin, Sweet 'n Sour

3 to 4 pounds pork tenderloin
2 cloves garlic, crushed
salt and pepper
¾ cup beef consomme
¾ cup orange marmalade
¼ teaspoon ground ginger
3 tablespoons vinegar

Place pork tenderloin in shallow glass dish. Combine remaining ingredients and pour over pork. Cover and refrigerate several hours or overnight. Remove pork from marinade and drain well. Place on grill over hot coals for 1¼ to 1½ hours, turning and basting with the marinade often. Or place pork on rack in 325° oven and cook, basting often, for two hours or until cooked through.
Serves 4 to 6.

ROSWELL REGISTER   MARCH 7, 1902

The Entre Nous Club

The Entre Nous Club met with Mrs. J. P. Patterson at 2:30 Tuesday afternoon. Each member was allowed the pleasure of inviting a guest and many ladies outside the regular attendants passed a delightful time. A guessing flower game occupied part of the afternoon, a solo by Mrs. J. E. McClane, sung very sweetly, and delicious refreshments were other enjoyable features.

Ham and Cheese Crepes #1 (Madeira)

12 slices (1 ounce each) boiled ham
2 pounds fresh asparagus, cleaned
   and trimmed
12 slices Swiss cheese
12 crepes

Mushroom Madeira Sauce:
8 ounces fresh mushrooms, sliced
3 tablespoons butter
3 tablespoons flour
¾ cup chicken broth
¼ cup Madeira wine
1 tablespoon chopped chives
1 teaspoon horseradish
¼ cup cream

Steam asparagus 10 to 15 minutes until crisp-tender. Place 1 ham slice, 1 cheese slice and 3 or 4 asparagus spears on each crepe and place in large shallow baking dish. Prepare sauce: in medium size saucepan, saute mushrooms in butter until tender. Stir in flour. Add chicken broth, wine, chives and horseradish. Cook over medium heat, stirring constantly, until thickened. Stir in cream. Spoon sauce over crepes. Bake in preheated 350° oven 20-30 minutes. *Serves 6.*

Ham and Cheese Crepes #2 (Puerto Vallarta)

1 jar (21 ounce) Ragu Spaghetti
   Sauce (divided)
½ teaspoon garlic salt
1 teaspoon oregano
¾ cup sour cream
1 can (10 ounce) green chiles
6 green onions, chopped
16 slices (1 ounce each) boiled ham
16 crepes
8 ounces Swiss or Monterey Jack
   cheese, grated (divided)

Combine Ragu sauce, garlic salt, oregano, and sour cream in processor and process until smooth. Add chiles and green onions. Place ham slice on each crepe. Spread with half the sauce, then half the grated cheese. Roll up, and top with remaining sauce and cheese. Bake at 350° for 10 minutes, then place under broiler to brown cheese. Serve with a burgundy and a fruit salad. *Serves 16.*

ROSWELL REGISTER   MARCH 7, 1902

HIGH FIVE CLUB

Friday afternoon, the High Five Club responded to the invitation of Mrs. Geo. M. Marshall to meet with her at the home of Mrs. G. A. Richards. Mrs. Geo. Slaughter and Miss Kellar were guests. Miss Patton won the prize, a silver shoe horn and buttoner. The refreshments served were very appetizing.

Luncheon Ham Baskets

4 tablespoons butter
¾ pound fresh mushrooms, sliced
4 teaspoons flour
2 tablespoons dry sherry
½ cup light cream
1 pound cooked ham, diced
2 tablespoons chopped chives
1 tablespoon chopped pimiento
12 frozen patty shells

In large frying pan, melt butter, add mushrooms and saute. Push mushrooms to one side of pan, then sprinkle flour over melted butter, and blend together. Stir in sherry, then mix in mushrooms. Add the light cream. Cook, stirring over medium heat, until cream thickens. Stir in ham, chives, pimiento; heat through. Meanwhile bake patty shells as directed on package. Spoon hot ham mixture into shells. Garnish with more pimiento and chives, if desired. Serve with fresh fruit platter.
Serves 12.

Ham Pate En Croute

2 cups ground cooked ham
1 tablespoon grated onion
1 clove garlic, crushed
2 tablespoons chopped parsley
2 tablespoons chopped chives
¼ pound butter
3 tablespoons heavy cream
1 tablespoon dry mustard
¼ teaspoon black pepper
1 tablespoon Worcestershire sauce
1 loaf French bread, 8 inches long
   and 3 inches wide

In food processor, process ham, onion, garlic, parsley and chives. Add butter, cream and seasonings. Refrigerate. If you don't have a processor, cream butter until light and fluffy in a large mixing bowl. Beat in ham, a little at a time. Then add remaining ingredients, except bread, beating to combine well. Refrigerate. Slice ends from bread. Remove inside of bread, leaving crust about ¼ inch thick. Stand bread on end; with a spoon, gently fill with ham mixture. Wrap in foil, refrigerate several hours. To serve, cut into ¼ inch slices.

Saucy Ham Loaf

Ham loaf:
2 cups shredded or ground cooked
    ham
2 eggs, well-beaten
½ cup bread crumbs
2 teaspoons Worcestershire sauce
salt and pepper
1 small onion, chopped
2 tablespoons catsup
¼ teaspoon prepared mustard

Raisin Sauce:
2 tablespoons butter
2 tablespoons flour
salt
1 cup apple cider
¼ cup raisins

Melt butter in skillet. Add onion and brown. Add to ham along with other ingredients. Shape into loaf. Place into greased baking dish and bake at 325º for about 40 minutes. Serve with raisin sauce. To prepare sauce: melt butter, add flour and salt and brown lightly. Add cider gradually, stirring constantly to make smooth sauce. Add raisins.
Serves 4.

Sausage Loaf

2 pounds bulk pork sausage
1 package (12 ounces) frozen rice
    pilaf, thawed
2 eggs, slightly beaten
1 cup rye bread crumbs (1½ slices)
⅓ cup milk
2 tablespoons chopped parsley

Glaze:
1 jar (4 ounce) strained plums (baby
    food)
1 tablespoon sugar
1 tablespoon lemon juice

Mix together sausage and rice. Add next 4 ingredients and shape into loaf on baking pan. Bake at 350º for 1 hour. Remove from oven and drain off fat.
Combine the glaze ingredients. Brush loaf with glaze and bake 15 more minutes.
Serves 8.

Sausage and Spinach Sandwich Loaf

1 loaf (1 pound) frozen bread dough
¾ to 1 pound Italian sausage
1 large onion, chopped
1 package (10 ounce) frozen
   chopped spinach, thawed
¼ teaspoon crushed red pepper
1 can (2¼ ounce) ripe olives, sliced,
   drained
⅔ cup grated Parmesan cheese
melted butter or margarine

Thaw bread dough as package directs. Meanwhile remove sausage casings and crumble meat into a frying pan with the onion. Cook over medium heat until meat is browned and onion is limp; discard fat. Squeeze water out of spinach; stir spinach and pepper into pan. On a floured board roll dough into an 11 x 15 inch rectangle. Scatter meat mixture onto dough to within 1 inch of edges. Sprinkle with olives and cheese. Starting with a long side, roll up tightly; pinch ends and seams. Place loaf seam side down on a greased baking sheet; tuck ends under. Brush with melted butter (or margarine) and slash top. Bake in a 350° oven until golden, about 35 minutes. Cut into thick slices. Good hot or cold.
Serves 6.

Jezebel Sauce

1 jar (16 ounce) apple jelly
1 jar (16 ounce) pineapple preserves
1 jar (5 ounce) horseradish
1 can (4 ounce) dry mustard
salt and pepper

Combine all ingredients and serve with meats. This is excellent when poured over cream cheese and served with crackers.

Marinara Sauce for Spaghetti

½ cup olive oil
4 cups coarsely chopped onions
2 small carrots, sliced
4 cloves garlic, finely minced
8 cups canned tomatoes
salt and pepper
2 teaspoons dried oregano
2 teaspoons dried basil

Saute onion, carrots and garlic in hot oil in skillet. Puree tomatoes in processor and add to vegetables. Add salt and pepper. Partly cover and simmer 30 minutes. Liquify by putting small batches in processor. Return to skillet, and add oregano and basil. Simmer partly covered 30 minutes or longer, depending on thickness desired.
This sauce can have meatballs or sausage added to it. It is delicious just as it is.
Yields 6 to 8 cups.

Madeira Sauce

3 tablespoons butter
1½ tablespoons flour
¾ cup beef stock
1 teaspoon Kitchen Bouquet
¼ cup Madeira wine

Melt the butter, stir in flour, and cook for 5 minutes. Add beef stock, Kitchen Bouquet, and madeira. Cook until thickened.

New Mexico Barbecue Sauce

1 medium onion, finely chopped
1 garlic clove, minced
¼ cup vegetable oil
2 tablespoons chili powder
2 cups catsup
1 cup cider vinegar
½ cup lemon juice
¼ cup Worcestershire sauce
⅓ cup brown sugar
2 tablespoons prepared mustard
1 tablespoon celery seeds, crushed
2 teaspoons cumin seeds, crushed
2 tablespoons butter

Saute onion and garlic in oil until golden and tender. Stir in chili powder and cook 1 minute. Add all remaining ingredients except butter, bring to boil, lower heat, simmer uncovered for 30 minutes. Stir in butter. This sauce will keep for several months in the refrigerator. It is excellent on brisket, spareribs, shortribs and chicken. *Yields 4½ cups.*

Roast Rub

6 garlic cloves, minced
1 tablespoon peppercorns
1 teaspoon salt
1 teaspoon summer savory OR 2
   teaspoons rosemary
1 teaspoon thyme

For roast pork, use the savory. For roast beef or lamb, use the rosemary. Mix all ingredients in a food processor. Rub well into the roast, and bake according to your favorite recipe.

ROSWELL RECORD   1901

The County Commission will meet Monday next as a Board of Equilization and he who thinks he has a kick acoming should be on hand.
Queen Wilhemina was married last Saturday. This is good news. Not that it makes any difference to us but because we will have a rest from reading about it.

JOYCE - PRUIT COMPANY

A large assortment of sizes and styles in corsets.
Former prices from 75¢ to $1.50, now------------------------------------25¢

IN THE SOCIAL WORLD

The ladies of the Independent Club surprised one of their members, Mrs. V. O. McCallum, at her home on N. Main Street, yesterday afternoon by calling in a body for an afternoon party. It was a "baby shower," the little son who arrived at the McCallum home on June 21st being the guest of honor. Every member took some dainty article of wearing apparel for the baby and it was a pretty collection.

The baby was made the center of attraction throughout the afternoon, and when the visitors served a nice punch, Baby McCallum was the centerpiece of the long table, and behaved beautifully.

Those present were Mesdames Barnett, Elza White, Estes, Wm. Alberts, Sam Jones, Ed Marable, Cottingham, J.B. Dilley, Buchly, Jack Martin and McCallum.

UNDERTAKER AND EMBALMER

Careful, Successful and Scientific
WORK DONE PROMPTLY AND AT REASONABLE PRICES
CLARENCE ULLERY
Phone 90 or 111

Regular Prices of Frank Snipes

Underwear
Ladies Ribbed Union Suites, 25¢, 35¢, 48¢ and up
Mens heavy Fleeced Underwear, suit . . . . . 90¢
Mens h'vy Ribbed Underwear, suite 80¢, 85¢, 90¢
Mens h'vy Ribbed Underwear, better grade . . .$1.40

Never was a cleaner or more fair primary election held in Chaves County than the one which occurred last week. The Republican organ's assertion that it was a day of carousal and drunkeness is only another exhibition of the Smart Alec in politics trying to be funny.

WANTED — Partner. Live man with brains, ability and some cash. Address "Partner," care Record.

Savoring Breads & Jams

OLD SETTLERS
"History of some of the Pioneers of the Pecos Valley"

M. L. Pierce is the first of the pioneers still living here who arrived full grown in the Pecos Valley. Mr. Bullard, mentioned yesterday, was born into the life of the pioneer days a helpless babe, requiring the care of a whole family to prevent his knowing anything of the hardships around him, that called for strong men to conquer.

In the early days there was a race track down Main street to the Hondo river, and when there was a horse race on all business was suspended until the fun was over.

Mr. Pierce tells the story of a trial by jury and hanging that took place in 1878 on the Pecos. A boy about 16 years of age traveling with the Chisum outfit, moving cattle, shot the foreman of the gang of cowboys in cold blood. A jury of the cow-punchers was selected, and Mr. Chisum acting as judge, the boy was tried and found guilty. There was no tree for hanging him, so a wagon tongue was propped high in the air, the boy was placed on a horse and after the rope was properly adjusted the horse was led out from under him, and he hanged until dead. So speedy justice was sometimes rendered without lawyers, warrants or officers, but no doubt the trial was as fair and the result as effective a warning to wrong-doers as though hedged about with all the majesty of the law.

ROSWELL RECORD, 1897
LUCIUS DILLS, Editor

Wealth is pretty evenly distributed in New Mexico. Per capita wealth is about $1500.00 a year.

The Pecos River never goes dry. The Pecos Valley is settled principally by American and Englishmen - all thrifty.

ROSWELL RECORD   DECEMBER 14, 1894

Everybody in New Mexico excepting the criminals and a few Republican Editors of the dirty class is proud of the record that Governor Thornton is making for himself and for the enforcement of the law in this territory.

We have nearly given up all hope of the passage of the statehood bill at this session of Congress. It may pass the lower house but those old gents who misrepresent their constituents in the Senate are opposed to an infusion of new blood into their august body of fossils.

The buffalo disappeared from this vicinity in 1877 and '78, and Mr. Dills theory is that the fool beasts, not knowing anything about quarantine lines, drifted too far south in winter and died of Spanish fever. He does not believe that the hunters killed them all.

ROSWELL RECORD   DECEMBER 14, 1894

A correspondent of an exchange wants to know what bifurcated skirts or bicycle dresses are. So far as the reporter has investigated the subject, a bicycle dress for ladies is a two-legged dress, similar to a pair of pants only a little more so. It is rather full about the hip pockets and a trifle loose in the region where a man generally strikes a match, while the bottom around the ankle is tied to keep out the mice. This kind of dress cannot be put on over the head, but the wearer must sit on the floor and pull it on the same as she does a pair of stockings, one on each foot. And she must be sure to get one foot in each skirt. She must also be sure to get the right part in front, and should remember and not get too gay imagining she is a man.

Butter Horns (Old World Kolachky)

4 cups sifted flour (preferably
  unbleached)
½ teaspoon salt
1¼ cups butter or margarine
3 egg yolks
¾ cup sour cream
1 teaspoon vanilla
1 cake fresh yeast

In large bowl work flour and salt into butter until crumbly. In small bowl beat egg yolks, sour cream and vanilla. Add yeast, blend well. Add to flour and butter mixture and mix well until smooth. Form into ball. Wrap in waxed paper and chill in refrigerator at least 1 hour (may be kept overnight). Divide dough ball into quarters, each quarter into thirds, to form 12 balls. Wrap each in waxed paper. Roll each ball into 8 inch diameter circle, on pastry cloth dredged with powdered sugar. Cut into 8 wedges. Place ½ teaspoon filling on each wedge, roll up from wide end to point. Bend to form into crescents. Bake on ungreased cookie sheet, about 1 inch apart, at 400° for 15 minutes or until golden brown. Optional: Sprinkle with powdered sugar while warm.

Traditional Fillings:

Nut:
3 egg whites, stiffly beaten
¾ cup sugar
1 cup ground nuts
½ teaspoon vanilla

Into stiffly beaten egg whites, gradually add sugar. Fold in ground nuts and vanilla.

Poppy Seed:
1 cup ground poppy seed
¼ cup butter or margarine
½ cup honey or sugar
¼ teaspoon cinnamon
1 teaspoon lemon juice
¼ cup water

Blend in saucepan and simmer about 5 minutes, until thick and smooth. Cool.

Cottage Cheese:
1 cup dry cottage cheese
½ teaspoon vanilla
½ tablespoon melted butter or
  margarine
1 teaspoon grated lemon rind
2 egg yolks
¼ cup sugar

Mash cheese, add all ingredients and mix well.

Continued on page 249

Bruce Connor

Bruce Connor was born in Campbellsburg, Indiana, May 5, 1909, and died in Roswell, New Mexico, April 1979. He attended schools in Peabody, Kansas; Roswell, New Mexico; Southern Methodist University, Dallas, Texas; Abbot Art School, Washington, D.C.; and Corcoran Gallery Art School; Washington, D.C.

After a twenty year residence in Washington, D.C., Mr. Connor returned to New Mexico in 1955 to live and paint. He made Roswell his home.

Early experimentation in subject matter, medium, and style evolved into the artist's unique and very personal expression of the Southwest scene. Mr. Connor painted nature both as he saw it and wished to see it.

He exhibited at the Museum of New Mexico, Santa Fe, New Mexico; The Roswell Museum and Art Center, Roswell; Corcoran Gallery of Art; Red Barn Gallery, Wichita Falls, Texas; and the Charles H. MacNider Museum, Mason City, Iowa.

THE PICNIC
Artist - Bruce Conner
28½" X 34"   1975
cassein
Courtesy of Mr. and Mrs.
S. H. Cavin

Butter Horns (Old World Kolachky)

Cottage Cheese Filling continued from page 245

Prune or Apricot:
1 pound pitted prunes or dry
   apricots
¾ cup sugar
1 cup water

Cook until soft, mash, mix well, cool.

Any prepared filling may also be used, or fruit preserves, as long as it is fairly thick and smooth. Dough and fillings may be frozen and thawed before using. Serve warm. Store in loose topped container in cool place. Store fillings separately.

Blueberry Savarin

2 cups flour
6 tablespoons warm milk
2 tablespoons sugar
1 envelope dry yeast
pinch of salt
6 tablespoons butter
4 eggs
2 tablespoons raisins, plumped in
   water, drained
Syrup

Syrup:
3 cups water
2¼ cups sugar
½ cup Cointreau
3 tablespoons Cognac

Apricot Glaze
1 jar (11 ounce) apricot preserves
¼ cup water
rind of 1 lemon, grated
2 tablespoons Cointreau
2 cups blueberries
1 pint strawberries, halved

Combine ½ cup flour, milk, sugar, yeast and salt in small mixing bowl, beat with wooden spoon until smooth, let stand until frothy. Combine remaining flour, butter and eggs in another mixing bowl and blend well. Add yeast mixture and beat for 3 to 4 minutes until dough is elastic. Add raisins, let rise for 45 to 60 minutes. Punch dough down. Butter 8-cup ring mold. Transfer dough to prepared mold and let rise 45 minutes. Then bake at 375° for about 20 minutes.

Prepare syrup: boil water and sugar for 3 minutes, remove from heat and add liqueur and Cognac.

When Savarin is done, remove to serving platter; make holes with fork over surface of cake and brush syrup over warm cake, repeating every 10 to 15 minutes until all syrup is absorbed.

Glaze: combine preserves, water and rind and cook slowly until preserve is melted. Remove from heat, stir in liqueur and strain. Spread evenly over savarin and fill center with blueberries and strawberries and serve with whipped cream.

THE ROSWELL REGISTER   *OCTOBER 24, 1894*

The O. K. Restaurant has moved to its new, large and convenient quarters on the corner of Main and Second Sts. Our board is first-class and our price is very low - $4.50 per week.

Casserole Cheese Bread

1 cup milk
3 tablespoons sugar
1 tablespoon salt
1 tablespoon butter
2 packages dry yeast
1 cup very warm water (105°-115°)
1 cup grated (full cup) Cheddar
  cheese
4½ cups sifted flour

Scald milk; stir in sugar, salt and butter. Cool to lukewarm. In mixing bowl sprinkle yeast into warm water. Stir until well dissolved. Add milk mixture, cheese and flour. Stir until blended. Cover and let rise until more than doubled in bulk (about 45 minutes). Stir batter down. Beat vigorously 4½ minutes. Turn into greased 2 quart casserole. Bake uncovered for 1 hour at 350°. If divided into 2 loaves, bake 35 minutes to 40 minutes. Use 1 large, 5⅜ x 9⅜ inch or 2 small 8½ x 4½ inch loaf pans.
Yields 1 large loaf or 2 small loaves.

Kolatch (Hungarian Christmas Bread)

Dough:
1 package yeast
¼ cup warm water
½ cup plus 2 tablespoons
  buttermilk
1 egg
2½-3 cups flour
¼ cup softened butter
¼ cup sugar
1 teaspoon baking powder
1 teaspoon salt

Nut Filling:
2 cups ground walnuts
½ cup brown sugar
¼ cup butter
¼ cup milk
½ teaspoon vanilla
½ teaspoon lemon extract

For dough: Dissolve yeast in water, add buttermilk, egg, 1 cup flour and butter, sugar and baking powder. Blend ½ minute on low speed, beat 2 minutes on medium speed. Add rest of flour. Dough should be soft and slightly sticky. Turn onto floured board and knead 5 minutes. Roll into rectangle 24 x 15 inch and spread with nut filling. Roll as for jelly roll, place seam side down in snail shape on greased 13 x 9 x 2 inch pan. Cover and let rise 1 hour. Bake at 375° for 30-35 minutes. While warm, brush with melted butter.

For Filling: Mix the ground walnuts with brown sugar until well-blended. Add rest of ingredients.
Freezes very well.
Yields 1 roll.

Oktoberfest Soft Pretzels

2 cups warm water (105⁰-115⁰)
2 packages active dry yeast
½ cup sugar
2 teaspoons salt
¼ cup softened margarine
1 egg
6½ to 7½ cups unsifted flour
1 egg yolk
2 tablespoons water
coarse salt

Measure warm water into large warm bowl. Sprinkle in yeast; stir until dissolved. Add sugar, 2 teaspoons salt, margarine, egg, and 3 cups flour. Beat until smooth. Add enough additional flour to make a stiff dough. Cover bowl tightly with aluminum foil. Refrigerate 24 hours. Turn dough out onto lightly floured board. Divide in half; cut each half into 16 equal pieces. Roll each piece into pencil shapes about 20 inches long. Shape into pretzels. Place on lightly greased baking sheets. Blend together egg yolk and 2 tablespoons water; brush pretzels with egg yolk mixture. Sprinkle with coarse salt. Let rise in warm place, free from draft, until doubled in bulk, about 25 minutes. Bake at 400⁰ about 15 minutes, or until done. Remove from baking sheets and cool on wire racks.
Yields 32.

Processor Yeast Dough for Bread

2 packages yeast
2 teaspoons sugar
¼ cup water (105⁰-115⁰ if using dry yeast)
4 tablespoons butter cut into 4 pieces
2 cups milk (warm if using dry yeast)
1 teaspoon salt
6 cups flour

Use plastic dough mixing blade in processor. Dissolve yeast in water, and combine with sugar in work bowl. Add 4 cups flour, salt, and butter. Push on and off. Add milk. Process until smooth. Add remaining flour in ⅓ cup amounts, processing until ball forms. Dough should be smooth and elastic. Place in oiled bowl. Cover, let rise until doubled. Punch down; divide into 2 loaves or rolls. Allow to rise. Bake at 375⁰ for 35 to 40 minutes for loaf. Bake at 350⁰ for 20 to 25 minutes for rolls.
Yields 1 loaf.

THE ROSWELL REGISTER   MARCH 14, 1902

Your health, your digestion, your complexion is improved by using Perfect Baking Powder.

One Hour Rolls

¾ cup milk
3 tablespoons oil
2 tablespoons sugar
½ teaspoon salt
1 package dry yeast
2 cups unbleached flour
3 tablespoons melted butter

Mix milk, oil, sugar and salt together. Heat until warm (105⁰-115⁰ for dry yeast). Add dry yeast. Transfer to large bowl. Blend in unbleached flour. Flour board and knead mixture about 5 minutes. Roll out to ½ inch thickness, cut with biscuit cutter, and dip each roll in melted butter. Stretch, and fold over. Place in pan touching each other. Let rise one hour. Bake at 350⁰ until brown.
A 2 inch cutter will make 21 rolls.

Orange Bow Knot Rolls

1½ cups scalded milk
½ cup shortening
⅓ cup sugar
1 teaspoon salt
1 package dry yeast, softened in ¼
   cup warm water (105⁰-115⁰)
2 eggs, well beaten
¼ cup orange juice
5 cups flour (measure before sifting)

Add shortening, sugar and salt to scalded milk. Cool to lukewarm. Add yeast and mix well. Add eggs, orange juice and flour, mix well. Cover and let stand 10 minutes. Knead lightly in bowl and place covered in refrigerator overnight. When ready to use, punch down. Roll out ½ inch thick and make bow knot rolls by cutting strips 7 x ½ inch and tie each strip into a knot. Let rise 2 hours. Bake in a 375⁰ oven for 15 minutes.

Glaze:
1 cup powdered sugar
1 tablespoon orange juice

Mix glaze ingredients and ice rolls before serving.
Yields 3 dozen rolls.

Sourdough Biscuits

1 cup warm water (115⁰)
1 package dry yeast
½ cup sugar
1 tablespoon salt
¾ cup cooking oil
½ teaspoon soda
2 cups buttermilk
6 cups flour
3 tablespoons baking powder

Mix together warm water, yeast, sugar and salt. When yeast is dissolved, add oil. Combine soda with buttermilk and add to yeast mixture. Sift together flour and baking powder. Combine dry and liquid ingredients. Place in air-tight container in refrigerator. Use as needed.
The longer this is kept the better it is. When ready to use, place in greased muffin tins, using 2 teaspoons to put dough into pans. Let rise until double in bulk. Bake in 350° oven about 30 minutes until brown.

Sourdough White Bread Starter

½ cup warm water
1 tablespoon dry yeast
¼ cup instant mashed potatoes
  (dry)
Flour
water

Dissolve yeast in water and mix in potatoes. Do not use a metal bowl. Allow to stand at room temperature for 3 days, stirring occasionally. On the 3rd day add ½ cup flour and ½ cup water, stir. After 8 hours add 1 cup flour and 1 cup water. This addition may be made every 8 hours until enough starter is made for needed recipe plus 1 cup. To keep starter going, add 1 cup flour and 1 cup water every 8 hours. The starter can be kept indefinitely if stored in the refrigerator, add 1 teaspoon sugar to starter when put in the refrigerator. Starter should be at room temperature when being used for any recipe.

Sourdough French Bread (whole wheat)

1½ cups warm water (105°-115°)
1 tablespoon or 1 package dry
  yeast
1 cup sourdough starter (To make
  starter see instructions under
  recipe for sourdough white
  bread.)
¼ cup honey (scant)
1 teaspoon salt
2 cups whole wheat flour
2 cups white flour for first rising
2 cups white flour for second rising
1 teaspoon soda
additional flour for kneading

Mix water, yeast, sourdough starter and honey. Add salt and whole wheat flour. Beat 3 minutes with a wooden spoon. Mix in white flour. Let rise in warm spot. Punch down, add the 2 cups additional flour and soda. Knead about 10 minutes, divide and place in 2 greased loaf pans, 9¼ x 5⅛ inch. Let rise again, until doubled in size. Bake in 350° oven about 50 minutes, or until golden and sounds hollow when you thump it. (Adding a pan of hot water during cooking makes a crisper crust.)
This bread freezes well. Don't forget to replenish (or feed) your starter when you take from it.
Yields 2 loaves.

Sue's Sourdough Starter

2 cups warm water
2 cups flour
1 tablespoon dry yeast

Mix ingredients together. Let stand in a warm spot 2-4 days. It is ready when it smells sour and is bubbly. To make starter more sour, add 2 or 3 tablespoons sour milk, after original starter has bubbled.
To renew starter after use, add 1 cup lukewarm milk or water, 1 cup flour and ¼ cup sugar.
Use for sourdough biscuits, pancakes, bread, muffins, cakes etc.
Yields 1 quart starter.

Sourdough White Bread

Starter Mixture:
1 cup Sue's sourdough starter
2 cups lukewarm water
2 cups flour

The night before making bread prepare the starter mixture for the bread. Mix 1 cup starter, water and flour. Cover and let stand in a warm place overnight, at least 12 hours. *Always reserve 1 cup of this starter mixture and place in refrigerator for next batch of bread.*

Bread Mixture:
2 cups milk, scalded
2 tablespoons butter
¼ cup honey
starter mixture
2 cups white bread flour
2 tablespoons sugar
2 teaspoons salt
2 teaspoons soda
4-5 cups flour

Add butter and honey to scalded milk, cool. Add starter mixture. Add white flour, sprinkle on sugar, salt and soda. Fold in lightly. Set in a warm place, cover with a cloth and let rise until light and bubbly (30 minutes to 1 hour). Add flour, more or less until dough is workable. Knead until smooth and springy. Put dough in 3 large greased loaf pans. Cover and let rise until double in size. Bake at 400° for 20 minutes. Pillsbury bread flour works best. Dough can be molded into any shape.
Yields 4 French loaves or
3 large rounds or
2-4 muffin tins or
3 bread loaf pans

Sourdough Pancakes and Waffles

2 eggs, separated
½ teaspoon salt
2 cups sourdough starter (see index)
2 tablespoons sugar
1 teaspoon baking soda
2 teaspoons water

Beat egg yolks with salt until thick and lemon colored. Beat egg whites until stiff, adding sugar gradually. Combine egg yolks with sourdough starter. Fold yolk mixture into egg whites. Dissolve baking soda in water and fold into batter. Bake on ungreased griddle. Waffles: Prepare as for pancakes. Before adding the soda and water mixture, add ½ cup melted butter, then add soda. Bake in waffle iron.
Yields 9 pancakes or 6 waffles.

Whole Wheat Bread

1 package active dry yeast
¼ cup warm water (110º-115º)
½ cup brown sugar
1 tablespoon salt
¼ cup shortening
2½ cups lukewarm water
3½ cups whole wheat flour
4 cups all-purpose flour

Sprinkle yeast on ¼ cup warm water, stir to dissolve. Mix brown sugar, salt and shortening in the 2½ cups warm water. Add whole wheat flour and yeast mixture. Beat to mix, add white flour to make a dough that leaves side of bowl. Turn dough onto floured board. Let rest covered 10 minutes. Knead until elastic about 10 minutes. Place in greased bowl. Cover and let rise until doubled (1½-2 hours). Punch down. Let rise again. Punch down, turn onto board and divide in half and make into balls. Cover and let rest 10 minutes. Shape into loaves and place in 5⅛ x 9¼ inch bread pans. Cover and let rise until dough is doubled or is well rounded in the pan. Bake in moderate oven 350º about 30-40 minutes. Cool on rack.
Yields 2 loaves.

Cheese Shortbread

½ pound butter or margarine
½ pound sharp Cheddar cheese
2 cups sifted flour
1 teaspoon Worcestershire sauce
½ teaspoon paprika
¼ teaspoon cayenne

Combine all ingredients. Mix well. Roll into 1 inch balls. Put on ungreased cookie sheet, mash criss cross with fork and bake for 30 minutes at 325º.
Freezes well.
Yields 4 to 5 dozen.

Freezer Biscuit

5 cups flour
¼ cup sugar
3 teaspoons baking powder
1 teaspoon salt
1 cup shortening
1 package dry yeast
2 tablespoons water (105°-115°)
2 cups buttermilk

Sift dry ingredients. Cut in shortening. Dissolve yeast in warm water and add to buttermilk. Add milk to dry mixture, mix well. Turn on lightly floured board, roll out about ½ inch thick and cut. Freeze on baking sheet. After frozen, store in freezer bags. About 45 minutes before baking, take from freezer, dip in melted butter. Bake at 375° for 10 minutes.

Buttermilk Doughnuts

2 eggs, beaten
1 cup sugar
¼ cup shortening, melted
1 cup buttermilk
4 cups flour
1 teaspoon baking powder
1 teaspoon soda
1 teaspoon salt
½ teaspoon nutmeg
vegetable shortening, for deep fat frying

Combine eggs and sugar and beat well. Add shortening and buttermilk. Sift together flour, baking powder, soda, salt and nutmeg and add to the first mixture. Mix very thoroughly. Roll out on a floured board and cut with doughnut cutter. Let the uncooked dough stand for 10-15 minutes. Deep fat fry at 375°, turning once. Drain on paper towels.
Best if eaten freshly made.
Yields 48 doughnuts.

One Old Settler's Bread

1 cake (or envelope) yeast dissolved in ¼ cup warm water (105°-115° if dry yeast used)
1 cup cream style cottage cheese heated to lukewarm
1 tablespoon butter, softened
2 tablespoons sugar
1 teaspoon salt
¼ teaspoon baking powder
1 tablespoon minced onion
2 teaspoons dill seed
1 egg
2¼ or 2½ cups flour

Dissolve yeast in warm water 10 minutes. Add butter to cottage cheese. Combine dry ingredients in large bowl. Add yeast and cottage cheese. Blend well. Cover and let rise in warm place until double in bulk. Knead down. Put in greased 1½-2 quart casserole. Let rise 40-45 minutes. Bake at 350° 35-40 minutes until golden brown. Brush with melted butter. Sprinkle with coarse salt if desired. Cool in casserole.
Yields 1 loaf.

Another Old Settler's Blueberry Muffins

2¼ cups flour
¾ cup sugar
1 tablespoon baking powder
¾ teaspoon salt
2 eggs
½ cup salad oil
¾ cup milk
1 cup fresh or frozen blueberries

Place dry ingredients in mixing bowl. Mix together eggs, salad oil and milk. Pour liquid into dry ingredients and mix lightly, just to moisten. Divide blueberries among 12 paper lined muffin tins. Spoon batter over blueberries. Bake in 400° oven for 20 to 25 minutes.

Spanish Corn Bread

2 eggs, well-beaten
1 package (8 ounce) cream cheese
1 cup cream corn
1 cup cornmeal
1½ teaspoons baking powder
1 teaspoon salt
⅔ cup oil
1 can green chiles, chopped
1 cup grated cheese

Mix well in order given. Bake at 325° for 45 minutes in an 8 x 8 x 2 inch pan or loaf pan, 3⅝ x 7⅜ inch.
Yields 1 loaf.

Spoon Bread

3½ cups milk
1 cup cornmeal
2 tablespoons butter
2 tablespoons sugar
¾ teaspoon salt
3-4 egg yolks, beaten
3-4 egg whites, stiffly beaten

Scald milk and add cornmeal mixing with wire whip until thick. Mix butter, sugar and salt and add to cornmeal. Gradually fold cornmeal mixture into egg yolks. Fold egg whites into mixture. Bake at 350° for 35-45 minutes. (until a little brown on top and tests done in the middle)
Use as potato substitute. Good with roast beef or ham.
Serves 8.

Apple-Raisin Loaves

3 eggs
1½ cups vegetable oil
1½ cups sugar
1 teaspoon vanilla
3⅓ cups flour
2 teaspoons baking soda
1 teaspoon baking powder
1 teaspoon cinnamon
1 teaspoon cloves
⅔ cup nuts, chopped
⅔ cup raisins
2 cups chopped unpared apples

Beat eggs, oil, sugar and vanilla on low speed, scraping bowl occasionally, for 1 minute. Add flour, baking soda, baking powder and spices. Beat on low speed 15 seconds and medium speed 45 seconds. Stir in nuts, raisins and apples. Spread in greased and floured loaf pans, 9 x 5 x 3 inch. Bake at 350° 55-60 minutes. Cool 10 minutes before removing from pan.
Dates may be used instead of raisins. Nuts can be pecans; almonds are also good. Refrigerate leftovers.
Yields 2 loaves.

Banana Nut Bread (Whole Wheat)

1½ cups whole wheat flour (sifted)
⅓ cup non-fat dry powdered milk
1 teaspoon salt
2 teaspoons baking powder
1 cup nuts, chopped
1¼ cup banana, mashed (2 large)
3 tablespoons vegetable oil
⅓ cup honey or molasses

Sift first 4 ingredients. Add nuts. Mix other ingredients with mashed banana and add to dry ingredients. Grease and flour pan, and line bottom of pan with brown paper. Stir batter well. Bake in 1 loaf pan, 3 ⅝ x 7 ⅜ inch or 3 miniature pans, 3 x 5⅛ inch at 350° for 45 minutes.
Freezes well.
Yields 1 loaf or 3 miniature.

Nana's Banana Bread

2 eggs, beaten
1 cup sugar
3 ripe medium sized bananas, mashed
2 tablespoons shortening, melted
4 tablespoons buttermilk
1 level teaspoon soda
1 level teaspoon baking powder
2 cups flour
1 cup chopped pecans

Mix together first 4 ingredients. Mix sour milk with soda. Add to first mixture. Add remaining ingredients. Bake in a well-greased 4½ x 8½ inch loaf pan for 1 hour at 325°.
A moist loaf that keeps well in the refrigerator.
Yields 1 loaf.

Cranberry-Orange Bread

1½ cups raw chopped cranberries
4 teaspoons grated orange peel
3 tablespoons sugar
3 cups sifted all-purpose flour
3 teaspoons baking powder
½ teaspoon baking soda
¾ teaspoon salt
¾ teaspoon nutmeg
1¼ cup sugar
2 eggs, beaten
¾ cup orange juice
¾ cup water
½ cup melted shortening
1 cup chopped walnuts

Combine cranberries, orange peel and 3 table-spoons sugar. Stir to mix and set aside. Sift together flour, baking powder, baking soda, salt, nutmeg, and sugar. Add eggs to orange juice and water; mix well. Add with cranberry mixture and shortening to dry ingredients. Stir just enough to blend and moisten all dry ingredients. Fold in nuts. Turn into two greased 9 x 5 x 3 inch loaf pans. Bake in moderate oven (350°) 1½ hours or until tested done. Cool 20 minutes. Turn bread out on wire rack and cool completely. (Do not cut for 24 hours.)
Yields two loaves.

Gingerbread Batter/Butter

1¼ cups margarine
1 cup white sugar
4 whole eggs
4 cups flour
¼ teaspoon cinnamon
1 teaspoon allspice
2 teaspoons soda
2 teaspoons ginger
1 cup buttermilk
1 cup Grandmother's Molasses
1½ cups chopped pecans

Cream margarine and sugar. Add eggs, one at a time. Mix together flour and spices. Alternate flour mixture with buttermilk, molasses and nuts. Bake at 400° for 20 minutes in small muffin tins.
The batter/butter will keep for 3 weeks in the refrigerator.
Yields 2 dozen muffins.

Gourmet Danish Pastry

½ pound butter or margarine
2 cups sifted flour
1 cup buttermilk

Filling:
2 tablespoons sugar
2 tablespoons almond paste
1 egg

Icing:
½ cup powdered sugar, sifted
water to spread

Cream butter and flour, add buttermilk. Knead on floured board 10-12 times. (Don't overhandle dough). Chill in refrigerator 30 minutes or longer (chilling makes flaky pastry). Divide into 3 balls. Roll each into very thin rectangle, about ⅛ inch thick and spread with filling. Fold 2 long sides to center, overlapping edges. Bake on cookie sheet in 350° oven 20-30 minutes until golden brown. While pastry is hot, spread with icing. To make filling: Cream sugar and almond paste. Add egg, cream well.
Serves 8

German Coffee Cake

2 cups flour
2 cups packed brown sugar
¾ cup chopped nuts
½ cup melted butter

½ cup buttermilk
1 teaspoon soda
1 teaspoon vanilla
1 egg

Mix first 4 ingredients together saving ½ cup to use as topping. Add soda to buttermilk. Mix together buttermilk, vanilla and egg and add to first mixture. Pour into greased and floured 8 inch square pan. Spread ½ cup topping mixture on top. Bake 35-40 minutes at 375° until done.

Lemon Bread

⅓ cup shortening
1⅓ cups sugar or honey
2 eggs
1½ cups sifted flour
1⅓ teaspoons baking powder
¼ teaspoon salt
½ cup milk
½ cup chopped nuts, optional
grated rind and juice of one lemon

Beat together shortening and 1 cup of sugar until light and fluffy. Add eggs, one at a time, beating well after each. Sift dry ingredients together and add alternately with milk to sugar mixture, beating well after each addition. Add nuts and lemon rind. Turn batter into greased 9 x 5 inch bread pan. Bake in preheated 350° oven 50-60 minutes. Blend remaining sugar and lemon juice. Pour over bread as soon as it comes from oven. *Yields 1 loaf.*

Mincemeat Bread

⅓ cup butter
¾ cup sugar
1 egg
¾ cup prepared mincemeat
2 cups flour, unsifted
2½ teaspoons baking powder
½ teaspoon salt
½ cup milk

Cream butter and sugar. Add egg, beat well. Add mincemeat. Mix dry ingredients. Add one half dry ingredients to egg, butter and sugar mixture. Add milk and other half of dry ingredients. Turn into a well greased 4 cup ring mold. Bake in a preheated 375° oven, 30-35 minutes.

Peanut Butter Bread

2 cups all-purpose flour
½ cup sugar
1 tablespoon grated orange peel
2 teaspoons double acting baking powder
1 teaspoon salt
1¼ cups milk
¾ cup chunky or creamy peanut butter
¼ cup softened butter or margarine
1 egg

Preheat oven to 375º. Grease 9 x 5 inch loaf pan. In medium bowl, with fork, mix flour, sugar, orange peel, baking powder and salt. In small bowl, with wire whisk or fork beat milk, peanut butter, butter and egg until well-mixed. Stir peanut butter and egg until well-mixed. Stir peanut butter mixture into flour mixture just until flour is moistened. Pour into pan. Bake 1 hour or until done. Cool on rack.
Make 1 day before serving.
Yields 1 loaf.

Pineapple-Coconut Bread

4 eggs
1½ cups sugar
2½ cups flour
2 teaspoons salt
2 teaspoons soda
1½ cups 3-minute oats
2½ cups (20 ounces) crushed, undrained pineapple
3 cups (10 ounces) flaked coconut

Combine eggs and sugar and beat until light (about 2 minutes). Sift flour, salt, and soda. Add to egg mixture and blend until smooth (about 2 minutes longer). Add remaining ingredients and mix very well. Spoon into greased and floured 9 x 5 inch loaf pan. Bake at 325º for 1 hour. Remove from pan immediately. It may be served warm or cold.
Yields 2 loaves.

Poppy Seed Bread

4 eggs, beaten
2 cups sugar
1½ cups salad oil
3 cups flour
1½ teaspoons baking powder
½ teaspoon salt
1 can (13 ounce) evaporated milk
1 box (2 ounce) poppy seeds
½ cup chopped nuts

Beat eggs in large bowl, add next 2 ingredients and beat. Add flour, baking powder and salt. Add evaporated milk, poppy seeds and nuts. Pour into a greased, floured angel food cake or Bundt pan. Bake at 350º for 1 hour and 15 minutes.
Can be frozen and kept for several weeks.
Yields 1 cake.

Prune Nut Bread

1½ cups sugar
1 cup vegetable oil
2 cups flour
1 teaspoon soda
1 teaspoon cinnamon
1 teaspoon nutmeg
1 teaspoon allspice
1 teaspoon salt
3 eggs
1 cup buttermilk
1 teaspoon vanilla
1 cup chopped cooked prunes
1 cup chopped nuts

Cream sugar and vegetable oil. Sift dry ingredients 3 times. Beat eggs well. Add eggs to sugar and vegetable oil. Then add dry ingredients, alternately with buttermilk. Beat well. Add vanilla, prunes and nuts. Bake in 3 small loaf pans, 3 x 5⅛ inch or 2 pans, 3⅝ x 7⅜ inch at 350⁰ for 40 minutes. Can be baked in tube pan at 350⁰ for about an hour and then iced if desired. Freezes very well.

Pumpkin Bread

2 cups sugar
3 cups flour
1 teaspoon nutmeg
½ teaspoon cloves
½ teaspoon ginger
2 teaspoons cinnamon
1 teaspoon allspice
2 teaspoons soda
1 teaspoon salt
1 cup cooking oil
4 eggs
2 cups fresh pumpkin or 1 (16 ounce) can pumpkin

Mix dry ingredients in order listed above, adding all the dry ingredients to the oil a little at a time. Add eggs, one at a time, beating well after each addition. Grease three 7⅜ x 3⅝ x 2¼ inch baking pans. Bake at 350⁰ for 1 hour or until done. Chopped nuts may be added to this bread.
Moist. Good with tea or coffee.
Yields 1 loaf.

Raisin Bran Muffins

1 box (15 ounce) Raisin Bran
5 cups flour
3 cups sugar
5 teaspoons soda
2 teaspoons salt
1 quart buttermilk
1 cup oil
4 eggs, well-beaten

Mix dry ingredients together. Mix liquid ingredients together and add to dry ingredients. Mix well. Fill muffin tins ¾ full. Bake at 425⁰ about 25 minutes. Dough will keep in refrigerator for 3 months, if in tightly sealed container.

Sour Cream Coffee Cake #1

6 tablespoons butter
¾ cup sugar
1 egg
1½ cups flour
1 teaspoon vanilla
1¼ teaspoons baking powder
¼ teaspoon soda
¼ teaspoon salt
¾ cup sour cream
½ cup chopped nuts
1 teaspoon cinnamon
2 tablespoons sugar
1 cup sifted powdered sugar
1 tablespoon milk
1 tablespoon vanilla
½ cup chopped nuts

Cream butter and sugar, add egg and vanilla. Add flour mixed with baking powder, soda and salt. Alternate with sour cream. Put one half of the batter in greased 9 inch tube pan, sprinkle with cinnamon and sugar and ½ cup nuts. Add remaining batter. Bake in 350⁰ oven 45 minutes. Make frosting by adding vanilla and milk to powdered sugar. Pour over cake. Press on chopped nuts.

Sour Cream Coffee Cake #2

1 cup margarine
2 cups sugar
2 eggs, well beaten
1 tablespoon vanilla
1 cup sour cream
2 cups flour
1 teaspoon baking powder
½ cup pecans, chopped
1 tablespoon cinnamon
2 tablespoons powdered sugar

Cream margarine and sugar. Add eggs and vanilla. Fold in sour cream. Sift together flour and baking power. Add to first mixture. Pour one third batter into greased Bundt pan or tube pan. Sprinkle with one half of the following mixture: pecans, cinnamon, and powdered sugar. Pour in one third of the batter and sprinkle the rest of the nut mixture. Pour rest of batter on top. Bake in a 325° oven for 1 hour and 20 minutes. DO NOT OPEN OVEN. Remove from oven and cool 10 minutes. Invert and sprinkle cake with powdered sugar. Freezes well.
Serves 8 to 10.

About Suzanne Mulkey

Suzanne was born in Rochester, Minnesota and died in Roswell, New Mexico in 1990. She lived in West Concord, Minnesota, until the age of ten when the family moved to Minneapolis; there she graduated from high school, studied art, ballet and ice skating.

In 1951 she enrolled as an art major at the University of Colorado where she met and married Dick Mulkey. They moved to Roswell in 1953 to make their home.

She studied with many artists in the area and at The Roswell Museum and Art Center and in the summers attended art workshops. Lia Nickson, her first teacher, had a great influence on her work, as did Jan Herring.

In 1968 she returned to college to complete her education and in 1972 received a Bachelor of Science degree, with Honors, majoring in fine art and psychology.

After graduation, she had four one artist shows, a four woman art show at The Roswell Museum and Art Center and painted five large wall-sized murals in different public buildings in Roswell.

Suzanne taught art at St. Andrew's Kindergarten and held art classes for children at The Roswell Museum and Art Center.

SCHIZOPHRENIC COFFEE CUP, painted in 1972, is a fantasy painting. Suzanne said, "I painted in this matter because I love to create the subject matter as I paint. This was my Surrealistic Period."

SCHIZOPHRENIC COFFEE CUP
Artist - Suzanne Mulkey
30" X 36"   1972
Courtesy of Mr. and Mrs.
Jimmy J. Hooper

Apple Butter

1 peck apples
sugar
2 tablespoons ground cinnamon
1 teaspoon allspice
1 teaspoon cloves

Peel and core apples. Cook in water just to cover until tender. Put through a colander. Use 4 cups apples to every 3 cups sugar. Add cinnamon, allspice and cloves. Cook very slowly until thick. Put into a hot sterilized jar. Seal while hot. Apple butter can also be cooked in a moderate oven.

Port Apple Butter

1 bottle (4/5 quart) California port wine
1 quart water
2 quarts peeled and sliced apples (Jonathan or other tart apple)
1½ cups sugar
¼ teaspoon salt
1 teaspoon cinnamon
½ teaspoon ground cloves
½ teaspoon allspice

Heat wine and water to boiling in large kettle. Add apples and cook slowly 1½ to 2 hours, or until mixture starts to thicken. Beat with electric mixer to break up apple slices. Add sugar, salt and spices. Cook, stirring occasionally until thick. It will take about 1 hour for this last cooking.

Apple Chutney

6 large apples, cut up
3 large, ripe tomatoes, cut up
2 large sweet peppers, cut up
2 hot peppers (red or green, size of middle finger), cut up
2 medium size onions, cut up
2 cups sugar
1 cup vinegar
1 tablespoon salt
1 teaspoon ground cinnamon
½ teaspoon ground allspice
½ teaspoon ground cloves

Combine first eight ingredients in saucepan. Mix together cinnamon, allspice, cloves, add to ingredients in saucepan and bring to boil. Boil for 5 minutes. Avoid letting it get too dark. Remove spices and continue to cook slowly, stirring well until mixture looks rather clear. Avoid overcooking.
Yields 3 pints.

Apricot Preserves

4 cups fresh apricots
3 cups sugar

Select apricots, seed and cook slowly to a mush. Add 3 cups sugar to apricots and simmer 20 minutes more. Pack into sterilized jars and seal.

Never Fail Cranberry Jelly

4 cups raw cranberries
2 cups boiling water
2 cups sugar

Wash cranberries. Put in pan with boiling water. Boil 20 minutes. Run through sieve. Return to pan. Add 2 cups sugar and cook 5 minutes longer. Turn into sterilized mold or glasses. Seal with melted paraffin.

Orange Marmalade

2 oranges
½ grapefruit
½ lemon
1 can (4 ounce) crushed pineapple
sugar

First Day:
Cut fruit in quarters and slice paper thin. Measure fruit and add twice as much water as fruit. Let stand overnight.
Next Day:
Boil, covered, for 45 minutes to 1 hour. Let stand overnight again.
Next Day:
Add 4 ounce can crushed pineapple and juice of ½ lemon. For every cup of fruit add one cup of sugar. Boil rapidly to jelly stage or 122°. Pour into sterilized jars and cover with paraffin.
Yields 8 half-pints.

Peach Chutney

4 quarts fresh ripe peaches, peeled,
  pitted and coarsely chopped
2 pounds dark brown sugar
2 cups cider vinegar
1 cup chopped onions
1 pound dark raisins
2 tablespoons mustard seed
4 tart apples, peeled, cored, and
  coarsely chopped
¼ cup minced fresh ginger or 3
  tablespoons powdered ginger
1½ tablespoons salt
2 tablespoons paprika
1 tablespoon cumin
juice of 2 limes
grated rind of 1 lime

Place the peaches in a large enameled pot. Cover with sugar and vinegar. Add the remaining ingredients and simmer, uncovered, stirring occasionally, for 2 to 3 hours or until thick. Pour into sterilized jars. Store in a cool, dark place.
Yields 6 to 8 pints.

Pickled Peaches

4 cups sugar
1 cup vinegar
1 cup water
4 quarts clingstone peaches, peeled
¼ ounce whole cloves
1 ounce can stick cinnamon

Boil sugar, vinegar and water together for 5 minutes. Press cloves in peeled peaches. Drop peaches into boiling syrup. Boil 20 minutes or until tender. Pack into sterilized jars with a stick of cinnamon in each jar. Seal while hot. Good served with chicken, tuna or shrimp salad for a luncheon.
Yields 4 to 5 quarts.

Peach Preserves

12 cups peeled, sliced peaches
6 cups sugar
¼ cup lemon juice

Combine ingredients and boil slowly for 15 minutes. Let set overnight or 12 hours. Next morning boil for 30 minutes. Pack into sterilized jars and seal.

Bread and Butter Pickles

4 quarts cucumbers
9 medium onions, sliced
1 green pepper, cut in strips
1 red sweet pepper, cut in strips
3 cloves garlic
⅓ cup salt
5 cups sugar
3 cups distilled white vinegar
1½ teaspoons tumeric
1½ teaspoons celery seed
2 tablespoons mustard seed

Wash and slice cucumbers thin. Do not pare. Add sliced onions, peppers and whole garlic. Sprinkle salt over layers as you work. Mix a tray of ice cubes through pickles. Put another tray on top. Let stand overnight or at least 3 hours in refrigerator. Drain thoroughly. Discard ice and salt water. Divide pickles in 2 kettles. Combine sugar, vinegar and spices and pour over cucumbers. Heat just to boiling. Ladle pickles into hot sterilized jars and seal. Let stand at least one month before eating.
Yields 8 pints.

Plum Jelly

1 peck damson plums
1 cup sugar to 1 cup of juice
water to cover plums

Place plums in kettle. Cover with water. Cook 25 minutes. Drain in a cheese cloth bag. Combine 1 cup juice to ¾ cup sugar. Cook until bubbles size of a dime or test until it syrups. Pour into sterilized jars. Seal with paraffin.

Sunberries

4 pints strawberries
8 cups sugar
¾ cup water
slices from 1 lemon

In large kettle combine 4 cups of the sugar and ¾ cup water. Boil for 5 minutes. Add half of the strawberries; boil 10 minutes. Add lemon slices, other half of strawberries and the other 4 cups sugar; boil 10 minutes more. Pour into long glass dish and put in a sunny window for 2 or 3 days, stirring occasionally. After 2 or 3 days, pour into sterilized jars and seal.
Yields 4 pints.

Green Tomato Crystal Slices

7 pounds green tomatoes
2 gallons water
2 cups pickling lime

Pickling syrup:
3 pints white vinegar
4½ pounds sugar (9 cups)
6 cinnamon sticks
1 teaspoon whole cloves
1 teaspoon celery seed
1 teaspoon whole allspice

Slice tomatoes ⅛ inch thick. Place in large crock or enamel container. In mixing lime with water, mix small amount of lime at a time. Stir well. (Never put lime down sink drain.) Cover tomatoes with lime water for 24 hours. Remove tomato slices. Wash through several waters. Let stand in clear, cold water for 3 hours. Drain. Boil pickling syrup for 5 minutes. Pour over sliced tomatoes and let stand for 24 hours. After 24 hours, simmer for 40 minutes. Pack into sterilized jars and seal.

Pear Preserves

12 ripe D'Anjou pears
6 cups sugar
8 slices of lemon

Combine ingredients and boil slowly, stirring constantly for 15 minutes. Allow to set 12 hours. Bring to boil and boil for 30 minutes. Pack into sterilized jars and seal.

Brandied Peaches

ripe, firm peaches
1 cup sugar for every pound of fruit
1 cup water for every pound of fruit
brandy

Weigh peaches. Peel. Simmer in sugar and water mixture for 5 minutes. Allow to set at least 6 hours. Drain. Boil syrup again. Pack peaches in sterilized jars. Pour boiling syrup over peaches. Pour 2-4 tablespoons brandy in each jar. Seal while hot. Process in boiling water for about 15 minutes. Place in quart jars, preferably big mouth jars.

These peaches should be stored in a cool dark place for at least 3 months before using. A delicious accompaniment for most any meal. Considered a delicacy.

Dill Pickles

½ bushel small to medium
   cucumbers
very cold water for soaking
5 quarts water, for brine
1 quart vinegar
1½ cups salt
grape leaves
heads of dill
alum
cloves of garlic
small chile peppers
6 quart jars or 12 pint jars

Soak cucumbers in very cold water overnight. Next day make brine and prepare jars.
Brine:
In a large kettle mix 5 quarts water, vinegar and salt. Bring to a boil. Place in each wide mouth jar (either quarts or pints) 1 grape leaf, 1 head of dill, 1 teaspoon alum, 1 clove garlic and 1 small chile pepper.
Drain cucumbers. Pack cucumbers into jars; pour boiling brine over cucumbers to cover. Seal while hot.

Pickled Okra

1 quart white vinegar
1 cup water
½ cup ice cream salt

Combine vinegar, water and salt and bring to a boil.

Okra, washed and outer stem
   removed

Pack into pint jars.

To each pint of packed okra, add:
2 small hot dried peppers
2 small cloves garlic
1 piece dill, dried or fresh
1 teaspoon dill seed
1 teaspoon mustard seed

Cover with vinegar mixture and seal.

Savoring Desserts

EPILOGUE

Each year, the National Municipal League sponsors a contest for the All America City Award. This is not a "pretty face" award; it is given on the basis of "Citizenship, effective organization and community involvement." In 1978, Roswell, New Mexico, was the recipient of this award.

Agriculture and ranching were the original bases of the economy until Walker Air Force Base was established during World War II. It was the first "permanent" Air Force installation in the nation until December 7, 1965, when Defense Secretary Robert McNamara announced the closing of the Base. The missiles were tucked away, the sites were closed. Over 15,000 people left town. The sound of engines, so long a financial symphony, became the silence of encroaching disaster. Forty-six percent of the City's work force and $25 million in payrolls were lost. Nearly 5,000 homes stood empty. Roswell's economic base was lost.

But Roswell was not the kind of town to take such a blow lying down. Everyone pitched in! Private investors pledged over $300,000 and the search for industry was launched.

On the very day the base closed, Longhorn Fireworks unloaded for business. Where SAC once stored atomic bombs, now firecrackers and roman candles could be found. The runways were silent only for a short time. A number of international airlines were attracted to train on one of the world's longest runways. The huge B-52 hanger became Transportation Manufacturing Corporation. Since 1974, all the Greyhound buses in the United States came from this Roswell company. At Christmas by Krebs, ornaments are assembled where air crews were once briefed in grim seriousness. The old officers' club, the barracks and administration buildings saw the greatest change of all. They became the Roswell Campus of Eastern New Mexico University.

A new municipal terminal was constructed at the air base.

New doctors have located in Roswell. A major addition to the Eastern New Mexico Medical Center was completed. Today, St. Mary's Hospital has the major trauma center in the area as well as a CAT/T Scanner and a 4 MEV Linear Accelerator.

Levi Strauss, who has dressed the world in jeans, became one of the largest employers in the city when they built their own factory.

A vigorous recruitment program brought thousands of retirees who helped to fill empty houses and boost the economy.

During the economic rebuilding, cultural development has not been ignored. The Roswell Museum and Art Center is unique for a city of 48,000. It houses the reconstructed original workshop of Robert Goddard, the father of modern rocketry, whose experiments have led us to the moon. Both a magnificient public library and an amphitheatre have been built. A symphony orchestra, community theatre and the Chaves County Historical Museum show that Roswell has not only survived but has grown culturally. The New Mexico Military Institute has grown to become the nation's largest military junior college.

The media, civic groups and service clubs have joined hands with bankers, doctors, educational people, city administrators and citizens to build a strong and going economy. Today, this Unique Southwestern city stands as a community which refused to quit. Its obstacles became opportunities; its problems became progress.

(Most of the preceding was taken from the text for All-America City presentation script.)

Baklava

1 pound walnut meats
¾ cup sugar
2 teaspoons cinnamon
1 teaspoon allspice
1 pound filo pastry sheets
1 pound butter, melted (you can start with ¾ pound)
honey syrup

Chop walnuts and mix with cinnamon and sugar and allspice. Cut the filo sheets to fit a 9 x 12 inch baking pan, 1½ inches deep. (If using an oblong pan, 11 x 18 inch, it is not necessary to cut the filo sheets.) Brush pan with melted butter. Place six sheets in bottom of pan, brushing each with melted butter. Then cover with a thin layer of the walnut mixture. Cover with another filo sheet, apply melted butter, and one layer of the nut mix. Continue to place alternately one pastry sheet, spread with melted butter and a layer of the nut mixture until you have only 6 filo sheets left. Place these, one sheet at a time, brushed with melted butter, on top to form the top of the baklava. With a sharp knife dipped in hot butter, cut the baklava into 1½ inch strips. Cut these strips diagonally to form small diamond shape pieces. (A yardstick or ruler is handy for cutting the diamond shape pieces). Heat remaining butter and pour into the knife slits between the strips. Bake in a slow oven at 300º for about 1 hour. Increase temperature to 400º for a few minutes longer until the top is golden brown. Remove and pour syrup over the top, as much as it will absorb. Let stand at least 3 hours before serving.

Honey Syrup:
1 cup sugar
1 cup water
1½ cups honey
2 teaspoons vanilla

Boil the sugar and water together; then add honey and vanilla. Cook all for 5 minutes.

Brandy Alexander Brownies

6 tablespoons melted butter
¾ cup sugar
2 eggs
1 square unsweetened chocolate, melted and cooled
2 tablespoons creme de cacao
2 tablespoons brandy
⅔ cup flour
½ teaspoon baking powder
¼ teaspoon salt
⅓ to ½ cup chopped walnuts
Sweet Brandy Frosting (recipe at end)

In a small bowl cream butter and sugar until fluffy; add eggs and beat well. Blend in the cooled chocolate, creme de cacao, and brandy. Sift together the flour, baking powder and salt. Add to the creamed mixture. Fold in the walnuts. Spread in a greased 9 x 9 x 2 inch pan and bake at 350º for 20 to 25 minutes. Cool; frost.

Sweet Brandy Frosting:
2 tablespoons margarine, softened
1 cup sifted powdered sugar
1 tablespoon creme de cacao
1 tablespoon brandy

Cream margarine and sugar. Add creme de cacao and brandy and blend to spreading consistency.
Yields 2 dozen bars.

Calcium Squares

¾ cup flour
½ teaspoon baking powder
¼ teaspoon salt
¼ teaspoon soda
1 cup dry milk
½ cup margarine
1¼ cups brown sugar
2 eggs
1 teaspoon vanilla
1 cup dates, diced
nuts, if desired

Sift flour, baking powder, salt, soda, and milk together. Melt margarine and add brown sugar, eggs and vanilla, then stir into dry ingredients. Add dates. Spread in a lightly buttered 9 x 13 inch pan and bake in 350º oven for about 30 minutes. Cool and cut into squares.

Carrot Bars

1 cup sugar
¾ cup oil
2 eggs
1 cup flour
1 teaspoon cinnamon
½ teaspoon soda
½ teaspoon salt
1 cup finely grated carrots
½ cup nuts, chopped

Cream sugar, oil, and eggs until well blended. Stir in flour, cinnamon, soda and salt. Fold in grated carrots and nuts. Pour into a well greased and lightly floured 9 x 13 inch pan. Bake at 350° in the oven until it tests done with wooden pick (25 to 30 minutes). Frost while warm with Brown Buttered Frosting.

Brown Buttered Frosting:
Melt 6 tablespoons butter until golden brown. Blend in 1½ cups powdered sugar. Stir in 2 to 3 tablespoons hot water for spreading consistency.
May be frozen.
Yields 27 (3 x 1 ½ inch) bars.

Chocolate Squares

1 cup butter or margarine
1 cup brown sugar, packed
1 egg yolk, beaten
1 teaspoon vanilla
1 cup flour, sifted
1 cup rolled oats
6 ounces real semi-sweet chocolate chips
½ cup nuts, chopped, or 48 pecan or walnut halves

Cream butter and sugar. Add beaten egg yolk and vanilla. Mix well. Combine flour and oats. Add to creamed mixture. Mix well. Spread thinly on ungreased jelly roll pan (10½ x 15 x 1 inch). Bake at 350° for 15-20 minutes. Sprinkle chips on hot cookie surface. Spread evenly as they melt. Sprinkle chopped nuts on and cut while warm, into 48 bars. If using nut halves, cut after chocolate is spread. Put one on each bar.
Yields 48 pieces.

Brownies

1 cup butter
4 squares chocolate
½ teaspoon salt
2 cups sugar
4 whole eggs
1½ cups flour
1 cup pecans
1 teaspoon vanilla

Melt butter, chocolate, salt and mix with the sugar. Add eggs one at a time and beat well after each addition. Add flour. Mix and add nuts and vanilla. Bake in jelly roll pan at 350° for 30 minutes.

Lemon Squares

1 cup butter
2 cups sifted flour
½ cup confectioners' sugar
2 cups granulated sugar
4 tablespoons flour
1 teaspoon baking powder
4 eggs
6 tablespoons lemon juice
⅛ teaspoon salt

Preheat oven to 350°. Melt butter. Add sifted flour and confectioners' sugar. Mix well and pack into an ungreased 9 x 13 pan. Bake 15 minutes. Mix together sugar, flour and baking powder. Add eggs, one at a time, lemon juice and salt. Pour this mixture over hot crust and return to oven and bake 25 to 30 minutes. Cool and cut in small squares. Sprinkle confectioners' sugar on top. *Yield: 4 dozen.*

Pumpkin Pie Squares

1 package yellow cake mix LESS 1 cup
1 egg
½ cup margarine, melted

Filling:
2 eggs, beaten
1 can (16 ounce) pumpkin
¾ cup sugar
½ teaspoon salt
1⅔ cup evaporated milk
½ teaspoon ginger
1 teaspoon cinnamon
1 teaspoon nutmeg
¼ teaspoon cloves

Topping:
1 cup cake mix
1 cup sugar
1 teaspoon cinnamon
¼ cup margarine
heavy cream, whipped to garnish

Combine cake mix (less 1 cup), egg and margarine in 9 x 13 inch pan. Press to make crust. Mix filling. Pour over cake mix. Top with 1 cup cake mix, sugar, margarine and spices. Bake for about 45 minutes at 350°. Cut in squares, and top with whipped cream.

Black Forest Cherry Cake

Cherry Filling
2 cans (16 ounce) pitted tart red
    cherries, drained reserving ⅔ cup
    juice
⅔ cup granulated sugar
¼ cup cornstarch

Chocolate Butter Cream
3 tablespoons butter
2 cups sifted powdered sugar
1 ounce unsweetened chocolate,
    melted and cooled
2 tablespoons light cream
1 teaspoon vanilla

Cake
2 egg whites
1½ cups granulated sugar
1¾ cups sifted cake flour
¾ teaspoon baking soda
1 teaspoon salt
⅓ cup cooking oil
1 cup milk
2 egg yolks
2 ounces unsweetened chocolate,
    melted and cooled
1 teaspoon unflavored gelatin
2 tablespoons cold water
3 cups whipping cream
½ cup Kirschwasser or cherry
    liqueur
¾ cup toasted sliced almonds
1 ounce semisweet chocolate,
    shaved

For Cherry filling: combine all ingredients and cook until mixture is thick and bubbly. Cool.

Chocolate butter cream: mix all ingredients until of piping consistency, one or two teaspoons of cream may have to be added.

For cake: beat egg whites, gradually add ½ cup sugar, beat until stiff peaks form. Sift flour, rest of sugar, soda and salt, add oil and ½ cup milk, beat 1 minute, add rest of the milk and egg yolks. Fold in egg whites. Pour ⅓ batter into lightly greased and floured 9 inch round cake pan. Add chocolate to remaining batter, pour chocolate mixture into 2 lightly greased and floured 9 inch cake pans. Bake all 3 layers in 350⁰ oven for 20 to 25 minutes. Cool.

To assemble cake: soften gelatin in water, heat just until dissolved. Whip cream, add gelatin, beat until soft peaks form. Place one chocolate layer on serving plate, fill pastry bag with chocolate butter cream. Pipe three rings of buttercream 1 inch apart, fill area in between with cherry filling, spread a thin layer of whipped cream on top. Place yellow cake layer atop, drizzle Kirsch very slowly over. Pipe a ring of whipped cream on outside of layer and fill center with cherry filling. Place second chocolate layer atop. Frost cake with remaining whipped cream. Press almonds onto side and sprinkle shaved chocolate on top. Make rosettes with whipped cream and garnish with maraschino cherries. Chill.
Serves 18.

Carrot Cake

1½ cups oil
2 cups sugar
4 eggs
2 cups flour
2 teaspoons baking powder
½ teaspoon salt
2 teaspoons soda
2 teaspoons cinnamon
3 cups grated carrots
1 cup pecans, chopped

Combine oil and sugar. Blend well. Add eggs, one at a time. Sift flour twice, adding dry ingredients second time. Add to sugar and oil. Add carrots and nuts and mix well. Bake in greased and floured 9 x 13 inch pan. Bake at 350° for 1 hour.

Icing:
6 ounces cream cheese, room
   temperature
5 tablespoons butter or margarine
⅔ box powdered sugar
½ cup nuts, chopped

Mix cream cheese and butter together until soft. Gradually add powdered sugar until smooth. Add nuts. Blend well and spread over cooled cake.

Cheesecake

Crust
1 cup sifted all purpose flour
¼ cup sugar
1 teaspoon grated lemon peel
½ teaspoon vanilla
1 egg yolk
¼ cup butter, softened

Filling
5 packages (8 ounce) cream cheese,
   softened
1¾ cups sugar
3 tablespoons flour
2 teaspoons grated lemon peel
1½ teaspoons grated orange peel
1 teaspoon vanilla
5 eggs and 2 egg yolks
¼ cup heavy cream

Topping
1½ cups sour cream
strawberries for decoration

Combine flour, sugar, lemon peel and vanilla. Add butter and egg yolk and make dough smooth with fingertips. Halve dough; cover one-half with waxed paper and roll dough on bottom of 9 inch springform pan. Remove paper and bake at 400° for 6 to 8 minutes. Divide other half of dough into 3 parts; cover with waxed paper and roll into three 2¼ by 9 inch strips. Assemble springform pan and line sides of pan with strips of dough. Remove waxed paper.

Filling: Blend cheese, sugar, flour, peels and vanilla at high speed; beat in eggs and yolks one at a time until smooth; beat in cream. Pour into pan and bake at 500° for 10 minutes. Lower oven to 250° and bake 1 hour longer. Cool; refrigerate for at least 3 hours or overnight.

Topping: Spread with sour cream and decorate with strawberries if desired.

Cherry Poundcake

¾ cup plus 2 tablespoons butter
1 cup sugar
1 teaspoon vanilla
¼ teaspoon salt
4 eggs
1½ cups flour
¼ cup cornstarch
1 teaspoon baking powder
3½ ounces almonds, ground
1 can (16 ounce) tart pitted cherries, drained
½ cup powdered sugar
2 tablespoons cherry liqueur (Kirschwasser)

Beat butter until light and fluffy. Add sugar, vanilla and salt. Beat in eggs, one at a time. Mix flour, cornstarch, baking powder and almonds together and add to mixture. Add drained cherries. Spoon batter into well greased Bundt pan and bake at 350⁰ for 1½ hours. While warm turn out of pan and top with glaze.

Glaze:
Mix powdered sugar and cherry liqueur until smooth.

Chocolate Gateau

1 cup unsalted butter
1 cup sugar
5 eggs, separated
1 teaspoon almond extract
7 ounces unsweetened chocolate, ground
7 ounces blanched almonds, ground
½ teaspoon cream of tartar
powdered sugar for decoration

Cream butter, sugar, egg yolks and almond extract until light and fluffy. Add chocolate and almonds and stir until well combined. Beat egg whites with cream of tartar until stiff. Add a small amount to butter mixture and stir, fold in remaining whites. Butter a 9 x 2 inch cake pan, line bottom with circle of wax paper. Put mixture into prepared pan and bake at 325⁰ for 40 to 45 minutes, center will be soft. Let cool and sprinkle with powdered sugar.

ROSWELL REGISTER   MARCH 7, 1902
A Geography Party

Mrs. W. G. Burrus gave a "Geography Party" to a number of lady friends on Tuesday afternoon at 2:30 at her pleasant home on the south Side. Twenty-five ladies were invited and nearly all were present. Each guest wore pinned to her dress or forming some part of her costume, a device indicating the name of some city, river, mountain, or other geographical object. Guessing the names represented formed the contest and gave the memories and wits of the guests some lively exercise.

Easy Does It Cake

2 cups sugar
2 eggs
½ cup salad oil
2 cups regular sifted flour
2 tablespoons cocoa
½ teaspoon salt
½ cup buttermilk
1 cup hot water
1 teaspoon vanilla
1 teaspoon soda

Mix sugar, eggs and oil. Sift flour, and add cocoa and salt. Add milk, water, vanilla and soda last. Bake in greased and floured long cake pan (9 x 13 inch). Bake at 325º for 55-60 minutes, until brown.

Topping:
5 tablespoons margarine, melted
1 cup brown sugar
1 cup coconut
½ cup evaporated milk
½ cup nuts, chopped

Mix all ingredients until softened. Pour over hot cake and place under broiler until coconut browns (2-3 minutes).

German Cheesecake

Crust:
¼ cup sugar
1 egg, beaten
½ cup margarine, softened
1 cup plus 4 tablespoons flour
¾ teaspoon baking powder

Mix sugar, egg and margarine together. Sift flour and baking powder together and mix in the other ingredients. Press into bottom and sides of 8 or 9 inch spring form pan.

Filling:
2 packages (8 ounce) cream cheese, softened
2 tablespoons flour
1½ cups sugar
2 eggs
1 teaspoon vanilla
1½ cups milk
cinnamon

Using an electric mixer beat cream cheese, flour and sugar. Add eggs and vanilla and mix until smooth. Add milk and pour into pan. Sprinkle with cinnamon. Bake 1 hour at 350°. Cool in pan. When cool, release from pan and refrigerate.

Hint: If cheesecake cracks, lower temperature to 325°.

Lincoln Town
Sidney Redfield
67

LINCOLN TOWN
Artist - Sidney Redfield
38" x 40"   1967
watercolor
Courtesy of Mr. and Mrs.
Ralph Burnworth

Sidney Redfield

Sidney Redfield was born in Minneapolis, Minnesota, in 1901 and died in Roswell, NM in September, 1985. He attended New Mexico Military Institute in Roswell, New Mexico, and later attended Stanford University, majoring in chemical engineering. Mr. Redfield followed this profession for a number of years, but then decided to return to an earlier interest in art.

He studied with Oscar Birninghaus in Taos in 1939. That was the turning point in his life. He made art his profession and displays skill and discipline in a variety of media. He has had five one man shows at The Roswell Museum and Art Center and numerous group exhibitions in the Museum of New Mexico, Santa Fe, New Mexico.

Mr. Redfield lived and painted in and around Roswell. He captured the arid beauty and hostility of the country with an insight rare in a self-taught artist. He painted primarily the rural area from Roswell extending to the Sacramento Mountains. The painting of LINCOLN TOWN is a fine example of his work. This painting is a pictorial record of this historical old Southwestern town.

Heavenly Sponge Cake

6 egg whites
1 teaspoon cream of tartar
½ cup sifted sugar
8 egg yolks
1 cup sifted sugar
¼ cup boiling water
1 tablespoon plus 1 teaspoon
   lemon juice
1 teaspoon vanilla
1 cup sifted flour
2 teaspoons baking powder
¼ teaspoon salt

Preheat oven to 325°; have ready ungreased 10 inch tube cake pan. Separate eggs. Put whites in the largest bowl of electric mixer. Put yolks in smaller bowl. Beat whites at high speed until frothy, add cream of tartar and continue to beat until the whites peak. Add ½ cup sugar very gradually beating until smooth and satiny; set aside. Beat the egg yolks at high speed until light. Beat in gradually 1 cup sugar, add boiling water, cool and beat in lemon juice and vanilla. Sift flour, salt and baking powder together. Add gradually to the egg yolks. Beat the batter until smooth. Pour the batter into the meringue and fold gently until all white disappears. Pour into tube pan. Cut through to remove bubbles. Bake 50 minutes. Cool 1 hour in the pan, upside down.

Mocha Cream

5 egg yolks
½ cup sugar
1 envelope unflavored gelatin
1½ cups milk
2 tablespoons coffee liqueur
1 ounce unsweetened chocolate,
   melted
2 teaspoons instant coffee powder
1 cup whipping cream

Decoration
1¼ cups whipping cream
2 ounces semisweet chocolate
1 tablespoon coffee liqueur

Beat yolks adding sugar gradually until thick and lemon colored. Add gelatin to milk in pan and simmer, stirring constantly. Add a small amount to yolks, stirring quickly to blend, return mixture to pan and bring to boil, whisking constantly. Remove from heat, stir in liqueur, melted chocolate and coffee powder and blend well. Cool to room temperature. Whip cream, add to gelatin mixture. Pour into lightly oiled 8 inch round cake pan, cover and refrigerate several hours or overnight. Place serving plate over top and invert mold onto plate. Chill again. For decoration, whip 1 cup cream stiff. Frost top and side with some of cream. Put remainder of cream in pastry bag and pipe flower pattern or six ovals on top. Heat remaining ¼ cup cream with chocolate until melted. Stir in liqueur. Cool and spoon chocolate mixture into ovals. Chill.
Serves 10.

Oatmeal Cake

1¼ cups boiling water
1 cup quick cooking oatmeal
½ cup margarine
1 cup sugar
1 cup brown sugar
2 eggs
1⅓ cups flour
¼ teaspoon salt
1 teaspoon soda
1 teaspoon cinnamon
½ teaspoon nutmeg
1 teaspoon vanilla

Pour boiling water over oats and margarine. Set aside. Mix together remaining ingredients. Add oatmeal mixture. Pour into well-greased and lightly floured 13 x 9 inch cake pan. Bake at 350⁰ about 35 minutes, or until cake tests done.

Broiled Icing:
¼ cup evaporated milk
4 tablespoons margarine
1 cup brown sugar
1 cup flaked coconut
½ cup nuts, chopped

While cake is baking, heat ingredients for icing until the sugar is melted. Spread over baked cake and brown under broiler.

Plum Cake

2 cups sifted self-rising flour
2 cups sugar
2 jars strained plums (baby food)
1 cup oil
3 eggs
1 teaspoon cinnamon
1 teaspoon ground cloves
½ teaspoon nutmeg
1 cup nuts, chopped

Combine all ingredients in a large bowl and mix with mixer at medium speed until well blended. Cook in greased and floured tube or Bundt pan at 350⁰ for 1 hour. While hot, top with glaze.

Glaze:
⅓ cup bourbon
½ cup powdered sugar

Mix ingredients until smooth.

Praline Cheese Cake

1 cup graham cracker crumbs
3 tablespoons sugar
3 tablespoons melted butter
3 packages (8 ounce) cream cheese
1¼ cups dark brown sugar, firmly
   packed
3 eggs
2 tablespoons flour
½ cup chopped pecans
1½ teaspoons vanilla
maple syrup

Mix crumbs, sugar, and butter, and press into 8 or 9 inch springform pan. Bake at 350° for 10 minutes. Cool. Beat the cream cheese and brown sugar until fluffy. Beat in eggs, one at a time. Sift in the flour, then add the pecans and vanilla. Pour mixture into pan, and bake at 325° for 55 minutes or until set. Cool in pan, then remove to serving plate, and brush with maple syrup and garnish with chopped pecans. Chill for at least 3 hours.

Pumpkin Torte

Crust:
1½ cups crushed graham crackers
½ cup butter

Cream Cheese Mixture:
2 eggs, beaten
½ cup sugar
8 ounces cream cheese, softened to
   room temperature

Pumpkin Mixture:
1 cup pumpkin
3 eggs, separated
½ cup sugar
1 cup milk
½ teaspoon salt
1 teaspoon cinnamon
1 teaspoon nutmeg
½ teaspoon ginger
1 envelope plain gelatin
2 tablespoons butter
¼ cup cold water

1 cup heavy cream, whipped

Mix crushed graham crackers and butter and press into 9 x 13 inch pan. Mix the two beaten eggs, sugar and cream cheese and pour over crust. Bake for 20 minutes at 350°. Beat egg yolks and mix with pumpkin, sugar, milk, salt and spices. Cook until thickened. Remove from heat. Add one envelope of plain gelatin dissolved in ¼ cup cold water. Cool. Beat 3 egg whites to soft peaks. Add ½ cup sugar gradually and beat until stiff. Fold into pumpkin mixture. Pour over crust and chill. Serve topped with whipped cream.
Serves 10 to 12

Rocky Road Cake

1 Angel Food cake
2 packages (12 ounce) chocolate
   bits
4 eggs, separated
1 pint whipping cream, whipped
½ cup nuts, chopped (pecans or
   walnuts)

Melt chocolate bits in the top of a double boiler. Add 4 egg yolks, beaten, and stir until mixture is creamy; cool. Beat 4 egg whites until peaks form, fold into chocolate mixture. Fold whipped cream into mixture. Tear cake into small pieces and place in a buttered jelly roll pan; reserve approximately 1½ cups. Pour mixture over cake and toss with 2 forks until cake is coated. Pour remaining mixture over cake and sprinkle with chopped nuts. Press down mixture and refrigerate overnight.

Vanilla Wafer Cake

1 cup margarine
1¾ cups sugar
6 eggs
½ cup milk
1 package (12 ounce) vanilla wafers,
   finely crushed
1 package (7 ounce) coconut flakes
1 cup pecans, chopped fine

Cream margarine and sugar in mixer until light and fluffy. Beat in eggs, one at a time, with mixer on high speed. At low speed add vanilla wafers alternately with milk. Fold in coconut and pecans. Spoon batter into a well greased tube pan and bake for 1 hour at 350⁰. Cool in pan and serve in thin slices.

White Fruitcake

4 cups candied fruit mix
½ to 1 cup dried apricots, chopped
1¼ cup white seedless raisins
2 cups slivered almonds
2 cups flaked coconut
2 cups sifted flour
1½ teaspoon baking powder
1 teaspoon salt
1 cup butter
1 cup sugar
1 teaspoon rum flavoring
5 eggs
½ cup pineapple juice

Mix fruits. Sift together flour, baking powder and salt. Sift a little of the flour mixture over fruits and nuts to coat. Cream sugar and butter; add flavoring. Beat in one egg at a time. Add flour and pineapple juice alternately to batter. Pour over fruit and nut mixture. Bake in a Bundt cake pan or line an angel food cake pan with brown paper. Bake at 275⁰ for 2 hours, cool and remove brown paper. Wrap cooled cake in cheese cloth dipped in either rum or brandy and let "ripen" for about 1-2 weeks. Slice thin.

Wacky Cake

1 cup sugar
3 tablespoons cocoa
1½ cups flour
1 teaspoon baking soda
¹⁄₁₆ teaspoon salt
6 tablespoons salad oil
1 tablespoon vinegar
1 teaspoon vanilla
1 cup cold water

Sift dry ingredients together into an ungreased 8 x 8 inch baking pan. Make 3 holes in dry ingredients. Pour oil in one hole, vinegar in one hole and vanilla in last hole. Pour cold water over all and stir with a fork until moistened. DO NOT BEAT. Bake at 350° for 30 minutes. Leave in pan and frost.

Frosting:
1 cup powdered sugar
2 tablespoons cocoa
2 tablespoons butter, melted
2 tablespoons cream or evaporated milk
¹⁄₁₆ teaspoon salt

Mix all ingredients together and pour over cake. *Serves 8.*

Whipping Cream Pound Cake

3 cups sugar
1 cup butter or margarine (room temperature)
6 eggs (room temperature)
3 cups sifted cake flour
½ pint whipping cream (room temperature)
1 teaspoon vanilla

Cream butter and sugar thoroughly. Add whole eggs, one at a time. Mix well. Add sifted flour and cream alternately, begin and end with flour. Add vanilla. Grease and flour tube pan, add batter. Put cake in cold oven before turning on heat. Bake for 1 hour and 25 minutes at 325°.

Papa's Birthday Cake

1 cup butter or margarine
3 cups granulated sugar
1 tablespoon lemon or orange extract
1 teaspoon almond extract
6 eggs
¼ teaspoon baking soda
3 cups unsifted, all purpose flour
1 cup commercial sour cream

Glaze:
¼ cup granulated sugar
2 tablespoons lemon or orange juice

In mixer bowl, beat together the first four ingredients. Add eggs, one at a time, beating well after each addition. Stir baking soda into flour and add this alternately with sour cream to mixing bowl until just mixed. Spoon batter into a *well greased* and *thoroughly* floured Bundt pan. Bake at 325° for 1½ hours or until cake begins to shrink from the pan and is golden in color. Cool in pan for 15 minutes, then turn out onto plate and glaze while still warm. Cool completely before cutting. *This cake freezes well.*

Baked Caramel Goodstuff (for nibbling)

8 cups puffed wheat cereal
½ cup walnut pieces
½ cup dry roasted peanuts
½ cup pecan pieces
½ cup butter or margarine
1 cup brown sugar, packed
¼ cup corn syrup
¼ teaspoon salt
¼ teaspoon soda
1 teaspoon vanilla

In large bowl combine first four ingredients. Melt butter in medium saucepan, stir in brown sugar, syrup and salt. Bring to boil, stirring constantly. Boil 5 minutes. Remove from heat and stir in soda and vanilla. Gradually pour over cereal mixture. Stir to coat thoroughly. On greased cookie sheet spread evenly. Bake at 300º for 15 minutes. Stir well and bake another 15 minutes more. Cool completely on pan. Break into desired size pieces and store in airtight container. (Set this near your cookie jar and you will find it cuts down on your cookie baking.)

Orange Pecans

Rounded tablespoon butter, melted
6 to 10 cups pecan halves
Grated rind of two oranges
2 cups sugar
⅔ cup water
1 cup milk

Butter large bowl with the melted butter, leaving remaining butter in bowl. Add grated rind and pecans. Mix well. In saucepan, mix sugar and water and cook until mixture spins a thread. Add milk and stir until soft-ball stage is reached. Pour this over pecan mixture and stir. When nuts are well-coated, pour on wax paper and rake apart when cool. (It crystalizes quickly). Let them get completely dry before storing in a tin.

Patience Candy

2½ cups sugar
1 cup light cream or milk
¼ cup white corn syrup
1 cup sugar
4 tablespoons butter
1 teaspoon vanilla
3 cups chopped nuts

Place first three ingredients in heavy pan and cook as for fudge. Caramelize 1 cup sugar slowly in another heavy skillet, add to first mixture. Cook to medium firm ball stage. Add butter and vanilla. Beat until creamy; add nuts. Beat until it is a firm praline when dropped on wax paper. Drop with teaspoon. If it gets too firm, either add 1 tablespoon boiling water or set pan on low heat to warm. When cool, store in covered tin.
Yields 2½ pounds.

Peanut Brittle

2 cups sugar
½ cup water
1 cup white Karo
1 tablespoon butter or margarine
2 cups raw peanuts
1 teaspoon soda
1 teaspoon vanilla
½ teaspoon salt

Cook sugar, Karo and water to softball stage. Add butter and peanuts, stir frequently and cook to hardcrack stage. Remove from heat and add soda, vanilla and salt. Pour quickly onto 4 *well* buttered cookie sheets. Spread thin with buttered utensils. Foil butter wrappers that are paper-lined may be used.

Sally's Fours

¾ pound butter
2 cups white sugar
2 cups brown sugar, packed
1 pint whipping cream
2 cups dark Karo
1 pint whipping cream
1 pound pecans
3 tablespoons vanilla

Bring first 5 ingredients to boil. When full rolling boil is reached, gradually add second pint of whipping cream. Cook to 238° (using candy thermometer). Remove from heat; add nuts and vanilla. Pour into buttered 15½ x 10½ x 1 inch pan. (DO NOT scrape pan when pouring as it might cause it to turn to sugar. Scrape out leftover in small saucer.) Let cool. Cut in 1 inch squares. Dip in dipping chocolate which has been melted over warm (not boiling) water.
It is very important to use a Taylor candy thermometer for accuracy.

Apricot Balls

8 ounces dried apricots, finely ground
1 cup coconut, flaked
⅔ cup pecans, ground
2 teaspoons orange juice
4 tablespoons powdered sugar or granulated sugar

Grind apricots and pecans together in food grinder on smallest blade. Combine ingredients and make into walnut size balls. Then roll in granulated or powdered sugar. If stored in tightly sealed container, will keep for months. *Yields 30.*

Danish Cookies

½ cup shortening
½ cup butter
1 cup sugar
1 teaspoon vanilla
1 egg
2 cups flour, sifted
½ teaspoon baking powder
½ teaspoon cream of tartar

Cream shortening, butter and sugar. Add egg and vanilla. Beat thoroughly. Add dry ingredients. Mix until blended. Use 1 teaspoon dough per cookie and roll into balls. Place on ungreased cookie sheet, bake at 350⁰ for 12 minutes. Cool cookies slightly before removing from cookie sheet. Raisins, chopped nuts or spices may be added to ingredients, if desired.

Elisen Lebkuchen

1 cup unblanched almonds, ground
1 cup hazelnuts or pecans, ground
2 tablespoons candied citron, ground
2 tablespoons candied orange peel, ground
1 tablespoon candied lemon peel, ground
½ cup sifted cake flour
1 teaspoon cinnamon
¼ teaspoon ground cloves
2 egg whites
1 cup sugar
½ cup apricot preserves
whole almonds
1 egg white
1 tablespoon water
chocolate icing

Mix first five ingredients in bowl with flour and spices; set aside. In a small mixing bowl beat egg whites until foamy. Beat in sugar until soft peaks form. Fold in fruit nut mixture, stir in apricot preserves. Spoon batter by rounded tablespoons onto greased cookie sheet. Spread to 2½ inch circles. Arrange 3 whole almonds on top of each cookie. Let stand uncovered for 2 hours to dry. Bake in 350⁰ oven 20-22 minutes. Combine egg white and water and brush over hot cookies or spread with chocolate icing. Cookies will keep up to 2 months. Flavor improves after 3 weeks. *Yields 2 dozen cookies.*

Chocolate Icing:
4 ounces sweet cooking chocolate
3 tablespoons butter
½ cup powdered sugar
3 tablespoons hot water

In a small saucepan, combine chocolate and butter and stir until melted. Remove from heat and stir in powdered sugar and water.
Blend well and ice cookies.

Lace Cookies

1 cup sugar
2 tablespoons butter
1 teaspoon vanilla
2 eggs
2 teaspoons baking powder
½ teaspoon salt
2½ cups quick-cooking oatmeal

Cream butter and sugar. Add vanilla, eggs, salt, baking powder and oats. Drop by teaspoonfuls on lightly greased cookie sheet. Bake at 350° for 15 minutes or until just brown around edges. Remove from sheet while warm. (Try a small number at a time to get used to handling them.) *Yields about 3 dozen.*

Lizzies

1 cup margarine
½ cup brown sugar
2 eggs
1½ cups flour
½ teaspoon nutmeg
1½ teaspoons soda
½ teaspoon salt
1½ teaspoons cinnamon
½ teaspoon ground cloves
1 pound raisins soaked in ½ cup apricot brandy overnight
1 pound pecans
½ pound citron or other candied fruit

Cream margarine, sugar and eggs. Add flour with soda, salt, cinnamon, nutmeg and cloves. Add raisins, candied fruit and nuts. Roll into balls and place on buttered cookie sheet close together. Bake at 325° for 15 minutes. Store in airtight container. Can be frozen. *Yields 10 dozen.*

Molasses Krinkles

¾ cup shortening
1 cup brown sugar
1 egg
¼ cup molasses
2½ cups flour
1½ teaspoons soda
½ teaspoon salt
1 teaspoon ginger
½ teaspoon cloves
½ teaspoon cinnamon

Cream shortening, add sugar, and cream well. Add egg, beat thoroughly, then add molasses. Sift flour, soda, salt, and spices together, and combine with creamed mixture. Chill several hours. Roll into balls the size of a walnut. Dip one side in granulated sugar. Place the unsugared side down on an oiled baking sheet. Bake at 375° for 12 minutes. (These have the appearance of old-fashioned ginger snaps!) *Yields 3 dozen.*

Roswell's Pecan Butter Cookies

1½ cups butter
2 eggs
1½ cups sugar
1 teaspoon vanilla
½ teaspoon salt
3 cups flour
1 cup pecan halves toasted lightly

Cream butter and sugar together well. Add eggs one at a time. Add vanilla. Sift flour and salt. Add to the creamed mixture. Drop by teaspoonful about 2 inches apart on an ungreased cookie sheet. Place a whole toasted pecan on top of each cookie. Bake at 350º for 10 minutes. To toast pecans melt 1 tablespoon butter in pie tin. Toss pecans in butter and lightly salt. Bake in 325º oven for 15 to 20 minutes.
Pecans can be toasted in microwave, 2 minutes on high.

Seven Layer Cookies

½ cup butter or margarine
1½ cups graham crackers, crushed
1 cup coconut
1 package (6 ounce) peanut butter bits
1 package (6 ounce) semi-sweet chocolate bits
1 can (14 ounce) Borden's Eagle Brand condensed milk
1 cup nuts, chopped

Melt butter in 9 x 13 inch pan. Add crackers. Mix well and press evenly in pan. Sprinkle a layer each of coconut, peanut butter bits and chocolate bits. Pour milk over all. Spread nuts over milk. Bake at 350º for 25 minutes. Cool and cut into bars.
Can be prepared ahead of time. Can substitute brickle chips for the peanut butter chips, if desired, for a different taste.

Roadrunners

1 package (6 ounce) chocolate chips
10 graham crackers, crushed
½ cup nuts, chopped
1 can (14 ounce) Borden's Eagle Brand condensed milk
1 teaspoon vanilla
⅛ teaspoon salt
sugar

Mix all ingredients except sugar together and pour into greased 8 x 8 inch pan. Bake at 350º for 25 minutes. Remove from oven, cool, cut into pieces and roll in sugar.

12 double graham crackers
2 cups miniature marshmallows
¾ cup sweet butter (do not use margarine)
¾ cup firmly packed brown sugar
1 teaspoon cinnamon
1 teaspoon vanilla
1 cup sliced almonds
1 cup flaked coconut

Place double crackers side by side in two rows (6 per row) on an ungreased 15 x 10 inch jelly roll pan. Sprinkle marshmallows evenly over crackers. In heavy 2 quart saucepan, combine butter, sugar, cinnamon and vanilla. Cook over medium heat stirring constantly until sugar is dissolved and butter is melted (4 to 5 minutes). Pour evenly over crackers and marshmallows. Sprinkle with almonds and coconut. Bake near center of 350º oven for 8 to 12 minutes or until lightly browned. Cool completely. Cut into 48 bars, each about 1 x 2 inch. These are best stored overnight in a tin container.
Yields 48.

Zimtsterne Cinnamon Stars

2 egg whites
1 cup superfine granulated sugar
1½ cups toasted almonds, ground
¾ cup toasted hazelnuts or pecans, ground
2 tablespoons all-purpose flour
1 teaspoon ground cinnamon
¼ teaspoon ground nutmeg
powdered sugar
1 egg white
1½ cups sifted powdered sugar
½ to 1 teaspoon water

Beat the 2 egg whites just until soft peaks form, beat in superfine sugar. Beat until stiff peaks form. Stir together nuts, flour and spices. Fold into beaten egg whites. Let mixture rest 30 minutes so nuts can absorb moisture. Roll out to ¼ inch thick on surface lightly sprinkled with powdered sugar. Cut with star-shaped cookie cutter and place on greased baking sheet. Bake in 325º oven for 10-15 minutes. Beat the one egg white slightly; stir in 1½ cups powdered sugar, add water. Spread icing on cookies.
Prepare ahead of time. Keeps in airtight container for as long as one month.
Yields 2 dozen.

Apple Crunch

1 cup sugar
½ cup flour
1 teaspoon cinnamon
2 tablespoons butter
½ cup corn flakes
6 apples, peeled
2 tablespoons sugar
1 cup orange juice

Cream together first 5 ingredients. Slice apples into buttered baking dish. Sprinkle with sugar and ½ of the orange juice. Sprinkle creamed mixture over apples. Pour remaining ½ cup orange juice over mixture and dot with butter. Bake at 350⁰ for 40 to 45 minutes.
This may be served hot or cold. It's good topped with ice cream.
Serves 6.

Apple Dumplings

8 apples, peeled and cut into
    quarters and sliced
4 cups flour
2 cups shortening
1 teaspoon salt
½ cup ice water
sugar
butter
cinnamon

Sauce:
½ cup butter
2 cups sugar
2 eggs
1 cup half and half

Make a dough of flour, shortening, salt and ice water. Roll dough thin. Cut into 6 inch round or square pieces. Place 3 apple slices on each pastry piece. Sprinkle with sugar and cinnamon and dot with butter. Press pastry around apples. Place on cookie sheet and bake at 425⁰ for 25 minutes, then reduce heat to 350⁰ for 30 minutes. Pour sauce over each dumpling at serving time.

Sauce: Cream butter and sugar. Add eggs. Cream again. Add half and half and cream again. Cook in double boiler until thick and clear, about 40 minutes. Cool. (You may add ¼ cup of bourbon if desired.)

Additional hot, cooked apple slices can be placed on top of dumpling before serving to add more apple flavor and moistness. Dumplings can be frozen right on cookie sheet, covered with foil. Take out night before and reheat on cookie sheet, still covered with foil, at 350° for 20 minutes prior to serving time.
Yields 20 dumplings.

Mrs. Pip's Apples

5 large golden delicious apples
½ cup white Karo
1 tablespoon butter
1½ cups sugar
5 cups cold water

Peel, halve and core apples. Put in large, flat-bottomed pan, uncovered. Pour in water; cook on burner at high temperature for 30 minutes, or until thoroughly tender, but not mushy. Add Karo, butter and sugar and continue cooking at high temperature for 20 minutes, or until juice has almost boiled out and is *very* thick. Spoon into flat bowl by halves.
Serves 6 to 8.

Apple Souffle

4 tart apples, sliced
3 tablespoons butter or margarine
1 cup sugar
2 tablespoons lemon juice
4 eggs, separated
1½ teaspoons grated lemon peel
1 teaspoon rum extract or 1-2
　jiggers of rum
½ cup sour cream
powdered sugar

Pare, core and cut apples into slices. Melt butter in large frying pan. Add ⅔ cup of sugar, lemon juice and apple slices. Cook over medium heat, turning apple slices until they are tender and glazed and the juice disappears. Place half the glazed apples in a 7 x 12 inch baking pan, souffle dish three inches high or an ovenproof 10½ inch round frying pan. Reserve remaining apple slices for a decorative topping. Beat egg whites until soft peaks form, then add the remaining ⅓ cup sugar, beating until stiff. In another bowl, beat egg yolks until thick and mix in the grated lemon peel, rum flavoring and sour cream. Fold into beaten egg whites. Spoon egg mixture over the apples in the pan and arrange the remaining poached apple slices in a pattern on top. Bake at 350⁰ for 25 minutes or until souffle is puffed and browned. Dust with powdered sugar. Serve hot or warm.
Serves 6 to 8.

Crepes Dominique

1½ cups flour
1 teaspoon sugar
⅛ teaspoon salt
3 eggs, beaten
1½ cups milk
2 tablespoons butter, melted and cooled
1 tablespoon brandy
1 teaspoon grated lemon rind

Sift flour, sugar and salt together in a bowl. Add eggs and mix together thoroughly. Mixture will form a thick paste. Add milk, gradually, beating thoroughly. Add melted and cooled butter. Add flavoring, allow batter to stand for at least 1 hour. Heat a small crepe pan, 5 or 6 inches across the bottom. Brush with butter or oil and when fat is hot but not smoking lift pan off heat and pour in 1½ to 2 tablespoons batter, depending on the size of the pan. Swirl quickly to cover bottom of pan. Return pan to heat. When crepe is golden brown (about 1 minute) turn it and cook on reverse side for about half a minute. Continue cooking crepes, adding butter to pan as needed. Turn crepes out on a clean towel or paper towels. If they are to be used immediately, stack on a plate and keep warm in a low oven. If they are to be held, stack with waxed paper between each after they have cooled and cover. If they are to be frozen, wrap stack in foil, freezer paper or freezer bags and freeze immediately. Two crepe pans are handy when cooking. Brown crepe in one pan on one side and flip out into the other crepe pan to brown other side. This speeds up the job.
3 filling choices following:

Apple Crepes Filling

3 tablespoons butter or margarine
2 cups finely chopped or sliced tart cooking apples (approximately 5 apples)
1 tablespoon flour
¼ to ½ cup sugar
½ teaspoon cinnamon
1 teaspoon lemon juice

Melt butter in saucepan, add the chopped raw apple, and cover. Cook over medium heat about 5 minutes, stirring once in a while, until apples are almost tender. Add flour, sugar, cinnamon mixed together and sprinkled over the top of hot apples. Add lemon juice. Fill crepes. Serve with sour cream topping or sprinkled with a little cinnamon and sugar.

Lemon Crepes Filling

3 tablespoons cornstarch
1 cup sugar
1 cup boiling water
3 egg yolks
1 tablespoon butter
grated rind of 2 lemons
½ cup lemon juice
12 crepes (5 inch)

Mix cornstarch and sugar, add boiling water slowly, stir and bring to boil over low heat. Continue to boil until liquid is clear. Beat the egg yolks. Pour some of the boiling liquid over the yolks and return all the egg mixture to the pan. Cook over very low heat or over boiling water until very thick, stirring constantly, about 5 minutes. Add butter, then grated rind and lemon juice, stirring to mix well. Cool. Then fill crepes and roll up. Top with whipped cream or sprinkle with powdered sugar.

Strawberry or Cherry Crepes Filling

2 cups sliced fresh strawberries or
   drained pitted dark sweet
   cherries
3 tablespoons sugar (or to taste)
⅛ teaspoon nutmeg

In small bowl, combine all ingredients and mix well. Fill crepes. Serve with sour cream and brown sugar.

Banana Split Dessert

1½ cups butter, divided
2 cups graham cracker crumbs
2 eggs
1 teaspoon vanilla
1 pound powdered sugar
1 can (8 ounce) crushed pineapple,
   drained, until dry
3 bananas, sliced
1 pint fresh strawberries, sliced
½ cup pecans, chopped fine
½ cup shredded coconut
1 carton (16 ounce) Cool Whip
chocolate shavings

Melt ½ cup butter and add graham cracker crumbs. Press into bottom of 8½ x 13 inch glass dish. Make filling of 2 eggs, 1 cup soft butter and 1 teaspoon vanilla. Beat until fluffy, at least 20 minutes. Add powdered sugar, gradually, and mix well. Pour over crust. Pour well-drained pineapple over filling. Slice 3 bananas on top and then put sliced strawberries on top. Sprinkle with pecans and coconut. Top with Cool Whip. Refrigerate 3 to 4 hours. Before serving, grate chocolate into shavings on top.

Dorothy Peterson

Dorothy Peterson's expressive paintings and graphics deal with the landscape and people of the Southwestern United States and Northern Mexico. Subject matter from her native New Mexico has always dominated her work. Visits to the Tarahumara Indians of Northern Mexico and several trips to Europe have given an added dimension to her imagery in recent years.

An award-winning painter in oils and aquamedia, she developed a series of original graphics in 1979 that combine the painterly qualities of her work with printmaking. All of her serigraphs and mixed-media multiples are hand-pulled in the studio, signed and numbered in small editions.

A working artist with over 20 years experience, she holds degrees from the University of New Mexico and the University of Texas of the Permian Basin. Her work has received numerous awards in national and regional competition and is represented in many collections across the country.

JUSTICE OF THE PEACE
Artist - Dorothy Peterson
40" X 40"   1983
mixed media
Private collection of the
artist

Date Pudding

1 cup dates, chopped
1 cup nut meats
1 cup bread crumbs
1 cup sugar
¾ cup milk
¼ teaspoon salt
3 eggs, well beaten
1 tablespoon baking powder
1 tablespoon flour
2 tablespoons water

Mix the dates, nutmeats, bread crumbs, sugar, milk and salt thoroughly. Cover and let stand for two hours or more. Before putting in oven add the eggs, baking powder, and mix the flour with the water and add. Stir thoroughly. Put in greased 8 x 11 inch glass dish or pan, and bake at 350° for 60 minutes over a pan of water. Before serving, add sauce or whipped cream.

Sauce:
1 cup brown sugar
2 tablespoons flour
½ cup water
2 tablespoons bourbon whiskey

Mix and cook until thick.
Serves 12.

Frozen Ambrosia

1 tablespoon orange juice
4 tablespoons mayonnaise
1 package (3 ounce) soft cream cheese
1 cup diced pineapple
½ cup Royal Ann cherries
1 cup Mandarin oranges
½ cup maraschino cherries
½ cup chopped pecans
3 tablespoons sugar
1 cup heavy cream
1 teaspoon grated orange rind

Blend first 3 ingredients thoroughly. Drain all fruit and add to cream cheese mixture. Whip heavy cream until stiff. Add grated orange rind. Fold whipped cream into fruit and cream cheese mixture and freeze. Let thaw a bit before serving. *Serves 6 to 8.*

Frozen Fruit Frappe

1 package (3 ounce) strawberry
  gelatin
1 can (16 ounce) crushed pineapple
  (drained; reserve liquid)
1 can (21 ounce) apricot or peach
  pie filling
1 pint strawberries, chopped
3 medium bananas, mashed

Add enough water to reserved liquid to make 1 cup. Bring to a boil and add to gelatin, stir to dissolve. Cool with 6 ice cubes. Add remaining ingredients, stirring well. Pour into a loaf pan and freeze 4 to 6 hours. Let stand at room temperature 15 minutes before slicing to serve. Serve with strawberry dressing.
Instead of a loaf pan, a 9 x 13 inch pan can be used and the servings cut into squares.

Strawberry Dressing:
1 cup crushed strawberries
2 tablespoons corn syrup
¾ cup mayonnaise

Blend and refrigerate.

Instant Spumoni

1 pint vanilla ice cream
1 tablespoon rum
¼ cup candied fruit, chopped
chopped nuts, optional
(red or green food coloring can be
  added for Christmas dinners)

Combine all ingredients and spoon into muffin pans lined with paper baking cups. Freeze just until firm (about 2 hours).

King Ludwig's Apricot Bavarian Cream

1 envelope plain gelatin
¼ cup cold water
2 cans (17 ounce) peeled apricots,
  divided or 18 fresh apricots
¾ cup sugar
juice of ½ lemon
1½ cups heavy cream, whipped
quarter sections (canned) apricots

Puree 12 canned or fresh apricots to make one cup. Soften gelatin in cold water and dissolve by setting in hot water; strain into the apricot puree. Add the sugar and lemon juice. Stir until the sugar is dissolved, then set into ice water and stir until the mixture begins to thicken. Add the cream which has been whipped, beating it evenly into the gelatin mixture. When mixture is chilled enough to hold its shape, turn into a fancy mold which has been lined with quarters of canned apricots. Serve chilled.
Serves 6.

Lemon Souffle

1 cup sugar
2½ tablespoons butter
2 teaspoons lemon rind
4 egg yolks
4 tablespoons flour
6 tablespoons lemon juice
1½ cups milk
4 egg whites

Cream butter and sugar and lemon rind. Add yolks and mix well. Stir in flour and add lemon juice and milk. Beat whites stiff and fold in. Pour into buttered custard cups or small souffle dish and bake surrounded with water for 45 minutes at 350º. Serve warm or cold.
Serves 4 to 6.

Blender Mousse or Pots de Cremes

1 package (6 ounce) semi-sweet dot chocolates
2 tablespoons sugar
1 egg
⅛ teaspoon salt
½ teaspoon instant coffee
¾ cup milk
whipped cream
grated orange rind

Into blender put chocolate bits, sugar, egg, salt, instant coffee. Heat milk to boiling point, add to chocolate. Blend for 1 minute on high. Pour into 4 pots de creme cups or into demi-tasse cups. Let chill for at least 2 hours. Serve with a bit of whipped cream with grated orange rind over that.
Serves 4.

Mousse Au Chocolat

2 egg yolks
1 cup chocolate chips
3 tablespoons brandy
1¼ cups half and half cream

Mix all ingredients in blender thoroughly. Pour into demi-tasse cups and chill well.
Serves 6.

Pineapple Bread Pudding

1 can (16 ounce) crushed pineapple,
  undrained
½ cup margarine
¾ cup sugar
4 eggs, beaten
1 teaspoon lemon juice
5 slices bread, toasted and cubed
½ cup raisins

Cream margarine and sugar. Add beaten eggs. Add all other ingredients. Pour into casserole, 1 ¾ quart size. Bake at 350° for 1 hour. *Serves 6.*

English Lemon Sauce

4 large lemons, use rind of one
  lemon
2 cups sugar
¾ cup butter
4 eggs, slightly beaten

Finely grate the rind of one lemon. Squeeze juice out of the 4 lemons, strain. Put juice, sugar and butter in saucepan and cook over low flame until sugar and butter are melted. Remove from heat, add slightly beaten eggs very slowly. Return to heat and cook until mixture coats spoon. Will keep well in refrigerator about three months. Use as a topping on ice cream and angel food cake, or in tiny tart shells with whipped cream on top. *Yields ¾ quart.*

ROSWELL REGISTER   APRIL 17, 1903

COURT NEWS
"Three Cases From Hagerman Disposed Of"

Monday was Hagerman day and Deputy Sheriff Wilson occupied the center of the stage with Judge Peacock.

Some weeks ago Lizzie Clancey was brought before Judge Peacock charged with enticing young girls from the straight and narrow path. She was given the choice of leaving the county or residing for sixty days in the County bastile. She chose the former, but only went as far as Hagerman. As a result she was taken up by Deputy Sheriff Wilson. Monday Judge Peacock sent her up to serve the sixty days. She has three children, two boys 11 and 12 years old and a girl of 14.

The next case was that of B. F. Kirby, who was also brought up from Hagerman, charged with being drunk and disorderly. He got $10 and costs, and not being able to put up the cash, was himself put up.

Also on Monday, Deputy Sheriff Wilson brought before Judge Peacock one R.C. Snow who was charged with running a disorderly house in Hagerman. He was fined $50, and not having the money was placed in his proper place, behind the bars.

Rhubarb Kuckero

1 cup flour, sifted
3 tablespoons sugar
1½ teaspoons baking powder
¼ teaspoon salt
6 tablespoons butter
1 beaten egg
2 tablespoons milk
½ teaspoon vanilla
⅓ cup sugar
1 package (3 ounce) strawberry
   Jello
3 tablespoons flour
1¼ pounds rhubarb (4 cups), sliced
⅔ cup sugar
⅓ cup flour

Combine first 4 ingredients. Cut in 3 tablespoons butter until mixture resembles crumbs. Combine egg, milk and vanilla. Add to flour mixture. Stir until moistened. Lightly flour hands. Pat dough on bottom and 1 inch up sides in a 9 x 9 x 2 inch baking pan. Combine Jello, ⅓ cup sugar and 3 tablespoons flour. Add rhubarb and mix well; pour into crust. Combine remaining sugar and flour. Cut in remaining 3 tablespoons butter until crumbly. Sprinkle over rhubarb. Bake at 350⁰ until rhubarb is tender and top is brown, 60 to 65 minutes. Cool slightly; cut into squares.

Sachertorte

¾ cup butter, softened
¾ cup semi-sweet chocolate
¾ cup powdered sugar
8 eggs, separated
¾ cup flour
½ cup apricot jam

Preheat oven to 350⁰. Line two 9 inch round pans with wax paper, grease with butter. Beat butter, melted chocolate, ½ cup sugar and add one by one the 8 yolks. Beat the 8 whites with the remaining sugar until stiff peaks form. Mix about one cup of whites to the yolk mixture, then pour mixture over remaining whites and carefully add flour. Divide batter evenly between the two cake pans, bake about 30 minutes or until cake tester comes out clean.

Chocolate Frosting:
3 ounces unsweetened chocolate,
   chopped
1 cup heavy cream
1 cup sugar
1 teaspoon vanilla
1 teaspoon corn syrup
1 egg, lightly beaten

Combine chocolate, cream, sugar and corn syrup in saucepan. Boil, stirring constantly, until temperature reaches 220⁰. Add 2 or 3 tablespoons of mixture to the lightly beaten egg, reduce heat to low and add egg mixture to pan; simmer for 3 to 4 mintues. Remove from heat, add vanilla and let cool to room temperature. Spread apricot jam on one cake, set the other on top. Pour the cooled glaze in a slow stream over the layered cakes. Refrigerate for about 3 hours; serve.
Serves 12.

Angel Pie

Meringue
4 egg whites
⅛ teaspoon cream of tartar
1 cup sugar

Beat the egg whites until frothy. Add cream of tartar and beat until stiff enough to hold a point. Gradually beat in sugar and beat until stiff and glossy. Spread in a well greased 9 inch pie plate. Bake at 275º for 20 minutes, then at 300º for 40 minutes. Remove from oven and let cool well.

Filling
4 egg yolks
2 whole eggs
½ cup sugar
3 tablespoons lemon juice
1 teaspoon lemon rind
¾ pint whipping cream

In a double boiler beat egg yolks and eggs together. Beat in sugar. Add lemon juice and lemon rind. Cook until thick, cool. Whip the cream. Spread half the whipped cream on meringue. Spread filling over this, spread the rest of the whipped cream over filling. Refrigerate for at least 24 hours.

French Coconut Pie

3 eggs, lightly beaten
1⅓ cups flaked coconut
⅓ cup buttermilk
1¼ cups sugar
1 teaspoon vanilla
6 tablespoons butter or margarine, melted
1 unbaked 9 inch pie crust

Mix all ingredients, in order given, and pour into unbaked pie crust. Bake at 350º for 40-45 minutes until brown.

Grandma's Fresh Coconut Pie

1 pie shell, baked and cooled
1 cup grated fresh coconut
¼ cup butter
1 cup sugar
3 large eggs
1 cup milk
1 tablespoon lemon extract
pinch of salt

Bake and cool pie shell. Grate coconut, spread on cookie sheet and toast in 350º oven for 2 to 5 minutes. Turn coconut while toasting. Set aside to cool. Cream butter and sugar. Add eggs, milk, lemon extract, salt and cooled coconut. Pour into cooled pie shell and bake at 350º for 30 to 40 minutes.

Chocolate Chess Pie

¼ cup butter or margarine
1½ (1 ounce) squares unsweetened
    chocolate
1½ cups sugar
1 tablespoon flour
½ cup undiluted evaporated milk
2 eggs
⅛ teaspoon salt
1 teaspoon vanilla extract
1 - 9 inch unbaked pie shell

Heat oven to 350º. Place butter and chocolate in a small saucepan over low heat and heat until melted, stirring constantly. Pour chocolate mixture into small bowl of electric mixer; add sugar, flour, evaporated milk, egg, salt and vanilla. Beat chocolate mixture at moderate speed for 5-7 minutes (do not over beat) until thick and creamy. Pour chocolate mixture into pie shell and bake 40-45 minutes, or until filling is firm. Serve cold.

Chaves Chocolate Surprise

¾ cup sugar
1 cup flour
2 teaspoons baking powder
⅛ teaspoon salt
1 square (1 ounce) chocolate
2 tablespoons butter
½ cup milk
1 teaspoon vanilla

Topping:
½ cup brown sugar
½ cup white sugar
4 tablespoons cocoa
1 cup cold water

Sift sugar, flour, baking powder and salt. Add chocolate and butter melted together over hot water. Add milk and vanilla. Pour into a greased 9 x 9 inch baking dish. Scatter, without mixing, the topping ingredients (except water). Pour water on top. Bake 40 minutes in a slow oven, 325º. Let stand at room temperature one hour or more, serve cool, but not chilled. *Whipped cream or ice cream is nice served with this. Serves 6.*

Lemon Chess Pie

2 cups sugar
1 tablespoon flour
1 tablespoon cornmeal
4 eggs
¼ cup melted butter
¼ cup cream (half & half)
¼ cup lemon juice
grated rind of 2 lemons
1 - 9 inch unbaked pie shell

Mix first 4 ingredients and beat well. Add other ingredients. Pour into unbaked pie shell. Bake 35 minutes at 350º. Place pan of water on shelf above pie while baking.

Lemon Meringue Pie

Filling
1 cup boiling water
2 tablespoons cornstarch dissolved in cold water
1 cup sugar
2 egg yolks, well beaten
grated rind and juice of 1 large lemon
1 tablespoon butter
1 pie crust baked and cooled (see index)

Stir the cornstarch mixture into the boiling water in the saucepan. Cook until mixture is clear. Cool. Add sugar, egg yolks, lemon juice and rind. Mix, cook until mixture is thick (do not boil). Add butter and cook 2 minutes longer; cool. Pour into cooled pie shell.

Meringue:
2 egg whites
2 tablespoons water
2 tablespoons sugar

Preheat oven to 400°. Have eggs at room temperature. In small bowl of mixer beat egg whites and water at high speed until egg whites form stiff peaks. Add sugar and blend the mixture by spoon. Spread over lemon filling. Put in oven and brown slowly for 5 minutes.

Lime Pie

½ cup key lime or Persian lime juice
1 can (15 ounce) sweetened condensed milk
5 egg whites
2 tablespoons sugar
1 tablespoon grated lemon rind
1 graham cracker pie shell (9 inch)

Combine lime juice and condensed milk, stirring until thick and smooth. Beat egg whites until foamy. Add sugar, one tablespoon at a time, and continue beating until stiff. Fold in lime - milk mixture. Sprinkle lemon rind on bottom of pie shell; turn filling into shell. Chill until set. Freeze and keep until time to serve or serve without freezing. For topping, swirl on sweetened whipped cream.

Key Lime Pie

4 egg yolks, beaten slightly
1 can (15 ounce) sweetened
   condensed milk
½ cup key lime juice (or Persian lime)
1 pie shell (9 inch), pastry or crumb
4 egg whites, stiffly beaten
4 tablespoons sugar

Combine egg yolks and condensed milk; mix well. Add lime juice; blend well. Turn into baked pie shell. Beat egg whites until stiff peaks form, gradually adding sugar. Swirl onto pie, spreading to edge of pie shell all around. Bake in 300° oven until meringue is pale honey colored.

Pecan Pie

1¼ cups sugar
½ cup light corn syrup
¼ cup butter or margarine
1 teaspoon vanilla extract
3 eggs, slightly beaten
1 cup pecans, cut up
1 unbaked pie shell (9 inch)

Combine sugar, corn syrup and butter in 2 quart saucepan. Bring to boil on high, stirring constantly until butter is melted. Remove from stove, gradually add hot syrup to beaten eggs, stirring constantly. Add pecans and cool to lukewarm; add vanilla to filling. Pour filling into pie shell. Bake in 350° oven for 40 to 45 minutes.

Strawberry Refrigerator Pie

2 cups sliced fresh strawberries
⅔ cup sugar
1 tablespoon lemon juice
⅛ teaspoon salt
2 teaspoons unflavored gelatin
½ cup water
1 cup heavy cream, whipped
1 teaspoon vanilla
1 pie shell (recipe below)
a few whole strawberries

Combine strawberries, sugar, lemon juice and salt. Chill. Soften gelatin in water 5 minutes. Dissolve over hot water. Fold gelatin, whipped cream and vanilla into strawberry mixture. Pour into pie shell and chill until firm. Garnish with whole strawberries.

Cereal Flake Pie Shell:
1½ cups fine cereal crumbs
¼ cup sugar
½ cup butter, melted

Mix crumbs, sugar together; stir in butter. Line pie pan with mixture. Chill 20 minutes or bake in moderate oven 350° for 10 minutes. Cool.

Graham Cracker Crust:
16 graham crackers, rolled fine
1 teaspoon flour
½ cup butter, melted
½ cup granulated sugar
1 teaspoon cinnamon

Mix all ingredients together until the mixture sticks together. Take ½ of the mixture and line the bottom of a pie plate. Bake at 300° for 5 to 6 minutes. Put filling in cooled baked shell, put meringue on top of filling, then put remainder of cracker crumbs over the meringue. Bake at 350° for 15 to 20 minutes.

Cream Filling:
¼ cup sugar
2 tablespoons cornstarch
2 cups milk
3 egg yolks, well beaten
1 teaspoon vanilla

In saucepan mix sugar and cornstarch together. Then add other ingredients and cook over medium heat until it thickens. Pour over cooled graham cracker crust.

Meringue:
3 egg whites
3 tablespoons water
2 rounded tablespoons sugar

Have eggs at room temperature. In small bowl of mixer beat egg whites and water at high speed until egg whites form stiff peaks. Add sugar and blend the mixture with a rubber spatula. Put on top of filling.

THE ROSWELL REGISTER-TRIBUNE   OCTOBER 12, 1909

WHAT ROSWELL HAS
"A paragraphed recital of the Varied Physical Resources of the Pearl of the Pecos"

Roswell is a great wool market, something like 2,000,000 pounds being sold here every year. A complete wool scouring plant is operated for the production of refined wool.

Roswell has a population of 9,000 people, counting the suburbs, 95 per cent American, and of the remaining 5 percent are Mexicans and the other 1 per cent knockers.

Roswell has the best water and sewer systems in the territory. Over $150,000 has been invested and it affords superb fire protection. Water sells under it as low as 12 1/2 cents per 1,000 gallons.

The merits of Roswell as a health resort, particularly for lung and throat patients, are becoming better understood each year, and there are several splendid institutions for the scientific care of patients.

Souffle Brandy Alexander

1 tablespoon unflavored gelatin
1 cup milk, divided
4 eggs, separated
⅔ cup sugar, divided
⅛ teaspoon salt
2 tablespoons brandy
2 tablespoons creme de cacao

Soften gelatin in ½ cup of milk in top of double boiler. In a bowl, beat together egg yolks and remaining ½ cup milk. Add to gelatin mixture. Place over boiling water and cook, stirring constantly, until gelatin dissolves and mixture thickens slightly, about 5 minutes. Remove from heat; stir in ⅓ cup sugar*, salt, brandy, and creme de cacao. Chill, stirring occasionally, until mixture begins to set. Beat egg whites until stiff, but not dry; gradually add ⅓ cup sugar and beat until stiff. Fold into gelatin mixture. Pour into 4-cup souffle dish and chill several hours.

*Use equivalent sugar substitute to equal ⅓ cup sugar to reduce calorie count for weight watchers. Will be approximately 100 calories per serving.
Serves 4 to 6.

Zabaglione

6 eggs
¼ cup confectioner's sugar
⅛ teaspoon salt
⅓ cup Marsala wine

Put eggs, sugar, and salt in the top of a double boiler, over hot water. Cook and beat constantly, for about 6 minutes, until mixture is very thick and light. Add wine and beat again until mixture is very thick. Pour into stemmed dessert glasses. This may be served warm or well chilled.
Serves 4.

Index

W

Y

Z

Savoring the Southwest

P.O. Box 3078
Roswell, New Mexico 88202-3078
(505) 623-7477

Please send me ___ copies of Savoring the Southwest   @ 18.95 each _____
   (U.S. Currency only)
Postage and handling in Continental U.S.   @   2.75 each _____
New Mexico residents add sales tax   _____
               Gift Wrap   @   2.00 each_____
Please make checks payable to RSG Publications, Inc.
Name _____
Street _____
City _____ State _____ Zip _____

See reverse for credit card use

Savoring the Southwest

P.O. Box 3078
Roswell, New Mexico 88202-3078
(505) 623-7477

Please send me ___ copies of Savoring the Southwest   @ 18.95 each _____
   (U.S. Currency only)
Postage and handling in Continental U.S.   @   2.75 each _____
New Mexico residents add sales tax   _____
               Gift Wrap   @   2.00 each_____
Please make checks payable to RSG Publications, Inc.
Name _____
Street _____
City _____ State _____ Zip _____

See reverse for credit card use

Savoring the Southwest

P.O. Box 3078
Roswell, New Mexico 88202-3078
(505) 623-7477

Please send me ___ copies of Savoring the Southwest   @ 18.95 each _____
   (U.S. Currency only)
Postage and handling in Continental U.S.   @   2.75 each _____
New Mexico residents add sales tax   _____
               Gift Wrap   @   2.00 each_____
Please make checks payable to RSG Publications, Inc.
Name _____
Street _____
City _____ State _____ Zip _____

See reverse for credit card use

If you would like to see *Savoring The Southwest* in your area, please send the names and addresses of your local gift or book stores.

_____

_____

_____

_____

_____

☐ Please charge to   ☐ Visa   ☐ Mastercard
Card number _____ Expiration Date _____
Authorization Signature _____

If you would like to see *Savoring The Southwest* in your area, please send the names and addresses of your local gift or book stores.

_____

_____

_____

_____

_____

☐ Please charge to   ☐ Visa   ☐ Mastercard
Card number _____ Expiration Date _____
Authorization Signature _____

If you would like to see *Savoring The Southwest* in your area, please send the names and addresses of your local gift or book stores.

_____

_____

_____

_____

_____

☐ Please charge to   ☐ Visa   ☐ Mastercard
Card number _____ Expiration Date _____
Authorization Signature _____